AF835986

THE OWNERSHIP OF GOODS AND CHATTELS

This book, for the first time, sets out in comprehensive and accessible fashion the law on acquiring, surrendering and transferring ownership rights in goods and chattels. These are issues that have the potential to present themselves in contentious and non-contentious matters of various kinds, for example in the contexts of testamentary and lifetime gifts and the law of mixtures, finding and bailment. It will therefore be of interest to a broad range of practitioners, as well as academics with an interest in property.

The Ownership of Goods and Chattels

Stephen Hackett

•HART•
OXFORD • LONDON • NEW YORK • NEW DELHI • SYDNEY

HART PUBLISHING

Bloomsbury Publishing Plc

Kemp House, Chawley Park, Cumnor Hill, Oxford, OX2 9PH, UK

1385 Broadway, New York, NY 10018, USA

HART PUBLISHING, the Hart/Stag logo, BLOOMSBURY and the Diana logo are trademarks of Bloomsbury Publishing Plc

First published in Great Britain 2020

Copyright © Stephen Hackett, 2020

Stephen Hackett has asserted his right under the Copyright, Designs and Patents Act 1988 to be identified as Author of this work.

All rights reserved. No part of this publication may be reproduced or transmitted in any form or by any means, electronic or mechanical, including photocopying, recording, or any information storage or retrieval system, without prior permission in writing from the publishers.

While every care has been taken to ensure the accuracy of this work, no responsibility for loss or damage occasioned to any person acting or refraining from action as a result of any statement in it can be accepted by the authors, editors or publishers.

All UK Government legislation and other public sector information used in the work is Crown Copyright ©. All House of Lords and House of Commons information used in the work is Parliamentary Copyright ©. This information is reused under the terms of the Open Government Licence v3.0 (http://www.nationalarchives.gov.uk/doc/open-government-licence/version/3) except where otherwise stated.

All Eur-lex material used in the work is © European Union, http://eur-lex.europa.eu/, 1998–2020.

A catalogue record for this book is available from the British Library.

Library of Congress Cataloging-in-Publication data

Library of Congress Control Number: 2019952046

ISBN: HB: 978-1-78225-856-8
ePDF: 978-1-78225-858-2
ePub: 978-1-78225-857-5

Typeset by Compuscript Ltd, Shannon
Printed and bound in Great Britain by CPI Group (UK) Ltd, Croydon CR0 4YY

FSC
www.fsc.org
MIX
Paper from responsible sources
FSC® C013604

To find out more about our authors and books visit www.hartpublishing.co.uk. Here you will find extracts, author information, details of forthcoming events and the option to sign up for our newsletters.

Preface

RIGHTS OVER CHATTELS are created, exercised and infringed day in, day out in ordinary life. There is perhaps no area of law more instinctively understood by the layman, yet less academically understood by the lawyer. Ask a man who has left his car parked in the driveway whether he still owns that car and he will say, 'yes'. Ask him if the dustman who has taken a broken old radiator on the same driveway has stolen that radiator and he will say, 'no'. Ask a lawyer why those two propositions are the case and he may struggle with the answer.

The idea of writing this book came to me first when arguing about the scope of a freezing order. The respondent, against whom the order had been made, took the position that a car did not form part of her frozen estate because on her case it had been gifted to her brother. A question arose ad hoc, albeit one that did not prove determinative, about whether and to what extent the car needed to be physically delivered to the brother in order to effect the gift. It struck me at the time as surprising that issues such as that so rarely seem to arise in practice.

Most litigation about personalty concerns high-value contexts such as shipping or the sale of substantial consignments of goods. Those types of disputes have enabled the law to be explored and developed, but only in the particular parts of the law of personalty that are relevant to those contexts. There are obvious and good reasons why more 'everyday' disputes about the ownership of chattels rarely make it to the civil courts. Perhaps most importantly the value of most chattels is so low that costs of litigating about ownership will rarely be merited. Also, where a chattel is damaged or taken without the consent of the owner, it is often the criminal rather than civil litigation machinery that is engaged, since the culprit may rarely have the means to give the compensation that the owner desires.

In the increasingly digitised spheres of finance and trade, and the increasingly service-oriented economy of the 21st-century West, wealth is ever the less likely to be reduced to hard currency or valuable objects. When Magna Carta was first sealed in 1215, insofar as it was concerned to protect the property of the king's commoner subjects, it overwhelmingly meant livestock, tools of trade and coinage. Now the assets of a British citizen (insofar as they are not real property) are likely to be cash in a bank, shares and derivatives. Trade tools are more likely than ever to be know-how or expertise, as opposed to tangible things like animal feed and artisanal implements.

This book therefore begins with a frank admission that its contents are at the more esoteric end of the issues that arise in practice. I make no apology for that, however. Were rights in chattels the regular subject of actions before the upper levels of the judiciary, it is certain that a vast amount more would have been written about them. As it is, what relatively little has been written in the last two decades has tended to focus on protecting rights in chattels through contractual principles and the various statutory torts prescribed by the Torts (Interference with Goods) Act 1977. Less attention is given to issues of creating, exercising and disposing of the rights of ownership in chattels. Those questions may have less practical application in the courts but they nevertheless remain an essential and fascinating part of the law of England and Wales.

As long as there has been the rule of law, there has been law protecting the right to personal property. The desire of humans to possess chattels, and the need to protect that possession to maintain an operable society, has always been at the centre of law making. When Draco the lawgiver first set out a written Constitution in Athens in the 7th century BC he treated personal property as a cornerstone (and the prescribed sentence of death for stealing a cabbage may justifiably be called 'draconian'). In contrast to intangible legal constructs such as trusts and estates in land, the existence of chattels is a legal brute fact. The law has not had the luxury of constructing a wholly synthetic framework to deal with chattels; it has had to do its best to make law to deal with the facts as they arise. This has led to some fascinating and at times curious outcomes, as we shall see.

This book began as a series of questions in my mind about ownership rights in chattels. The more I thought about them, the more questions there seemed to be. Is every apple growing on a tree a separate chattel? If so, when does a bud cease to be a part of the tree and start to be a chattel? If not, does the act of being picked or falling cause a new chattel to burst into being? If so, can my scrumping neighbour cut most of the apple off the tree but leave the stalk without converting it? If I tell my neighbour he can have as many apples as we wants from my tree, am I allowed to pick one myself or am I converting his property? There are five questions on apple trees alone.

It quickly became clear that it was beyond me to address all the questions I could think of, and that many would turn on their own facts. I hope, however, that this short book sets out some principles that will allow anyone interested to form a view about what the law of England and Wales says about these matters.

I would like to take this opportunity of thanking my wife Catherine for her unwavering support in the writing of this book. Time spent writing, coupled with a full-time professional practice, has led to great impositions being placed upon her and I am enormously grateful to her for shouldering them. She has made me happy for as long as I have known her and ever more since we were married.

Table of Contents

Preface .... *v*
Table of Cases .... *ix*

1. **What is a Chattel and When Does it Become Capable of Ownership?** 1
   The Development of Goods and Chattels as Legal Concepts 1
   Differentiating Chattels from Other Types of Property 6
   Ownership of Chattels 14
   Mixtures and Combinations 26

2. **Obtaining and Keeping Title to Property that is Bona Vacantia** 42
   Animals 42
   Plants, Natural Features and Things on Land 46
   Human Tissue 48
   Wreck, Salvage and Treasure 54
   Bona Vacantia in the Narrow Sense – Special Circumstances in which Ownership Reverts to the Crown 59

3. **Obtaining Title to a Chattel from a Third Party** 62
   Sale 62
   Gifts 68
   Failed Gifts 73
   Conditional Gifts 78
   Rejecting a Gift 94
   Failure of Transfer of Goods Obtained by Fraud 95
   Equitable Interests in Personalty 96
   Security Over Personalty 96
   Future Goods 107
   Money 108

4. **Giving Up Rights in Chattels and Acquiring Chattels that have been Surrendered** 119
   Abandonment 119
   Bona Vacantia 127
   Bailment Created when Possession has been Abandoned 130

5. Protecting the Rights of Owners and Possessors of Chattels 134
The Historical Context 134
Statutory Developments Since the 1970s 143
The Major Modern Rights Available to Protect Interests in Goods 146
Trespass to Goods and Conversion 151

Index *157*

Table of Cases

Abingdon RDC v O'Gorman [1968] 2 QB 811 140
Albermarle Supply Co v Hind and Company [1928] 1 KB 307 101–02
Anonymous (1698) 91 ER 118 114
Armory v Delamirie (1721) 93 ER 664 .... 79, 120, 126
Armstrong DLW GmbH v Winnington Networks Ltd [2012] EWHC 10 (Ch); [2013] Ch. 156 155
Arthur v Anker [1996] 2 WLR 602 at 571 142–43
Ashby v Tolhurst [1937] 2 KB 242 (CA) 135, 146–47
Att Gen v Sir Henry Constable (1600) 77 ER 218 54
Attorney-General of the Duchy of Lancaster v GE Overton (Farms) Ltd [1980] 3 All ER 503 57
Attorney-General v Trustees of the British Museum [1903] 2 Ch 598 57
Avonwick Holdings Ltd v Shlosberg [2017] Ch 210.......................................99
Bain v Brand (1876) 1 App Cas 762...10
Baker v Barclays Bank Ltd [1955] 1 WLR 822...25
Barclays Bank Ltd v Quistclose Investments Ltd [1970] AC 567 87
Barker v Strickney [1919] 1 KB 9
Blades v Higgs (1861) 142 ER 634..15
Blades v Higgs (1865) 144 ER 1087 44
Borden (UK) Ltd v Scottish Timber Products Ltd [1981] Ch 25............... 30–32
Bridges v. Hawkesworth (1851) 21 L. J. (Q. B.) 75 122
British Road Services Ltd v Arthur V Crutchley & Co Ltd [1968] 1 All ER 811 CA 151
Broadwood v Granara (1854) 10 Ex 417.. 100
Brown v Peck (1758) 1 Eden 140 84
Bullen v Swan Engraving (1904) 23 TLR 258 CA... 150
Burn v Morris (1834) 2 Cr. & M. 579 155
Burn v Morris (1864) 149 ER 891.. 116
Butler v Butler [2016] EWHC 1793 (Ch) 24–25
Butterworth v Kingsway Motors Ltd [1954] 1 WLR 1286 65
Campbell v MacLennan (1888) 1 White 604.. 128
Canadian Pacific Wine Company v Tuley and others [1921] 2 AC 417.......... 140
Case of Swans (1591) 7 Coke Reports 15b.. 43, 45–46
Chambers v Warkhouse (1692) 3 Lev 336...48
Chantrey Martin v Martin [1953] 2 QB 286 98
Chesworth v Farrar [1967] 1 QB 407... 131
Chettiar v Chettiar [1962] AC 294 75

Chillingworth v Esche [[1924] 1 Ch 97 82
City of London Corporation v Appleyard [1963] 1 WLR 982; 2 All ER 843 .... 59, 121
Clayton v Le Roy [1911] 2 KB 1031 136–37
Clayton v Ramsden [1943] AC 320 .... 82, 84
Clough Mill Ltd v Martin [1985] 1 WLR 111 80
Cochrane v Moore (1890) 2 QBD 57 68
Coggs v Bernard (1703) 2 Lord Raymond 909; 92 ER 622 .... 96, 148, 150–51
Collier v Collier [2002] EWCA Civ 1095 75
Conservative and Unionist Party v Burrell [1982] 1 WLR 522 88
Crosse v Gardner (1688) 90 ER 656 64
Day v Royal Collage of Music [2014] Ch 211 70
De Mattos v Gibson (1859) 4 De G & J 276 and Lord Strathcona Steamship Co v Dominion Coal Co [1926] AC 108 9
Delgoffe v Fader [1939] Ch 922 92–93
Devise (1580) Brook New Cases 59 79
Dewar v Dewar [1975] 1 WLR 1532 70
Dobson v North Tyneside Health Authority and another [1997] 1 WLR 597 51–52
Donald v Suckling (1866) LR 1 QB 585 97
Doodeward v Spence [1908] 6 CLR 40 50–53
Draycot v Piot (1600) 78 ER 1045 115
Duffield v Elwes (1827) 4 ER 959 93
Dyke v Walkford (1846) 13 ER 557 128
Elwes v Brigg Gas Co (1886) 22 Ch D 562 47–48
Eyland and Sons Ltd v TSL Turton [2015] EWHC 3942 (QB) 141–42
Falcke v Scottish Imperial Insurance Co (1886) 34 Ch D 234 104–06
Five Steel Barges (1890) 15 PD 142 56
Foley v Hill (1848) 2 HLC 28 .... 112, 155
Foster v Dodd (1867) LR 3 QB 67 50
Fouldes v Willoughby (1841) 151 ER 1153 154
Franklin v Neate (1844) 153 ER 200 11
Fraser v Kershaw (1856) 2 K & J 496 26
Gamba Holdings v Minories Finance [1989] BCLC 115 98
Gardner v Parker (1818) 56 ER 478 92
General and Finance Facilities Ltd v Cooks Cars (Romford) Ltd [1963] 1 WLR 644 137
Gibbs v Cruikshank and Others (1872–73) LR 8 CP 454 139
Gilchrist Watt & Sanderson Pty Ltd v York Products Pty Ltd [1970] 1 WLR 1262 (PC) 58, 130
Gill and Duffus (Liverpool) Ltd v Scruttons Ltd [1953] 1 WLR 1407 40
Glencore International AG v Metro Trading International [2001] CLC 1732 .... 28, 31
Gregson v Gilbert (1783) 3 Doug 232 48–49

Hall v Dean (1599) 78 ER 1068 115
Hammond v Mitchell [1991] 1 WLR 1127 22
Hamps v Darby [1948] 2 KB 311 43
Handyside's Case (1749) 2 East PC 652 50
Hanley v J C & A Solicitors [2018] EWHC 2592 (QB) 98
Hannah v Peel [1945] KB 509 122
Hartley v Moxham (1842) 114 ER 675 151
Hatton v Car Maintenance Company [1915] 1 Ch 621 100
Haynes's Case (1613) 12 Coke Reports 113 .... 50, 119–20, 125
Heseltine v Heseltine [1971] 1 All ER 952 21–22
Hibbert v Mckiernan [1948] 2 KB 142 126
Hobbs v Petersham Transport Co Pty Ltd (1971) 124 CLR 220 at 241 151
Holiday v Hicks (1598) 78 ER 900 115
Holland v Hodgson (1871–1872) LR 7 CP 328 11
Holroyd v Marshall (1862) 10 HOLC 191 108
Houghland in Sutcliffe v Chief Constable of West Yorkshire [1996] RTR 86 151
Houghland v RR Low (Luxury Coaches) Ltd [1962] 1 QB 694 CA 150
Hunter v Moss [1994] 1 WLR 452 41
Hussey v Palmer [1972] 1 WLR 1286 105
In re Caborne [1943] Ch. 224; [1943] 2 All E.R. 7 85
Indian Oil Corporation v Greenstone Shipping Company SA, The Ypatianna [1988] QB 345 37
International Factors Ltd v Rodriguez [1979] Q.B. 351 117
Isaack v Clark (1613) 80 ER 1143 131–33
Jarvis v. Williams [1955] 1 W.L.R. 71 .... 118, 137
Jones v Garnett (Inspector of Taxes) [2007] 1 WLR 2030 49
Karlshamns Oljefabriker v East Port Navigation Corp (The Elafi) [1981] 2 Lloyd's Rep. 679 67
Kearry v Pattinson [1939] 1 All ER 65 45
Kinaston v Moor (1626) 79 ER 678 .... 116, 155
King v Victoria Insurance Co Ltd [1896] AC 250 13–14
Kirk v Gregory (1876) 1 Ex D 55 138–39
Kwei Tek Chao v British Traders and Shippers Ltd [1954] 2 QB 459 79
L.A. Pye (Oxford) Ltd v Graham [2002] 3 WLR 221 at 233 .... 120, 147
Lancashire and Yorkshire Railway Co v MacNicoll (1918) 88 LJKB 135, 154
Legg v Evans (1840) 6 M & W 36 101
Leicestershire CC v Michael Faraday & Partners [1941] 2 KB 205 98
Leigh and Sillavan Ltd v Aliakmon Shipping Co Ltd [1986] A.C. 785 67
Lipkin Gorman v Karpnale [1991] 2 AC 558 at 559 155
Lipkin Gorman v Karpnale Ltd [1991] 2 A.C. 548 .... 114, 116–17
Lock v Heath (1892) 8 TLR 295 71
Lord Advocate v Aberdeen University 1963 SC 533, 549 127
Lord Petre v Heneage (1706) 88 ER 1491 154

Lord v Price (1873) L.R. 9 Ex. 54 155
Lunn v Thornton (1845) 1 Common Bench Reports 379 107
Martin v London County Council [1947] KB 628 131
Mayhew v Herrick (1849) 7 CB 229 25
McGruther v Pitcher [1904] 2 Ch 306 9
Mercantile Credit Co Ltd v Hamblin [1965] 2 Q.B. 242 18
Mercer v Craven Grain [1994] CLC 328 35–36
Merwe v Goldman [2016] EWHC 790 (Ch), [2016] 4 W.L.R. 71 73
Metall Market OOO v Vitorio Shipping Co Ltd [2014] QB 760 101
Microbeads v Vinhurst [1975] 1 WLR 218 63
Middleton v Spicer (1783) 2 ER 1083 128
Miller v Race (1758) 97 ER 398 113–14
Milroy v Lord (1862) 45 ER 1185 75–78
Moffatt v Kazana [1968] 3 All ER 271 120–21
Moorgate Mercantile Co Ltd v Finch [1962] 2 All ER 467 135
Morgan v Marquis (1853) 9 Ex 145 25
Morley v Attenborough (1849) 154 ER 943 64
Morris v CW Martin and Sons Ltd [1965] 3 WLR 147–48
Morrison v Robertson 1908 SC 332 19
Moss v Hancock [1899] 2 QB 111 17
Mulliner v Florence (1878) 3 QBD 484 (CA) 100
National Coal Board v JE Evans & Co (Cardiff) Ltd [1951] 2 KB 861 152
Neill v Duke of Devonshire (1882) 8 App Cas 135 46
Newman v Bourne and Hollingsworth (1915) 31 TLR 209 133
Nyberg v Handelaar [1892] 2 QB 202 25
Oakley v Lyster [1931] 1 KB 148 (CA) 154
OBG v Allan and others [2008] 1 AC 1 .... 6, 14, 154–55
Pacific Motor Auctions pty Ltd v Motor Credits (Hire Finance) Ltd [1965] AC 867 18
Parker v British Airways Board [1982] QB 1004 (CA) 57–59, 122–23, 131–33
Patel v Mirza [2017] AC 467 85–86
Perrin v Morgan [1943] AC 399 109–10
Pettitt v Pettitt [1970] AC 777 75
Pitt v Holt [2013] UKSC 26, [2013] 2 A.C. 108) 73
Pusey v Pusey (1684) 1 Vern 273 .... 8, 10
R & H Tresize v Bilato Nominees Pty Ltd (1986) 83 FLR 44 104
R v Ashwell (1885) 16 QBD 190 at 223 148
R v Forty-Nine Casks of Brandy (1836) 166 ER 401 54
R v Kelly [1999] 2 WLR 384 52–53
R v Peters (1843) 1 Car & K 245 125
R v Price (1884) 12 QB 247 50
R v Reed (1842) Carr & M 307 .... 125, 129
Rawlinson v Mort (1905) 93 LT 555 71
Re Allen [1953] Ch 810 83

Re Beddoe [1893] 1 Ch 547 at 558 104
Re Bishop [1965] 2 WLR 188 21
Re Biss [1903[2 Ch 40 28
Re Cole [1964] Ch 175 .... 21, 70–71, 75
Re Cosslett (Contractors) Ltd [1998] Ch. 495 101
Re Dillon (1890) 44 Ch D 76 93
Re Elliott [1952] Ch 217 83
Re Figgis [1969] 1 Ch 123 21
Re Frame [1939] Ch 700 87
Re Gape's Will Trusts [1952] Ch 743 84
Re Gillie ex parte Cornell M. Gillie [1996] 1 FCA 974 25
Re Gillingham Bus Disaster Fund [1958] Ch 300 60
Re Goldcorp Exchange Ltd [1995] 1 AC 74 (PC) 35, 40
Re Goodwin [1924] 2 Ch 26 89
Re Greenwood [1903] 1 Ch 749 82
Re Hewett [1894] 1 Ch 362 19
Re Johnson's Will Trusts [1967] Ch 387 84
Re Neeld [1962] Ch 643 86
Re Organ Retention Group Ltd [2005] QB 506 53
Re Paradise Motor Co [1968] 1 WLR 1125 94–95
Re Piper [1946] 2 All ER 503 83
Re Pumfrey (1882) 22 Ch D 255 104
Re Stapylton Fletcher Ltd [1994] 1 WLR 1181 .... 34–35, 41
Re Stoneham [1918] 1 Ch 149 81
Re Wells, Swinburne-Hanham v Howard [1933] Ch. 29 128–29
Re West Sussex Constabulary's Widows, Children and Benevolent (1930) Fund Trusts [1971] Ch 1 61
Re Whitting ex parte Hall (1879) 10 Ch D, 615 13
Reynolds v Ashby & Son [1904] AC 466 47
Rowland v Divall [1923] 2 KB 500 64–66
Samson v Samson [1960] 1 WLR 190 20
Sanderson v Marsden (1922) 10 Ll. L. Rep. 467 at 472 136
Sen v Headley [1991] Ch 425 92
Shelmer's case (1725) Gilb 109
Shirlaw v Taylor (1991) 102 ALR 551 104
Shogun v Hudson [2004] 1 AC 919 95–96
Sifton v Sifton [1938] AC 656 82
Sinclair v Brougham [1914] AC 398 37
Smith v Littlewoods Organisation Ltd [1987] AC 241 HL at 271 150
Somes v British Empire Shipping Co (1860) 8 HLC 338 101
South Staffordshire Water Co [1896] 2 Q. B. 44, 47 122
Sparks v Southall [1920] 1 Ch. 122 84
Spaul v Spaul [2014] EWCA Civ 679 82
Spence v Union Marine Insurance Company Ltd (1868) LR 3 CP 427 36–38

Stack v Dowden [2007] 2 AC 432 21
Standing v Bowring (1885) 31 Ch.D. 282 .....69, 75, 80
Staniland v Willott (1852) 42 ER 416 93
Strong v Bird (1874) LR 18 Eq 315 73
Swiss Bank Corp v Lloyds Bank Ltd [1982] A.C. 584 at 595 103
Tancred v Allgood (1859) 158 ER 910 143
Tappenden v Artus [1964] 2 QB 185 (CA) 100
Taylor v Popham (1782) 28 ER 1059 89
The Colonial Bank v Frederick Whinney (1886) 11 App Cas 426 12
The Future Express [1993] 2 Lloyd's Rep. 542 155
The Lusitania [1986] QB 384 .....42, 126
The Pioneer Container [1994] 2 AC 324; 3 WLR 1 .....132, 147, 151
The Playa Larga [1983] 2 Lloyd's Rep 171 64
The Russland [1924] P. 55 56
The Veritas [1901] P.304 56
The Winckfield [1902] P.42 16
The Winkfield [1902] P 42 26
The Winson [1982] AC 939 HL at 960 150–51
Thomas v Times Book Co [1966] 1 WLR 911 72
Thunder Air Ltd v Hilmarsson [2008] EWHC 355 (Ch) 155
Tinsley v Milligan [1993] 3 WLR 126 75
Tinsley v Milligan [1994] 1 AC 340 85–86
Transco plc v United Utilities Water plc [2005] EWHC 2784 (QB) 139
Tucker v Farm and General Investment Trust Ltd [1996] 2 WLR 1241; 2 All ER 508 .....28–29, 43
Tulk v Moxhay [1848] EWHC Ch J34 9
USA v Dollfus Mieg et Cie SA [1952] A.C. 582, 611 153
Ward v Macauley (1791) 4 T.R. 489 at 490 152
Waverley Borough Council v Fletcher [1996] QB 334 .....59, 62, 122
White v Withers LLP [2009] EWCA Civ 1122 .....138, 152
Whitebread & Co v Watt [1902] 1 Ch 835 103
Wilbraham v Snow (1668) 2 Wms. Saund. 47a 155
Wilkes v Allington [1931] 2 Ch 104 92
Williams v Phillips (1957) Cr App R 5 53
Williams v Williams (1882) 29 Ch D 659 49–51
Wilson v Lombank [1963] 1 WLR 1294 152
Wilson v South Kesteven District Council [2001] 1 WLR 387 142

1

What is a Chattel and When Does it Become Capable of Ownership?

THE DEVELOPMENT OF GOODS AND CHATTELS AS LEGAL CONCEPTS

THE WORD 'CHATTEL' is Norman in origin. It is sometimes said to have derived from the word 'cattle' since cattle were at the time the most common form of personal property. Appealing though this notion is, it appears more likely that the word 'cattle' did not give rise to 'chattel', but instead both are from the same etymological root, namely the Latin, *capitale*, meaning 'property'.

Clearly the term 'property' has an extremely wide meaning in English law. Most lawyers would be comfortable in saying that property is either real or personal; and that the former concerns interests in land and the latter interests in other types of property. They may be less sure of their ground if asked to attempt a precise definition of both types of property and the theoretical distinctions between them.

There can be no doubt that the law of England evolved with the protection of real property as its primary focus. As Sir William Blackstone wrote in the eighteenth century:[1]

> Under the name of things personal are included all sorts of things moveable, which may attend a man's person wherever he goes; and therefore, being only the objects of the law while they remain within the limits of its jurisdiction, and being also of a perishable quality, are not esteemed of so high a nature, nor paid so much regard to by the law, as things that are in their nature more permanent and immoveable, as lands, and houses, and the profits issuing thereout. These being constantly within the reach, and under the protection of the law, were the principal favourites of our first legislators: who took all imaginable care in ascertaining the rights, and directing the disposition, of such property as they imagined to be lasting, and which would answer to posterity the trouble and pains that their ancestors employed about them; but at the same time entertained a very low and contemptuous opinion of all personal estate, which they regarded only as a transient commodity. The amount

[1] *Commentaries*, second edition, chapter 24.

> of it indeed was, comparatively, very trifling, during the scarcity of money and the ignorance of luxurious refinements, which prevailed in the feudal ages. Hence it was, that a tax of the fifteenth, tenth, or sometimes a much larger proportion, of all the moveables of the subject, was frequently laid without scruple, and is mentioned with much unconcern by our ancient historians, though now it would justly alarm our opulent merchants and stockholders. And hence likewise may be derived the frequent forfeitures inflicted by the common law, of all a man's good and chattels, for misbehaviours and inadvertencies that at present hardly seem to deserve so severe a punishment.

Even by Blackstone's time, then, (and of course certainly in the modern age) the idea of personal property being restricted to 'things moveable, which may attend a man's person wherever he goes' was greatly outmoded. Additionally, the emergence of a merchant class had vastly increased the quantity and value of personal property in circulation. In consequence, the law could no longer deal with personal property in its previous relatively dismissive manner. Thus Blackstone continues at chapter 24 to describe how the courts of his day 'regard a man's personalty in a light nearly, if not quite, equal to his realty'.

So far as the question of defining personal property is concerned, Blackstone offers the following:

> But things personal, by our law, do not only include things moveable, but also something more. The whole of which is comprehended under the general name of chattels, catalla; which, Sir Edward Coke says, is a French word signifying goods. And this is true, if understood of the Norman dialect; for in the grand coustumier,[2] we find the word chattels used and set in opposition to a fief or sued: so that not only goods, but whatever was not a feud,[3] were accounted chattels. And it is, I apprehend, in the same large, extended, negative sense, that not sufficiently comprehensive to take in every thing that our law considers as a chattel interest. For since, as the commentator on the coustumier observes, there are two requisites to make a fief or heritage, duration as to time, and immobility with regard to place; whatever wants either of these qualities is not, according to the Normans, an heritage or fief; or, according to us, is not a real estate: the consequence of which in both laws is, that it must be a personal estate, or chattel.

Thus Blackstone's definition of personal property is essentially, 'any property that is not real property'. While this negative definition may appear somewhat unsatisfactory, the reality is that it remains the best definition available. In order to understand more of the development of the law of personal property, it is therefore necessary to say something of the development of ownership rights in real property.

[2] ie *Le Grand Coutumier de Normandie*, which is a French-language version of *Summa de legibus in curia laicali* – 'A summary of the laws of the lay court'.

[3] ie a right under the feudal system.

The Development of Ownership Rights in Real Property

It has been said that the origin of the law of real property is the origin of the common law.[4] The phrase 'common law' meant judge-made law that was common to the whole kingdom, as distinct from varying local customs and laws. By about the middle of the thirteenth century the common law meant, in effect, the judgments of the judges of the three royal courts: the Court of Common Pleas, the Court of the King's Bench and the Court of the Exchequer.

The fundamental principles of English land law are feudal in origin. The feudal system was imposed following the Norman Conquest. As is well known, under the feudal system the king granted the use of land to his followers and to cooperative Anglo-Saxons. Importantly it was only the use of the land that was granted (ie a 'tenure' – meaning 'holding'), not an absolute transfer of ownership of the land. Persons who were granted 'tenure' were known as 'tenants'. A person who received such a grant of land from the king was known as a 'tenant in chief'. They were in essence the senior nobles of the land.

Tenants in chief were entitled to grant the use of parts of their land to others. The grantees of the tenants in chief were in their turn entitled to grant the use of the land to others, and so on. The effect was a pyramid with the king at the top and the actual occupants of the land at the bottom. The actual occupants of the land were known as 'tenants in demesne'. Those between the king at the top of the pyramid and the tenants in demesne at the bottom were known as 'mesnes', meaning 'intermediates'.

Every tenure of land was granted subject to an obligation that the tenant provided some service to the mesne lord or the Crown as the case may be. For example, a tenant might agree to provide a certain number of fighting men for a certain time per year. Over time the different services one might provide under the tenure became relatively standardised. So, for example, the requirement to provide fighting men was known as the 'knight's tenure'. Another common form of tenure was 'socage', under which a tenant would provide some non-military, non-religious service, which might have been a contribution of farm produce, say, but over time became typically a payment of cash.

Both socage and knight's tenure were examples of 'free' tenure. There was a separate species of tenure known as 'unfree' tenure. The most common unfree tenure was 'villeinage' (being a form of serfdom – indentured servitude under which tenants were required to work the land of their mesne lord).

Whatever tenure of land was granted, it could be granted for different periods of time, known as 'estates' (from the word 'status'). There were three different types of estate. The least estate was a life interest, which, as the name suggests, ended on the death of the holder of the tenure. The greatest estate was called a 'fee simple'. This meant that the tenure could be bequeathed by the tenant to

[4] *Megarry and Wade: The Law of Real Property*, 8th edition, 1-014.

any heir he wished. In between the fee simple and the life interest was an estate called a 'fee tail'. Like a fee simple, a fee tail was capable of being inherited on the death of the original tenant, but a fee tail could only pass to a descendant of the tenant and not to any heir the tenant wished. It will be noted that leasehold interests as we now understand them are not among the three possible estates in land listed here. That is because, as is discussed further below, leasehold interests are not strictly real property interests at all, but rather are personal property, even though in practice they are always treated as being part of the law of real property.

The feudal system described above has engendered two principles that have been historically fundamental to the law of real property: the doctrine of tenure and the doctrine of estates. The former describes the conditions subject to which land is held; the latter describes the time period for which the land is held.

The concept of tenure gradually decayed in the centuries following the institution of the feudal system. By the Tenures Abolition Act 1660 the number of possible tenures was in effect reduced to two:[5] socage (later known by its modern name 'freehold') and copyhold (being the old unfree tenure of villeinage as altered over time). The Law of Property Act 1922 converted all copyhold tenures into freehold tenures.

By 1925 the only meaningful feudal right that mesne lords continued to enjoy was the right of escheat, which is to say the reversion of the freehold to the mesne lord on the death of the tenant who has not disposed of it by will and has no descendants. In practice even this right was not always easy to enforce as the tenant's entitlement to alienate his freehold made it difficult to establish status as mesne lord of that property. In any event, the Administration of Estates Act 1925 provided by ss 45 and 46 that the right of escheat was abolished and, in the event of a tenant dying without heirs or issue, the property reverts to the Crown (or the royal duchies of Cornwall or Lancaster, depending on the location of the property). That remains the law.[6]

The doctrine of tenure therefore endures to the modern time in the principle that all land is owned by the Crown. Therefore all land falls into two categories. First, there is the small amount of land that is actually occupied by the Crown (ie royal residences and Crown estate land). The term 'demesne' land is used to describe such land (see, for example, ss 79–81 Land Registration Act 2002).[7]

[5] A third tenure, frankalmoine (essentially an obligation to say prayers for the mesne lord), also survived. It became obsolete, however, as any alienation of land converted a tenure of frankalmoine into socage and only the Crown was entitled to create a new tenure of frankalmoine pursuant to the Statute of Quia Emptores 1290.

[6] Albeit chattels belonging to a person without heirs or issue can still pass to the Crown under the quite different principle of *bona vacantia* as discussed later in this work.

[7] The term 'demesne' had previously referred to land held by a mesne lord for his personal use, rather than 'sub-enfeoffed' to persons further down the feudal pyramid. Prior to the Land Registration Act 2002 the term 'demesne' did not refer to land in the Crown's possession, and in fact no recognised term existed to describe such land.

The second category of land is land that is held by other parties under the tenure of freehold (or socage as once was). The person referred to conversationally as the 'owner' of a property is strictly speaking a 'tenant' since all property is held on tenure from the Crown. This is so even though the term 'tenant' is invariably used, even in professional legal circles, to refer to a person who has been granted a lease. The true ownership of land being with the Crown rather than the freeholder is a matter of great theoretical significance but very little practical importance given the wide entitlement of a freehold tenant to deal with his tenure as he wishes.

Of the doctrine of estates, over time the fee simple estate began to acquire ever more of the characteristics of what we would now call 'ownership'. By s 1(1) Law of Property Act 1925 fee simple was made the only legal estate that was capable of subsisting, being created or being transferred (except for a leasehold interest, which is strictly not a real property interest, as discussed further below). Fee tails and life interests continue to be possible in equity as interests under trusts.

By the Statute of Quia Emptores 1290, holders of a tenure in fee simple were able to alienate their estate to a third party and, in doing so, the third party became obligated to perform the original tenant's feudal duties. In spite of its great antiquity, the Statute of Quia Emptores remains not only good, but also essential law. It operates every time a person conveys their freehold title to another person so as to ensure that the recipient assumes the status of tenant.

The Contrasting Ways of Protecting Ownership Rights in Real and Personal Property

The English law appears always to have drawn a distinction between real property on the one hand and personal property on the other. The very term 'real property' alludes to this distinction. 'Real property' is a term that originally meant the type of property that could only be recovered by a 'real action' if possession were lost. A 'real action' was a form of action that was the English law's equivalent of the Roman legal concept of an *actio in rem* as distinct from an *actio in personam*.

The concepts of actions *in rem* and *in personam* are still relatively familiar to modern lawyers. An action *in rem* is an action to assert a right to a thing or status, which right can be asserted against the whole world. By contrast, an action *in personam* is an action against an individual to enforce a right or obligation. The simplest example is that an action *in rem* would allow the recovery of a thing, whereas an action *in personam* would only allow the recovery of damages to compensate for the loss of the value of the thing.

The real actions began as mechanisms to enforce feudal customs.[8] In the Baronial courts following the Norman Conquest, local mesne lords were sovereign and able to deviate from these customs without a remedy. The first real action was the 'writ of right', which was a means of compelling the mesne lord to 'do right' by his tenant and restore the land. Until about 1179 it appears that the writ of right would generally be tried by battle, and thereafter by the 'Grand Assize' of royal justices. Other real actions developed in due course, all of which were designed to establish and enforce title to land.

Those real actions could be contrasted with, for example, the writ of trespass. That writ was concerned to protect land and goods (and indeed the person), but in all cases it was an action *in personam*. If the trespasser was content to pay damages, the writ of trespass would not restore any property (be it land or goods) that was being trespassed on.

Thus 'real property' emerged as a term to describe the property that could be recovered by (and only by) the real actions. Since the real actions were ways of enforcing feudal customs, it was only feudal property (ie land) which could be real property.

In fact, *in personam* actions that enabled title in land to be effectively protected developed relatively quickly. By the start of the 16th century the convenient action of ejectment had developed. Ejectment was a type of trespass writ with the effect of removing a person from land. It was therefore a remedy *in personam*, but in practical terms allowed a land owner to enforce his title. Ejectment was a far more convenient remedy than the old real actions and so began to eclipse them.

The advent of ejectment meant it was no longer easily possible to say that 'real property' was property recoverable only by the 'real actions'. Nevertheless, the use of the term 'real property' has endured as a description of land – ie the kind of property that was at one time recoverable only by the real actions.

DIFFERENTIATING CHATTELS FROM OTHER TYPES OF PROPERTY

A modern description of property was offered by Lady Hale in *OBG v Allan and others* [2008] 1 AC 1 at paragraph 309:

> The essential feature of property is that it has an existence independent of a particular person: it can be bought and sold, given and received, bequeathed and inherited, pledged or seized to secure debts, acquired (in the olden days) by a husband on marrying its owner.

This definition is useful to the modern practitioner, who operates in a legal system whereby property of all kinds can be dealt with much as Lady Hale

[8] *Megarry and Wade: The Law of Real Property*, 8th edition, chapter 4 part 2.

describes. The description, if correct now, by no means holds good throughout all legal history as discussed further below. Although useful as far as it goes, it was not intended as a forensic definition of property of all sorts, and in particular makes no effort to identify the distinction between real and personal property; and the sub-sections of personal property. These distinctions are of interest, however, and in some cases of great practical importance.

Distinctions between Real and Personal Property

As described above, by way of a definition of chattels, we can achieve nothing more satisfactory than describing them as that property that is not real property. That being so, it is sensible to consider some of the differences between real and personal property.

In the middle of the nineteenth century, three main distinctions were observed between real and personal property.[9]

First, as noted above, real property is subject to the doctrine of tenure and the doctrine of estates. That is to say, real property is owned by the Crown and only a tenure in real property can be held by anyone else. Furthermore, any tenure in real property is subject to an estate, which in principle dictates the length of time for which the tenure is held, though in practice since the Law of Property Act 1925 only a fee simple absolute and leasehold estate are capable of existing. By contrast, personal property is capable of being owned absolutely, rather than in tenure and subject to an estate.

Secondly, the remedies to protect rights in the real property on the one hand and personal property on the other were originally different (ie the historic real actions described above).

Thirdly, and most complex to modern readers, real property on the one hand and personal property on the other were circumscribed by differing requirements as to succession after death. It is useful to provide some further explanation of this third point.

Before 1897 fee simple estates in land passed under common law directly to the heir of the deceased. The term 'heir' is used in the modern age to describe anyone who is entitled to inherit property. In the nineteenth century and earlier, however, it was a specific status, conferred upon a person uppermost in a predetermined order of succession, starting with the eldest son. A fee simple estate was also capable of being bequeathed by a will (as distinct from a fee tail, which could only pass to an heir).

Personal property, by contrast, would in the first instance vest with the deceased's personal representatives (ie the executors of a will or, if there was no

[9] Joshua Williams, *Principles of the Law of Personal Property*, 1848 edition, as quoted in the 5th edition of *Crossley Vaines on Personal Property*, 7.

will then the deceased's administrators). The personal property would thereafter be applied according to the terms of the will or, if there was no will, in accordance with the rules of intestacy, which did not provide for the personal property to pass to the heir but rather to different individuals specified by statute.

After 1897 the Land Transfer Act provided that a fee simple (ie real property capable of being devised under a will) would, like personal property, vest in the first instance with the personal representatives of the deceased. In cases of intestacy, however, the historic distinction remained: a fee simple would pass to the heir whereas personal property would pass under a separate order of succession.

With the passage of the Administration of Estates Act 1925, however, the concept of the 'heir' was abolished and the succession arrangements for both real and personal property were synthesised. There was thereafter, and still is, an identical order for succession in circumstances of intestacy, whatever is the nature of the property that is being passed.

It will be apparent from the above that the three key legal distinctions between real and personal property observed in the middle of the nineteenth century are largely redundant. The legal distinctions as to the actions used to enforce the rights and succession to the property have been swept away. The doctrines of tenure and estate remain, but they have little if any practical impact on the way in which real property is dealt with. There do remain, however, three distinctions between real and personal property that are of significance to the modern practitioner.

First, and contrary to the position with real property, the common law does not permit possession of personal property to be recovered as of right. This has been a feature throughout the history of the law of personal property; only a remedy in damages has been guaranteed. The courts of equity have long since been more flexible,[10] but only in circumstances where in the discretion of the court the return of the chattel is particularly merited. The modern position is contained in s 3 Torts (Interference with Goods) Act 1977. In essence, a claimant can bring a claim (i) demanding that the chattel be returned but giving the defendant the option of paying damages instead; or (ii) simply seeking damages. Under that statute the court retains the power to order that a chattel be delivered up without giving the defendant the option of paying damages, but it is entirely a matter for the court's discretion and not a remedy on which the claimant is entitled to insist.

Secondly, different formalities are required for the creation and transfer of interests in real as opposed to personal property. In particular, by s 52 Law of Property Act 1925 the conveyance of a legal estate can only be achieved by deed (subject to minor exceptions); by s 53(1)(a) Law of Property Act 1925 no interest in land can be created or conveyed other than in writing; and by s 2 Law of Property (Miscellaneous Provisions) Act 1989 a contract for the sale or

[10] See for example *Pusey v Pusey* (1684) 1 Vern 273.

disposition of land or an interest in land must be in writing and must incorporate all terms expressly agreed in one document. By contrast, the transfer of ownership of personal property is a great deal more straightforward. Certain intangible pieces of personal property, for example shares, have formalities attached to their transfer, but generally all that is required to transfer ownership of a chattel is delivery and the intention to transfer ownership.

Thirdly, and perhaps furthest from the forefront of the modern lawyer's mind, personal property is not of a type that permits the attachment of restrictive covenants that are capable of running with the chattel. By contrast, per the doctrine of *Tulk v Moxhay* [1848] EWHC Ch J34, real property can be encumbered with a restrictive covenant that binds all future owners if they have notice of the covenant (or do not give value for the property).

By way of example of this rule, in *McGruther v Pitcher* [1904] 2 Ch 306 the Court of Appeal held that a retailer was not bound by a minimum sale price covenant included in the agreement between the manufacturer and the wholesaler from whom the retailer purchased the products.[11] Another example can be found in *Barker v Strickney* [1919] 1 KB, in which Scrutton LJ held that the purchaser of copyright was not bound by contractual stipulations entered into by the creator and the vendor. The court stated as follows at page 132 of the judgment: 'a purchaser of chattels is not to be bound by mere notice of stipulations made by his vendor unless he was himself a party to the contract in which the stipulations were made'. By contrast, there is a line of authority to the effect that restrictive covenants can run with a chattel.[12] That proposition has on the whole been viewed sceptically, and is generally considered either to be wrong, or to be correct only within the limited context of shipping, by virtue of the particular law of liens in that area.[13]

Property Falling Within the Scope of Personal Property

As noted above, the best available definition of personal property is that it is all property that is not real property. It is possible to sub-divide personal property further, beginning with the division of all personal property into 'chattels real' and 'chattels personal'.

Chattels real are chattels that are closely connected with real estate. There appears to be only one chattel real known to modern English law and that is a leasehold interest. Notwithstanding the fact that s 1 Law of Property Act 1925 provides that a lease (ie a term of years) is one of only two possible legal estates

[11] The rule as applied in this specific context has received qualification over time by statute specifically governing price maintenance practices.

[12] *De Mattos v Gibson* (1859) 4 De G & J 276 and *Lord Strathcona Steamship Co v Dominion Coal Co* [1926] AC 108.

[13] See *Palmer and McKendrick, Interests in Goods*, 2nd edition, 498–504.

in land,[14] in its origins a lease was personalty rather than realty. That is because a term of years was outside the scope of the feudal system and therefore was not enforceable by the real actions.[15] Rather leases were understood to be private business arrangements between individuals; they were enforceable in a claim for damages but did not create interests in the land itself (in that respect they seem to have been similar to modern licences). Over time leases began to enjoy increased protection and, as noted above, by the time of the Law of Property Act 1925 they were recognised as estates in land, but not before being classified as 'chattels real'.

Some commentators maintain[16] that the term 'chattels real' only ever properly describes leasehold interests. At least one other type of property seems to have been described as a 'chattel real' in relatively recent times, however, and that is the tenancy acquired by a judgment creditor under the writ of *elegit*[17] (being a means of enforcing a judgment against a debtor by recovering rents from his land). The writ of *elegit* ceased to be available by operation of s 34(1) Administration of Justice Act 1956.

Going further back into legal history, other types of personalty seem to all intents and purposes to qualify as chattels real. The principal example is 'heirlooms', which were those items of personal property that were by immemorial custom affixed to the land and passed with the land in accordance with the rules of succession that governed the land. So, for example, in *Pusey v Pusey* (1684) 1 Vern 273 the court found that a drinking horn, supposedly granted with the manor to the Pusey family by King Cnut, properly passed with the real estate to the heir, rather than with other chattels to the deceased's personal representatives.[18]

Chattels real must be distinguished from chattels personal that are attached to the land in such a way as to actually become part of the real estate. As is well known, the court will apply a twofold test to determine whether a chattel has become part of the real estate, looking first at whether there is a substantial physical connection between the chattel and the land and secondly at the purpose of the annexation.

If there is a substantial physical connection between the chattel and the land, the chattel will ordinarily form part of the land.[19] That is not the end of the story, however, and the court will take account of the purpose of the annexation. Based on the purpose of annexation the court will in some instances construe a chattel as part of the land even if it is not fixed by substantial means and

[14] The other being fee simple absolute.

[15] *Megarry and Wade, The Modern Law of Real Property*, 8th edition, paras 1-011–1-012.

[16] ibid.

[17] *Crossley Vaines on Personal Property*, 5th edition, 8–9.

[18] The Pusey horn is now on display in the Victoria & Albert Museum, where it is dated to around the start of the fifteenth century and therefore, contrary to the court's finding in *Pusey v Pusey*, cannot be the very article gifted by King Cnut.

[19] *Bain v Brand* (1876) 1 App Cas 762.

conversely will construe something fixed to the land as nevertheless a chattel. The classical exposition of that second principle is from Blackburn J in *Holland v Hodgson* (1871–1872) LR 7 CP 328, which has been quoted on many occasions since:

> Thus blocks of stone placed one on the top of another without any mortar or cement for the purpose of forming a dry stone wall would become part of the land, though the same stones, if deposited in a builder's yard and for convenience sake stacked on the top of each other in the form of a wall, would remain chattels. On the other hand, an article may be very firmly fixed to the land, and yet the circumstances may be such as to show that it was never intended to be part of the land, and then it does not become part of the land. The anchor of a large ship must be very firmly fixed in the ground in order to bear the strain of the cable, yet no one could suppose that it became part of the land, even though it should chance that shipowner was also the owner of the fee of the spot where the anchor was dropped. An anchor similarly fixed in the soil for the purpose of bearing the strain of the chain of a suspension bridge would be part of the land. Perhaps the true rule is, that articles not otherwise attached to the land than by their own weight are not to be considered as part of the land, unless the circumstances are such as to show that they were intended to be part of the land, the onus of showing that they were so intended lying on those who assert that they have ceased to be chattels, and that, on the contrary, an article which is affixed to the land even slightly is to be considered as part of the land, unless the circumstances are such as to show that it was intended all along to continue a chattel, the onus lying on those who contend that it is a chattel.

'Chattels personal' describes all chattels that are not chattels real. 'Chattels personal' can themselves be divided into two categories: choses in action and choses in possession. 'Chose' in this context means nothing more than 'thing'.

Choses in action consist of intangible property, being essentially those rights and incorporeal things that are neither real property nor chattels real. Here again there has been an evolution of the legal concept over time, and one that is not entirely satisfactory. So it appears that in the seventeenth or early eighteenth centuries a chose in action was defined as 'a thing incorporeal and only a right; as an annuity, obligation for debt, a covenant ... and generally all causes of suit for any debt or duty, trespass or wrong are to be accounted choses in action'.[20] In other words, choses in action were debts and causes of action. As such they were personal rights, for which compensation was given in damages only.[21] Over the following two centuries, however, the scope of the term 'chose in action' had

[20] *Blount's Law Dictionary* as cited in *Crossley Vaines on Personal Property*, 11.

[21] It should probably be mentioned for completeness that *Blackstone's Commentaries* at chapter 24 (pp 396–97) attempts a definition of chose in action that includes the right of an owner of a chattel who is out of possession. If this aspect of the definition was correct at the time, it was incorrect at the latest by 1844, when the Court of Exchequer ruled that a pawnor was entitled to assign the property in his pawned watch without it being an (at the time unlawful) assignment of a chose in action: *Franklin v Neate* (1844) 153 ER 200.

broadened to include all manner of intangible property that, although unknown to early law makers, became an essential part of modern life.

Thus, as early as 1886, the House of Lords[22] was in a position to describe rights under insurance policies, rights in a partnership, and shares as choses in action. There had been no formal evolution of the term 'choses in action' to encompass these items of intangible property, but as their Lordships stated at 439–40:

> in Ex parte Agra Bank, Wood L.J. in speaking of an assignment of shares, uses the phrase 'whether in an assignment of a chose in action.' He had no need to inquire whether it was a strictly correct phrase, but to him it appeared, as it had done before to Lord Thurlow and Lord Denman, that the phrase expressed the idea. And I think it was hardly disputed that, in modern times, lawyers have accurately or inaccurately used the phrase 'choses in action' as including all personal chattels that are not in possession.

It may appear to the modern reader that the absence of a consistent theory of choses in action is of only the most academic interest. In one sense that is true because there is no doubt that familiar forms of intangible property such as shares and intellectual property rights can properly be described as choses in action. On the other hand, circumstances continue to arise in which law makers use the phrases, 'chose in action' or 'thing in action' and doubt remains about the scope of that phrase.

For example, s 283 Insolvency Act 1986 (read with reference to the interpretive provisions at s 436) provides a definition of a bankrupt's estate as including all 'things in action'. The significance of the point is that anything that is part of the bankrupt's estate passes to the trustee in bankruptcy on his appointment. A considerable amount of case law has arisen in connection with whether a given intangible right properly falls within the definition of property. At paragraph 3-617 of *Muir Hunter on Personal Insolvency* the authors give some examples of the more unusual types of property that have been found to fall within the definition at s 436:

> Some less obvious examples of property that has been held to fall within *s.436* are milk quota (*Swift v Dairywise Farms Ltd [2000] 1 W.L.R. 1177*), a waste management licence granted under the *Environmental Protection Act 1990* (*Re Celtic Extraction Ltd (In Liquidation) [2001] Ch. 475 CA*), the right of a songwriter to distributions from the Performing Rights Society (*Performing Rights Society Ltd v Rowland [1997] 3 All E.R. 336*), the entitlement of the holder of a fishing licence granted under the *Sea Fish (Conservation) Act 1967*, invalidated as a consequence of the holder's bankruptcy, to be considered for the grant of a new licence (*Re Rae [1995] BCC 102*), a right of pre-emption over land (*Dear v Reeves [2001] EWCA Civ 277; [2001] 3 W.L.R. 662*) and a right in equity, by virtue of a proprietary estoppel arising from a testamentary promise, to have land conveyed to the promisee on the death of the

[22] *The Colonial Bank v Frederick Whinney* (1886) 11 App Cas 426.

> promisor (*Webster v Ashcroft [2011] EWHC 3848 (Ch); [2012] 1 W.L.R. 1309*). On the other hand, it has been held that the ability to resort to the machinery of the *Retention of Registration Marks Regulations 1993* to obtain the transfer of a vehicle registration mark from one vehicle to another is not a species of property and cannot properly be described as a 'right' to a vehicle registration mark (*Goel v Pick [2006] EWHC 833 (Ch); [2007] 1 All E.R. 982*).

A more consistent approach to choses in action in English law would remove much of this uncertainty and the courts would not have to approach every novel intangible entitlement and right and try to do its best on the facts.

Historically, the key practical difference between choses in action and choses in possession was that only choses in possession were assignable. That distinction has long since ceased to have practical force. Choses in action became generally assignable by the Judicature Act 1873; the present governing law is s 136 Law of Property Act 1925. In addition, certain commonly occurring examples of choses in action, for example shares, are transferrable in accordance with a specific regime of prescribed formalities.

A distinction ought to be noted between chattels real on the one hand and choses in action touching on land on the other. A leasehold interest, as noted above, is one of the very few examples of a chattel real. A right to receive rent from the lease, however, is a contractual right and therefore a chose in action.[23]

Finally, as a matter of principle there ought to be a distinction between choses in action on the one hand and equitable rights on the other. That is because the concept of a chose in action developed in the common law courts rather than the courts of equity. Into the category of what might be called 'equitable choses' are of course interests under a trust and other rights that the common law courts would not recognise.

It appears that equitable choses had always been assignable and the courts of equity would allow an assignee to bring an action in his own name.[24] More relevantly to the modern practitioner, soon after legal choses in action came to be assignable under the Judicature Act 1873, equitable choses were recognised by the court (albeit perhaps a little tentatively) as also assignable by operation of those provisions. In *King v Victoria Insurance Co Ltd* [1896] AC 250 at 254 Lord Hobhouse stated as follows:

> The learned judges below consider that the term 'legal chose in action' includes all rights the assignment of which a Court of Law or Equity would before the Act have considered lawful, and that the right in question is a right of that kind.

This conclusion was adopted at page 256 as follows:

> Their Lordships do not express any dissent from the views taken in the Court below of the construction of the Judicature Act with reference to the term 'legal chose in

[23] *Re Whitting ex parte Hall* (1879) 10 Ch D, 615.
[24] Crossley Vaines on Personal Property, 5th edition, 264.

action.' They prefer to avoid discussing a question not free from difficulty, and to express no opinion what limitation, if any, should be placed on the literal meaning of that term.

The House of Lords in *King* could have been more emphatic in adopting the Court of Appeal's interpretation of 'legal chose in action' as including equitable choses. Nevertheless, it does not appear that that interpretation is in any dispute and the assignment of equitable choses is therefore permissible under the same law that permits the assignment of legal choses in action.

Having dealt with legal choses in action, that leaves choses in possession, also known as pure personalty. Choses in possession are quite simply tangible and moveable property. The name derives from the fact that choses in possession are supposedly always in the possession of someone (when one considers that 'possession', properly interpreted, includes a right to possession). In fact it is somewhat doubtful that notion is correct when exposed to scrutiny, as is discussed further below.

OWNERSHIP OF CHATTELS

Ownership in English Law

The concept of 'ownership' at English law is an uneasy one because English law does not have a clear theory of ownership, or at least not a consistent one (except perhaps in the case of the Crown). Under Roman law, for example, there was a proprietary cause of action called *vindicatio*, which enabled a litigant to assert a right of absolute and unfettered ownership.

English law, by contrast, which developed through the mechanism of resolving disputes between litigants, had no equivalent to *vindicatio*.[25] Real property, as has already been discussed, is incapable of absolute ownership and only estates in land can be owned, which are themselves in principle subject to tenure. The law is only really concerned to protect the right to possession of land (and to pass that right to possession to others) rather than engaging itself with any concept of absolute ownership.

As for personal property, the law developed specific causes of action in the form of trespass, detinue and trover/conversion, which originally provided remedies respectively for taking away, keeping or disposing of another's personalty. As noted above, those remedies were remedies *in personam*, which is to say they gave rise as of right only to damages, and delivery up of a good was, if available at all, in the discretion of the court. Thus the law does not recognise and protect any right of absolute ownership or even of possession.

[25] *OBG v Allan and others* [2008] 1 AC 1 308.

Sir John Salmond[26] stated as follows of the concept of ownership at English law:

> So long as we remember that the ownership of a material thing is nothing more than a figurative substitute for the ownership of a particular kind of right in respect of that thing, the usage is one of great convenience; but so soon as we attempt to treat it as anything more than a figure of speech, it becomes a fertile source of confusion of thought.

Some consideration of the supposed 'particular kind of right' enjoyed by an 'owner' reveals that the rights of an 'owner' are not consistent as between different types of property (even as between different types of choses in possession). As is stated by the authors of *Crossley Vaines on Personal Property*:[27]

> You can still wear your watch as you please, or throw it away if so minded, but when you attempt similar freedoms of user or disposition with respect to your motor car you are in immediate danger of infringing the law. Thus we have to fall back on Sir Frederick Pollock's definition of ownership as 'the entirety of the powers of use and disposal allowed by law'.[28]

This definition still appears to be the best working definition of ownership at English law and, throughout this work, the terms 'owner' and 'ownership' will be used in reliance on this meaning.

What Rights Are Ordinarily Available to an Owner?

The differences between ownership rights over real property and personal property are dealt with above. The most striking point is that the legacy of the feudal system is such that only estates in land are capable of ownership. By contrast, chattels are capable of outright ownership.

A less well-known distinction in ownership rights arises in the context of recovery of possession. Since the late fourteenth century there has been statutory protection for those in possession of land, such that a person cannot be forcibly dispossessed (ie without due legal process) even by someone with a better right to possession. By contrast, the common law permits a person to use force, although applying no more violence than is necessary, to recover possession of a chattel. Authority for that proposition can be found, for example, in *Blades v Higgs* (1861) 142 ER 634. Perhaps surprisingly, this case appears never to have been overruled, nor its reasoning expressly countermanded by statute. Nevertheless, it is hard to believe reliance on it could avail a modern litigant, particularly against the background of the Human Rights Act 1998.

[26] *Salmond on Jurisprudence*, 8th edition, 279.
[27] Fifth edition, 39.
[28] Sir Frederick Pollock, *A First Book of Jurisprudence for Students of the Common Law*, 179.

As is perhaps implied in the paragraph above, the right to possession of a chattel (or real property) is an essential part of the bundle of rights that make up ownership at English law. This is so much so that the concepts of right to possession on the one hand and ownership on the other are sometimes considered as interchangeable. This can be seen, for example, in the case of real property, where the ultimate vindication of a superior title is, and always has been, to be awarded possession.

Distinction and Overlap between Ownership and Possession

It does not take a great deal of reflection to appreciate that ownership and possession are different things, however. After all, a person who hires a chattel enjoys at least some of the possessory rights of ownership without ever being able to lay claim to the ownership of the item. It is therefore beyond doubt that the right to possession, important though it is to the collection of rights comprising ownership, is not the same thing as ownership. There are a number of areas, however, in which there is a considerable overlap between possession and ownership. These are worth considering.

First, possession has always been a root of title. The term 'possessory title' is generally used to describe title deriving from possession (or in some cases perhaps from the mere right to possession). In *The Winckfield* [1902] P.42, for example, the Court of Appeal confirmed that a bailee is entitled to sue in conversion in reliance on his possessory title: 'the right of the bailee to bring his action rests … as against a wrongdoer, on his possessory title, and he recovers on the strength of his possession just as in the case of a finder'. This principle is the explanation for the law's protection of a converter of chattels (or real estate) as against anyone who cannot show a better title. That is to say, where a person takes possession of a chattel, he has acquired possessory title, even where he has acquired that possession by conversion or indeed theft. The law will vindicate that possessory title by granting the possessor a remedy for wrongful interference with goods[29] against anyone but a person with a better title.

Secondly, possession is prima facie proof of ownership of a chattel (or at least a chose in possession). This is purely a practical point rather than one of theory. As will be discussed below, transfer of ownership of a chose in possession can be (and almost invariably is in non-commercial situations) effected simply by delivery and the intention to transfer ownership. Given the absence of the formalities attendant on the transfer of title in, for example, real property, possession remains as one of the few and perhaps the most reliable indicators of title in a chose in possession.

[29] Which is to say, per s 1 Torts (Interference with Goods) Act 1977, conversion, trespass to goods or negligence affecting goods.

Thirdly, there are certain circumstances in which the possession of chattels (or certain specific chattels) is sufficient to allow the possessor to convey a good title in the chose to a third party, even where the transferor is not the owner. There are two main areas in which this may happen, the first being the transmission of currency and the second touching on certain circumstances in which goods are sold by a party in possession who does not in fact have title to them.

Currency

As to currency (by which is meant coin of the realm and negotiable instruments (essentially bank notes)), there is a distinction to be drawn between currency that passes into circulation and currency that is treated as a chattel. In the former case, a transferee will acquire good title to the currency where it is taken in good faith for value without notice of the defect in title of the transferor. Where coinage is treated as a chattel, however, mere possession of the coin is insufficient to enable a person to transfer good title to a third party. So in *Moss v Hancock* [1899] 2 QB 111 a thief stole a special edition £5 Jubilee gold piece and sold it on to a dealer as a curiosity. In those circumstances the court found it had not passed into circulation and so good title had not been transferred.

Goods Sold by a Person Who is Not the Owner

The ancient common law principle of *nemo dat quod non habet* (no one can give what he does not have) was given statutory force in a sale of goods context by s 21(1) Sale of Goods Act 1979:

> Subject to this Act, where goods are sold by a person who is not their owner, and who does not sell them under the authority or with the consent of the owner, the buyer acquires no better title to the goods than the seller had, unless the owner of the goods is by his conduct precluded from denying the seller's authority to sell.

Of now merely historical interest was the exception to this principle contained until 1995 in s 22(1) Sale of Goods Act 1979 for goods sold in 'market overt'. The concept of market overt is an ancient one, dating back to the thirteenth century in England. Essentially it was a provision of law allowing good title to be passed by vendors operating from shops in the City of London and legally constituted markets outside it, even where the vendor did not have good title to pass. Its origins lay with the privileges of market owners, who were able to generate substantial profit from their entitlement to hold markets. Clearly those markets were more attractive to vendors and purchasers alike if a purchaser could be sure that good title could be obtained from the transaction, without having to worry about whether the vendor himself had obtained good title. The survival of the market overt exemption to s 21(1) Sale of Goods Act 1979 was quite remarkable. It has been said:

> It was an exception which could be politely characterised as an obsolescence. More accurately it could be characterised as an ugly medieval relic, the only benefit of which was to assist in the sale of stolen goods. Whichever is chosen, its retention was a good example of the difficulty of reforming even the most blatant legal absurdities.[30]

Although the concept of market overt has been consigned to history, a small number of other exceptions to the general rule in s 21(1) Sale of Goods Act 1979 remain.[31] One such exception is at s 24(1). It provides that, where a seller remains in possession of goods after their sale, and then sells them on to a third party, that third party will acquire good title to the goods. This exception is not available, however, where there has been a completion of the original sale by delivery, and the seller simply happens to come back into possession of the chattel.[32] A similar exception exists in s 25(1) Sale of Goods Act 1979 for the benefit of buyers who come into possession of goods they have agreed to buy.

Another exception to the rule in s 21(1) is estoppel. The wording of s 21(1) is expressly drafted to continue to permit the common law principles of estoppel to take effect. An estoppel under this statutory exception is somewhat unusual in that it not only has an affect as between the true owner and the recipient of the goods, but also sets up a genuine transfer of title that is good against the world (see, for example, *Mercantile Credit Co Ltd v Hamblin* [1965] 2 QB 242 at 275).

Section 23 Sale of Goods Act 1979 provides a further exception to s 21(1) in circumstances where a vendor has a voidable title to goods; the goods are then sold to a third party; and the title to the goods is voided thereafter. In those circumstances, provided again that the recipient receives the goods in good faith, he will take a good title to those goods. This principle may come into effect, for example, where a person obtains goods from their original owner by fraud and then sells those goods on to a third party. In those circumstances the original owner will be able to void the transaction to the vendor, but this will have no effect on the good title received by the ultimate recipient. Other examples of circumstances that can give rise to a voidable title are duress, misrepresentation and undue influence.

It must be stressed that the s 23 exception is available only in respect of a *voidable* title. This must be contrasted with a *void* title, such as is created where goods pass from one person to another under a contract entered into under a mistake or because of a lack of coincidence between the terms of the offer

[30] *Palmer and McKendrick, Interests in Goods*, 2nd edition, 337.

[31] See chapter 7 of the 9th edition of *Benjamin's Sale of Goods* for more detail.

[32] *Pacific Motor Auctions pty Ltd v Motor Credits (Hire Finance) Ltd* [1965] AC 867, decided on the statute preceding the Sale of Goods Act 1979 but no doubt still applicable.

and acceptance.[33] Where a title is void rather than merely voidable, it never passes from the original owner of the goods to the original recipient. Therefore, that recipient has no title of any kind to pass on to a third party and the exception in s 23 is not available.

Co-ownership of Chattels

While lawyers are accustomed to dealing with the joint ownership of real property, joint ownership of a chattel is a less familiar notion. This is perhaps because the tangible nature of chattels (or at least chattels in possession) so naturally lends itself to the control of a single individual. Nevertheless, the law recognises the possibility of joint ownership and it must be considered.

Just as with real property, joint ownership of personal property can be by way of a tenancy in common or joint tenancy. Those terms are familiar from the world of real property, but have a somewhat distinct meaning in the context of personal property. In particular, ss 1, 34 and 36 Law of Property Act 1925, which require any jointly owned land to be held as joint tenants in law, do not apply to personal property. The consequence is that it is possible for a chattel to be owned legally in tenancy in common.

Just as is the case with real estate, joint ownership of a chattel entails a single indivisible ownership jointly held by two or more people. Where a joint tenant dies the other joint tenant will enjoy a right of survivorship. Where a chattel is transferred to joint ownership without more said on the matter, the kind of ownership that will arise is joint tenancy. Similarly, where a chattel is purchased by more than one person those purchasers will hold the chattel as joint tenants except to the extent that they have expressed to each other an intention jointly to own the chattel in a different way.

Again as with real estate, a tenancy in common in a chattel can be created by the severance of a previous joint tenancy (see, for example, *Re Hewett* [1894] 1 Ch 362). Tenancies in common in chattels can also be created in other ways familiar from the law of real property: namely, where a chattel is transferred on terms that it is jointly owned in unequal shares; or where a tenancy in common is the expressed intention of the joint owners.

Chattels Owned within Marriage

An interesting body of law concerns the joint ownership of chattels within marriage. While there is extensive jurisprudence on the question of joint ownership of real property, the law has not kept pace in respect of personal property.

[33] Such as happened in *Morrison v Robertson* 1908 SC 332.

The result is a number of decisions in support of propositions, some of which seem rather surprising to the modern reader.[34] As well as seeming in some cases to lack modern relevance, they take no account whatever of civil partnerships and same-sex marriage. As valid propositions of law likely to carry weight in the courts, they must be treated with extreme caution, and yet they remain the law so far as it can be ascertained.

Chattels owned by a person before marriage continue to be the sole property of that person after marriage. In other words, there is nothing in the law of personal property that operates to vest joint ownership of an individual's chattels in his or her spouse in the event of marriage. Naturally, a person may convey a share of a chattel to his or her spouse, but only in the usual way.

More surprisingly, there is no presumption that wedding presents are gifted to the couple jointly. The critical issue is the intention of the donor. In any given case it may be that there is specific evidence that a donor intended to make a gift to one or other of the newlyweds, or to them both jointly. In those circumstances that is the effect that the gift will have. Where there is no such evidence, however, the law presumes that the friends and relatives of a given spouse intend to make a gift to that spouse alone. This principle was upheld by the Court of Appeal as recently as 1960 in *Samson v Samson* [1960] 1 WLR 190 in which Lord Justice Hodson said as follows:

> I do not think that, as a matter of law, any intention is to be attributed to the donor. Where there is evidence of intention on the part of the donor, it may well be that wedding presents may be found to have been given to one spouse, or the other, or to both; but where no intention is clear, the court is fully entitled, in my judgment, to draw the inference that money and gifts in kind originating from one side of the family were intended for the husband, and those from the other side, from friends of that party, were intended for the wife. Another possible position may arise – that property which is given at the time of the wedding to one spouse or the other may become joint property by the conduct of the parties.

So far as chattels acquired by way of gift during a marriage are concerned, the starting point is once again that the gifts are owned by the spouses jointly or individually as per the intention of the donor insofar as that can be ascertained. Although it does not appear that the point has ever been tested in the courts, it would appear logical that, as with wedding presents, where no evidence of the donor's intention is available, the court will presume that a gift by the friends or relatives of one spouse is intended as a gift solely to that spouse.

So far as the purchase of chattels by a married couple is concerned, various presumptions are applied by the courts, all of which can be displaced by evidence about the true intentions of the parties acquiring the chattel.

[34] *Palmer and McKendrick, Interests in Goods*, 2nd edition, 252 onwards provides an analysis of these principles from which I have borrowed, updating them so far as necessary.

First, a chattel will generally belong to the person who provided the purchase price.[35] This principle echoes the presumption that once existed that a person who provided the purchase price of real property would own the equitable interest of that property under a resulting trust. That presumption has been largely abandoned since *Stack v Dowden* [2007] 2 AC 432, and it remains to be seen whether the comparable presumption in *Re Cole* would withstand testing in the appellate courts.

Secondly, if a chattel is purchased from a joint bank account to which both spouses contribute roughly equally, the law presumes not that the chattel is owned jointly, but that the purchasing spouse owns that chattel solely. The rationale for this rule is explained in *Re Bishop* [1965] 2 WLR 188 as being that the purpose of a joint account is to enable each spouse to draw upon it for their own purposes just as much as for joint marital purposes.

Where a chattel is purchased from a joint account funded mainly by the wife, legal title will be presumed to belong to the person who purchased the chattel or on whose behalf it was purchased. Equitable title, on the other hand, will be presumed to belong to the wife.[36]

There is a contention by the authors of *Palmer and McKendrick*[37] that the matters stated in the paragraph above are to be contrasted with the position of a husband who has contributed the majority of the monies to a joint account. The contention is that, whereas the wife is presumed to be the sole equitable owner, the husband only benefits from a presumption that he is joint equitable owner. This analysis appears to gain some support from the case of *Re Figgis* [1969] 1 Ch 123.

It is respectfully submitted, however, that the proper reading of *Re Figgis* and *Heseltine* is not that husbands and wives are presumed to enjoy different equitable interests in chattels depending on which of them it was who funded the joint account. The law was stated in *Heseltine* at 347 by Lord Denning as follows:

> In some cases where husband and wife each contribute to a joint account, the proper inference is that they are putting their moneys into the account with the intention that they should belong to them both jointly. If the marriage breaks down, investments made out of that account belong to them jointly, usually half-and-half, although in the name of one only: see *Jones v. Maynard* [1951] Ch. 572. But there are other cases where one party provides all the money in the joint account, and it is only opened and used as a matter of convenience of administration. In such cases, if the marriage breaks down, the moneys belong to the one who provided them. So do any investments made with those moneys.

In other words, the law at the time of *Heseltine*, and surely still, is that the person who solely funds a joint account is presumed in the absence of evidence

[35] *In Re Cole* [1964] Ch 175.
[36] *Heseltine v Heseltine* [1971] 1 All ER 952.
[37] Second edition, 253.

as to the intention of the parties at the time of purchase. The idea of husbands and wives being presumed to enjoy different equitable interests does not appear to have been the law at the time of *Heseltine* and is most unlikely to be found to be the law now. Moreover, the courts have expressed understandable reluctance to have disputes between spouses as to the ownership of chattels brought before them. In *Hammond v Mitchell* [1991] 1 WLR 1127 at 1138 the court stated as follows:

> While no one suggests that English law recognises or should develop a doctrine of community of property regarding the household goods of those who settle for an unmarried union, the parties must expect the court in ordinary cases to adopt a robust allegiance to the maxim that 'equality is equity,' if only in the interests of fulfilling the equally salutary maxim 'sit finis litis.' If it is really necessary to bring issues of disputed ownership of household chattels to adjudication, the proper way of doing it is a claim for a declaration or inquiry as to the beneficial interest, supported with appropriate affidavit evidence, on lines similar to the procedure for resolving disputes under *section 17 of the Married Women's Property Act 1882 (45 & 46 Vict. c. 75)*. It is not normally appropriate to proceed by actions framed in conversion or detinue.

It must be stressed that, whatever force if any these presumptions continue to enjoy at law, they are in any event readily rebutted by evidence before the court as to the true intentions of the parties at the time of acquisition as to how ownership is to be arranged.

Disposal of Jointly Owned Interests in Chattels

The rule of *nemo dat quod non habet* (ie the rule that a person cannot give better title than he has, subject to the few exceptions discussed above) applies to a joint interest in chattels as much as it does to any other property. Thus, where one co-owner purports to sell good title to an entire chattel, the purchaser will simply acquire a tenancy in common in the chattel with the other co-owner.[38]

This principle appears apt to have potentially significant consequences in the sphere of insolvency. Under s 306 Insolvency Act 1986 a trustee in bankruptcy is vested with the bankrupt's property on his appointment. By virtue of the *nemo dat* principle, if a chattel is only part owned by a bankrupt then the trustee will only be vested with that partial ownership. Naturally the onward sale of a tenancy in common in a chattel, while possible at law, is unusual and would have a limited market, thereby making it difficult to realise a significant amount for the bankrupt's creditors.

[38] The act of purporting to sell the chattel would no doubt imply a warranty on the part of the seller as to his good and sole title, but such a warrantee would not assist the purchaser against a co-owner.

As discussed further below, the scope for a co-owner to force the sale of a whole chattel is limited. Therefore, the most plausible purchaser of a bankrupt's share of a co-owned chattel will almost inevitably be the co-owner, who in turn is perhaps most likely to be the bankrupt's spouse. A sale at a low value to a spouse would probably be better for the bankrupt's creditors than no sale at all. One might imagine, therefore, that disputes would arise as to the sole or co-ownership of valuable chattels in a bankrupt's estate. In practice, however, such disputes appear to arise very seldom or at all. Those advising insolvent individuals who own valuable chattels, however, might do well to consider whether those chattels might in reality be co-owned by a person friendly to the bankrupt.

Rights of Joint Owners Against Each Other

Practitioners are used to co-owners of land availing themselves of the regime under the Trusts of Land and Appointment of Trustees Act 1994 to police their mutual interests. No equivalent provisions exist in respect of chattels and the rights of co-owners are a great deal more restricted.

In particular, a co-owner of a chattel does not have an automatic right to force a sale of that chattel, and in some or perhaps all cases there is no jurisdiction for the court to make such an order. An interesting jurisdiction exists at s 188 Law of Property Act 1925. That section permits a claimant who jointly owns 'any chattels' with some other person to make an application to the court, but only if the claimant owns a half share or better. On such an application the claimant can seek a 'division of the chattels or any of them' and the court can, 'make such order as it thinks fit'. This section gives rise to a number of interesting issues.

First, and on any view, it leaves an owner of a minority share of a chattel without any kind of entitlement against a co-owner to force a division. Given the inability to obtain exclusive possession of a co-owned chattel discussed below, there may be situations in which a minority interest in a chattel is virtually worthless.

Secondly, the wording of the section appears to envisage persons jointly owning collections of chattels. There is doubt about whether the jurisdiction is available to people who co-own a single chattel with another person. There is further doubt about whether the wording 'or any of them' in respect of the division of chattels can mean that a jurisdiction exists to order some kind of division of a single chattel.

The authors of *Palmer and McKendrick* consider that the court would accept jurisdiction under s 188 to deal with a single chattel.[39] No authority is

[39] Second edition, 255.

cited for this contention, which, it is submitted, is not as self-evident as appears to be suggested. Presumably if Parliament had intended the section to apply to a single chattel as easily as to a collection of them it could have drafted it in those terms without difficulty. The fact it has not, but has instead couched s 188 in what appears to be the language of division of collections of chattels, perhaps tends to suggest it is to be read as conferring a jurisdiction only in respect of collections.

The final doubt about the section is whether it confers a power of sale on the court.

Section 188 made one of its extremely rare appearances before the court in the recent decision of *Butler v Butler* [2016] WTLR 1519. That decision was made by Judge Simon Barker QC sitting as a deputy High Court judge. It also happened to be in a case where the chattels at issue were a collection and the most just outcome was found not to involve a sale. The judgment does, however, contain some potentially useful clarification about the scope of s 188.

At paragraph 71, the judge stated that the High Court had the inherent jurisdiction to make an order for sale regardless of the correct construction of s 188. No authority is cited in support of this proposition, which does not appear to have been a matter of submissions. If correct that the High Court has such a jurisdiction, it can evidently be exercised without reference to s 188 (and therefore is presumably open to even the owners of a minority interest in a chattel). If it exists, that inherent jurisdiction of the High Court would not in any event be available to the County Court (as the judge acknowledged in *Butler*) because the County Court has no inherent jurisdiction.

At paragraph 73 of *Butler* the court stated as follows:

> I take as a reasonable starting point that Parliament will have enacted section 188 as a provision to assist the courts in doing justice as between co-owners unable to agree between themselves what is to become of their jointly owned property … Parliament also recognised that for co-owners valuation or commercial interests might not be the only or the appropriate criteria for doing justice. Beyond that, the only fetter to the court's power to make any order it thinks fit is the word 'division'. Moreover, the criteria for deciding upon a division are very wide: 'or otherwise'. From this I take the view that the court is empowered by section 188 to take a flexible and case by case approach aiming to deliver justice according to the particular circumstances of the case. Should it become necessary to decide the point, I would prefer Mr Brisby QC's submission that the language of section 188 is wide enough to enable a court intent upon making an order as between co-owners not to be forced to make either no order or an incomplete order thereby leaving one or more chattels unaddressed, and possibly causing ongoing expense to, the co-owners. Whether an order made by the court directing a sale should, for example, permit a co-owner to have conduct of the sale or to be a purchaser, or permit a combination of division between co-owners (and on what basis) and sale would be fact sensitive. I do not consider that the partnership dissolution cases provide a direct analogy or compelling guidance. I do hold the view that the aim of Parliament will have been to enable the court to achieve practical justice between co-owners of chattels who have fallen out over what is to become of their jointly owned asset(s).

This, then, is support, albeit possibly obiter, for the proposition that the court does enjoy a power of sale under s 188. Additionally, the use of the phrase 'jointly owned asset(s)' suggests that the judge felt that a single asset was amenable to an application under s 188. So far as can be ascertained at the present time, these two propositions as stated in *Butler* represent the law as to s 188.

Leaving s 188 aside, what other rights does a co-owner enjoy against his fellow owner? Both joint owners of a chattel have the right to possession of the chattel but they do not have an exclusive right to possession unless they have reached an agreement to that effect.[40] The consequence of this is that a co-owner can take possession from another co-owner (or retain possession against the co-owner's will) without giving rise to a right of action in conversion.[41]

Since neither co-owner enjoys exclusive possession, however, an action in conversion is possible where an act is taken that is only permissible where an owner enjoys exclusive possession. As Devlin, J said in *Baker v Barclays Bank Ltd* [1955] 1 WLR 822 at 827:

> I think it is quite clear that one co-owner can commit an act of conversion in respect of joint property. Of course, the mere fact that he takes possession of it will not be sufficient to amount to a conversion, because he is entitled to the possession of it. Neither party, however, is entitled to exclusive possession, and, if one of the two does an act which can be justified only by the right to exclusive possession, then he converts.

The most obvious example of an act that can be justified only by exclusive possession is the destruction of a chattel.[42] In any collection of chattels, ownership of each chattel is joint (hence the need for s 188 Law of Property Act 1925 discussed above). In consequence, if one joint owner of, for example, a herd of cattle appropriates and destroys half of the herd and leaves the other half for his co-owner, that will amount to a conversion.[43]

An action for conversion also lies against a co-owner where a co-owner sells a chattel to a third party in such a way as to bring the sale into one of the exceptions to the *nemo dat* rule discussed above.[44] In principle, this is no more than an extension of the concept that a co-owner has an action in conversion in the case of construction of a chattel. After all, the sale of a chattel in circumstances in which the purchaser takes free of a co-owner's interest amounts in effect to the destruction of that interest.

By parity of reasoning, one would expect that, in disposals of chattels in which there was no exception to the *nemo dat* rule available, an action for conversion is not available by one co-owner against the other. For many years that appears to have been the case in spite of a degree of judicial doubt.[45] Justice

[40] *Nyberg v Handelaar* [1892] 2 QB 202.
[41] ibid.
[42] *Morgan v Marquis* (1853) 9 Ex 145.
[43] As happened in the Australian case of *Re Gillie ex parte Cornell M. Gillie* [1996] 1 FCA 974.
[44] For example *Mayhew v Herrick* (1849) 7 CB 229.
[45] ibid.

was served at that time by a duty in equity on the wrongful seller to account to his co-owner from the proceeds.[46]

The position was resolved by the Torts (Interference with Goods) Act 1977. Section 10(1)(b) provides that there is no defence available in conversion where a co-owner

> (b) purports to dispose of the goods in a way which would give a good title to the entire property in the goods if he was acting with the authority of all co-owners of the goods.

Much as this provision has helped to introduce clarity to the law, it relates only to the disposal of the 'entire interest' in a chattel. No mention is made of actions that would stop short of such a total disposal, for example pledging a chattel by way of a pawn. It appears likely that in such circumstances no action for conversion would be available, although that point has not been tested. The same point may be made in respect of an action in trespass to goods, to which s 10 applies just as it does in conversion.

The 1977 Act has also made provision to deal with issues arising from a single joint owner bringing actions against third parties. Section 8(1) operates so as to enable a defendant to a claim brought by a person in possession of a chattel to add any person who has a better right than the claimant to all or part of the chattel. Thus a co-owner out of possession can be joined and the court may allocate damages as appropriate between those two.

Section 8 has a wider application, however, and can be used to enable a defendant to add as a party a person with better title than the claimant. Thus, for example, where a bailee sues a person in reliance on his possession of the chattel, the defendant can add the bailor as a party. This is a major qualification to the previous common law position that

> possession with an assertion of title, or even possession alone (which is the case of a bailee), gives the possessor such a property as will enable him to maintain an action against a wrongdoer: for possession is prima facie evidence of property.[47]

MIXTURES AND COMBINATIONS

In the sphere of mixing or combining chattels one encounters some of the most ancient, arcane and uncertain law in the sphere of personal property.

The term 'combinations' is used to describe any circumstances in which multiple chattels are brought together so as to join or interact in some way. The term 'mixtures' is a term of art, which describes a particular kind of combination. It is perhaps the type of combination that most commonly comes before

[46] *Fraser v Kershaw* (1856) 2 K & J 496.
[47] *The Winkfield* [1902] P 42.

the courts, and certainly the type giving rise to the most established and complex law, but that does not alter the fact that other kinds of combinations do appear to exist.

The different kinds of combinations are addressed in turn below. In at least some cases they are doctrines that derive from Roman law. Their status in English law is not always certain, although the position as it can best be ascertained is described below. It will also be noted that the principles governing mixtures are also able to explain the way in which new chattels come into being.

It should also be added that there is often immense scope for argument as to what kind of combination a particular arrangement constitutes. Nevertheless, the fact remains that the different combinations have different law attaching to them, and so the distinction would in principle need to be drawn by the court as best it can. The phrase 'in principle' is used because as a matter of fact the application of the various doctrines discussed below is extremely rare, as the sparsity of case law testifies.

Accessio Cedit Principali

The doctrine of *accessio* is originally a part of Roman law. It is the principle that additions to property by growth or increase belong to the owner of that property. It appears to apply to real and personal property. As part of the principle of *accessio*, where an 'accessory thing' becomes part of a 'principal thing' the accessory thing ceases to exist and it becomes part of the principal thing, with the consequence that it is owned by the owner of the principal thing.[48]

Thus, insofar as *accessio* is a part of English law, there are two separate areas of law in which it is a potentially useful concept. First, it would be the basis for the proposition that the owner of a piece of property that grows or generates additional property also owns the additional property. For example, it would explain why the owner of an apple tree owns the apples that grow on the tree and continues to do so once those apples are separated from that tree (it presumably only being at that time at which each apple becomes a separate chattel). This invocation of the principle of *accessio* is unlikely ever to prove controversial.

Secondly, and with slightly more scope for controversy, *accessio* would operate to deal with a situation in which an accessory chattel is combined with a principal chattel to confer ownership on the owner of the principal chattel. By way of example, if a thread is sewn into a piece of cloth to repair it, the principle of *accessio* would operate to confer ownership of the thread onto the owner of the cloth.

[48] This description is indebted to the relevant definitions in the 4th edition of *Jowitt's Dictionary of English Law*.

This application of the principle of *accessio* does have the potential to be in tension with the law of granular or fluid mixtures. In the law of mixtures (discussed in greater detail below) the contributors of the component chattels enjoy ownership rights in the mixture (albeit the precise nature of those ownership rights may be uncertain as a matter of English law). In the case of *accessio* the owner of the accessory chattel loses all ownership rights in it when the combination occurs.

Insofar as it can be understood, the distinction between a mixture and an *accessio* combination appears to be that an *accessio* will be engaged when there is a principal and an accessory chattel, whereas a mixture requires meaningful contributions to the final product. In some circumstances, such as the thread example given above, or the example of glue being used to repair a chattel, the principal and accessory relationship seems intuitively obvious. One can, however, imagine a whole range of factual scenarios in which there would be a dispute as to whether one element of the combination was merely an accessory or whether it was sufficient to constitute a component part of a mixture. There is a total absence of English authority to assist in resolving that question.

There remains the question of whether the principle of *accessio* is even a part of English law. On balance it appears that it probably is (certainly this appears to be assumed by commentators generally). For example, in *Re Biss* [1903] 2 Ch 40 at 51 the court appeared to acknowledge the existence of the doctrine, conflating it in effect with the comparable real property doctrine of accretion. Additionally (and as discussed in more detail below), in *Glencore International AG v Metro Trading International* [2001] CLC 1732 Moore-Bick J (as he then was) appeared to acknowledge the existence of the doctrine of *accessio* in English law (see especially paragraphs 178–79).

In *Tucker v Farm and General Investment Trust Ltd* [1996] 2 WLR 1241 the court found that the person in possession of livestock is the person entitled to ownership of its progeny. In reaching that decision the court consciously followed the civil law in determining that the person in possession of a domestic animal (and indeed an apple tree) was entitled to the progeny of that animal. *Tucker* is cited by the authors of the fourth edition of *Jowitt's Dictionary of English Law* as an example of the implementation of the principle of *accessio*. That is somewhat doubtful, however, as in fact the court appeared to be relying on the doctrine of *partus sequitur ventrem*.[49] Lord Denning quoted favourably from Blackstone at page 426 as follows:

> Of all tame and domestic animals, the brood belongs to the owner of the dam or mother; the English law agreeing with the civil, that 'partus sequitur ventrem' in the brute creation, though for the most part in the human species it disallows that maxim. And therefore in the laws of England, as well as Rome – then I will translate

[49] 'That which is brought forth follows the womb', being (among other applications) the common law principle establishing that the child of a slave was him- or herself also a slave.

the Latin into English – 'if your stallion makes my mare become pregnant, then the foal belongs not to you but to me who am the owner of the mare.' And, for this Puffendorf gives a sensible reason: not only because the male is frequently unknown, but also because the dam, during the time of her pregnancy, is almost useless to the proprietor, and must be maintained with greater expense and care: wherefore as her owner is the loser by her pregnancy, he ought to be the gainer by her brood.

Specificatio

Specificatio is a principle whereby one person becomes the owner of a chattel by manufacturing it from the chattels of another. Thus, to use the classic example, where one person makes wine out of another person's grapes, the person who has made the wine (as opposed to the owner of the grapes) owns the wine under the principle of *specificatio*.

The principle of *specificatio* stands in contrast to the approach adopted by the Roman jurists of the school of Masurius Sabinus. That approach held that the new chattel simply belongs to the person who owned the materials from which the chattel was made. The principle of *specificatio* appears to have been advanced by the Justinian school.[50]

The 'manufacturing' situation is to be distinguished from circumstances (discussed above in the context of *Tucker*) in which one piece of personal property naturally produces another. The example dealt with in *Tucker* involved the ownership of livestock born of a parent, but by parity of reasoning it must be uncontroversial at English law that the same principle would apply, for example, to other naturally developing chattels. Thus, for example, where an apple grown on a tree is picked, English law must allow the apple to belong to the person who owned the tree.

'Manufacturing' of the *specificatio* type must also be distinguished from the combination of the *accessio* type. Here there is clearly a substantial possibility of overlap. In fact, it appears that Blackstone treated *specificatio* as a sub-set of *accessio*.[51] Nevertheless, as *accessio* and *specificatio* have the potential to produce different outcomes, the distinction is a meaningful one (assuming both principles are in fact a part of English law). There is no guidance that is capable of providing the answer and the matter would inevitably turn on the perspective of an individual judge.

Peter Birks[52] has given the example of butter, flour and eggs being made into a cake. The principle of *specificatio*, in his view, would have the effect of vesting ownership of the finished cake with the baker. This is an intuitively

[50] Justinian, Institutes 2.1.25, with gratitude to Professor Birks's analysis in chapter 9 of *Palmer and McKenrick, Interests in Goods*, 2nd edition.

[51] See the definition of 'specification' in the 4th edition of *Jowitt's Dictionary of English Law.*

[52] *Palmer and McKenrick, Interests in Goods*, 2nd edition, 228.

uncontroversial observation. He goes on to say that placing icing on the cake would be an example of *accessio* since the icing serves only to improve the cake, rather than to alter its form. It may be that some judges would take a different view of this conclusion. If icing on top of a cake is merely an accessory chattel that accedes to the whole, one might wonder if the position is any different if the icing is structurally integral to the cake as a whole, as, for example, in the case of a Victoria sponge.

To illustrate the potential significance of the question, one can extend Professor Birks's example. Suppose that person A bakes two sponge cakes and person B takes those cakes and applies icing to them to turn them into a Victoria sponge. If the principle of *accessio* is at work then the Victoria sponge becomes the property of the baker. If the principle of *specificatio* is at work, the Victoria sponge becomes the property of the icer.

Trivial though this example is, it highlights the potential importance of the distinction between *accessio* and *specificatio*. In theory this is fertile ground for the perspective of individual judges, perhaps in the context of a somewhat more valuable chattel. In practice, however, disputes of this kind have been virtually non-existent.

The next question, then, is whether the principle of *specificatio* is actually a part of English law. As mentioned above, authorities that are capable of providing assistance in determining this question are very few.

The most useful authority is the Court of Appeal's decision in *Borden (UK) Ltd v Scottish Timber Products Ltd* [1981] Ch 25. In that case the plaintiff had supplied the defendant with resin for the manufacture of chipboard. The chipboard was then manufactured with the resin. When the defendant did not make payment for the resin the plaintiff brought a claim seeking to enforce a charge over the resin.

The Court of Appeal found that the act of using the resin in the manufacturing process meant that it ceased to exist and became one with the chipboard. In those circumstances it was impossible for the vendor to assert a charge over it. Bridge LJ held as follows at 41–42:

> Some extreme examples were canvassed in argument. Suppose cattle cake is sold to a farmer, or fuel to a steel manufacturer, in each case with a reservation of title clause, but on terms which permit the farmer to feed the cattle cake to his herd and the steelmaker to fuel his furnaces, before paying the purchase price. Mr. Mowbray concedes that in these cases the seller cannot trace into the cattle or the steel. He says that the difference is that the goods have been consumed. But once this concession is made, I find it impossible to draw an intelligible line of distinction in principle which would give the plaintiffs a right to trace the resin into the chipboard in the instant case. What has happened in the manufacturing process is much more akin to the process of consumption than to any simple process of admixture of goods. To put the point in another way, if the contribution that the resin has made to the chipboard gives rise to a tracing remedy, I find it difficult to see any good reason why, in the steelmaking example, the essential contribution made by the fuel to the steel manufacturing process should not do likewise.

> These are the principal considerations which have led me to the conclusion that the plaintiffs are not entitled to the tracing remedy which they claim. But I am fortified in that conclusion by the further consideration that if the remedy were available in such cases, a most intractable problem could, and in many cases would, arise in quantifying the proportion of the value of the manufactured product which the tracer could claim as properly attributable to his ingredient. In the instant case, a breakdown of the actual costings of chipboard over a period of seven months to July 29, 1977, has been agreed, attributing 17 per cent. of the total cost to the cost of resin, subject to a reservation with respect to wastage and over-usage. But one can well see that in many cases where the cost of materials and labour involved in a particular production process were constantly fluctuating, it might be quite impossible to assign a proportion of the total cost properly attributable to one particular ingredient with any certainty at all.[53]

It has to be said that Bridge LJ did not in his reasoning make any reference to specification (or to *accessio*). In forming his view he acknowledged (at 36) that there was virtually no authority directly on point to provide guidance. There was no indication that the Court of Appeal had its attention drawn to the various academic works that had at the time suggested the existence of *specificatio* within English law. In its reasoning, the Court of Appeal appealed to analogous principles of equity and tracing.

It is, therefore, probably going too far to vest *Borden* with the status of an authority confirming that the principle of *specificatio* applies to English law. It does seem, however, that in *Borden* the Court of Appeal arrived at a conclusion that is the same as the principle of *specificatio*, even if it did so without knowing of that principle and by way of analogy with other legal principles.

The question of the status of *specificatio* in English law was considered expressly by Moore-Bick J (as he then was) in *Glencore International AG v Metro Trading International* [2001] CLC 1732, albeit his conclusions were somewhat equivocal. At paragraphs 178–79 he said as follows:

> … Mr Smith's submission was essentially a simple one: if goods have ceased to exist because they have been turned into something completely new, the person who made that new thing automatically acquires title to it by virtue of the fact that he made it, is in possession of it and can exercise dominion over it. There is much to be said for that proposition and the doctrine of *specificatio* is well established in Scots law: see *International Banking Corporation v Ferguson, Shaw & Sons*. However, it is less clear that it forms part of English law, at any rate in its full rigour. The principle for which Mr Smith contended would, I think, offend many people's sense of justice in a case where the original materials belonged entirely to someone other than the maker of the new commodity, even if he were unaware of the fact; it is even more likely to do so in a case where the maker of the new commodity knew that he had no right to take and use them. It was for this reason that from early times English law allowed the original owner to recover his goods even though in one sense they had been turned into something new, for example, leather into shoes (Case of Leather YB 5 Hen VII fol. 15) or standing trees into sawn timber (Anon Moore 20, 72 ER 411) … The courts did

[53] See also Templeman LJ at 44.

> recognise, however, that there would come a point at which the original materials could not be sufficiently identified in the new article to permit recovery by the owner. None of the examples I have given are cases involving mixing, of course, but they do show that it is necessary to approach the proposition that a new commodity automatically belongs to its manufacturer with some care. The old authorities support the conclusion that merely working the original materials to produce a new article is not enough to vest title in the manufacturer if he is a wrongdoer; nor … is the mere addition of other materials belonging to the manufacturer himself.
>
> 179 The cases to which I have referred proceed on the principle that the owner of goods which are wrongfully taken and used to make a new commodity can recover them from the wrongdoer, even in their altered form, if he can identify them in that new commodity and show that it is wholly or substantially composed of them. In such cases the work carried out on the goods by the wrongdoer, as well as additions of small amounts of his own materials, are treated as attaching to the goods by accession. This appears most clearly from the judgment in Jones v De Marchant.[54] Under this approach title depends not on the creation of a new commodity, but on the ability of the original owner to identify his goods in the new commodity. Viewed in that way it is difficult to see why the owner of the leather should be able to recover the shoes, or the owner of the trees the boards, but the owner of the stolen ingredients should not be entitled to recover the cake into which they have wrongfully been made, even if their physical presence is less obvious. There are, of course, limits to the extent to which it is possible to identify the original materials in the new commodity, but in my view that is essentially a matter of fact in each case. The examples of the cattle cake and the fuel oil canvassed in Borden[55] can, I think, properly be treated as cases where the goods can no longer be regarded as remaining in existence as a substantial component of the product with the result that property in them must be considered to have passed to the farmer or the steelmaker, as the case may be, by accession. Historically English law has not considered that a wrongdoer who has improved the goods by his labour or by providing additional materials of a relatively minor nature, such as the thread used to turn leather into shoes, should be entitled to property in the new commodity or compensation for his labour or materials. The position would probably be different, however, if the new commodity substantially represented work or materials provided by the wrongdoer.

It appears to follow from the above that certain principles can cautiously be ventured with respect to the application of *specificatio* in English law.

1. There is no basis for the view that *specificatio* applies to English law in the full way in which it appears to apply, for example, to Scots law.

[54] A Commonwealth case in which four beaver skins belonging to a wife were combined with 18 beaver skins belonging to the husband and made (by the husband) into a coat for his mistress.

[55] Ie circumstances in which cattle cake is fed to cows or fuel is used in production of steel, such that the cattle cake and the fuel are consumed – see 41 of *Borden*. Moore-Bick, J's application of the principle of accession in this context is hard to argue with. The Court of Appeal in *Borden* did not have that principle drawn to its attention and did not refer to it, but surely Moore-Bick, J is right to infer that it was in the Court of Appeal's mind or would have been applied had it been drawn to their attention.

2. Nevertheless, English courts do have some sympathy for *specificatio* and appear willing to apply it in appropriate circumstances.
3. In particular, there does appear to come point where a sufficient amount of work has been done and/or a sufficient amount of additional materials have been provided by the manufacturer that title to the newly manufactured commodity does pass to the manufacturer.
4. Whether that happens is a question of fact for any given case. It may be a permissible inference, however, that the nature and extent of wrongdoing on the part of the manufacturer will be taken into account.

Mixtures

'Mixtures' are combinations of chattels that do not lead to the manufacture of a new chattel (as is dealt with by *specificatio*), nor is the combination one in which one of the chattels is so much an accessory that it merely becomes part of the principal chattel (as is dealt with by *accessio*). 'Mixtures' is therefore a term that can be applied to any other combination of chattels leading to some form of co-mingling.

Again the point must be stressed that there is substantial scope for argument over whether a given combination gives rise to a mixture or an *accessio* or a *specificatio*. That is ultimately a dispute that will turn on the facts of a given case.

As with *accessio* and *specificatio*, the current English law is best understood with an awareness of the Roman background. In particular, Roman law recognised two different kinds of mixtures, which are generally referred to in modern English as 'granular' and 'fluid' mixtures.

As the names may suggest, granular mixtures are those mixtures in which the component parts keep their physical integrity, such that as a matter of theory (no matter how difficult in practice) they could be separated out from each other. Grain is an obvious example of such a mixture, although the component parts could be any chattels, regardless of size.

A fluid mixture is a mixture in which the component parts lose their identity and become co-mingled in a way that makes them impossible to extract. As well as applying to fluids that remain fluid, the concept of a fluid mixture was extended to molten metals that solidified.

The Roman law is set out in Justinian's Institutes 2.1.27–28:[56]

> If materials owned by two people are deliberately blended together, the resultant mass becomes the common property of both. Examples are where two people blend together their wine or melt together their ingots of silver or gold. The same applies where the materials are different, and their fusion produces a new substance, for

[56] With gratitude to Professor Birks's analysis in chapter 9 of *Palmer and McKenrick, Interests in Goods*, 2nd edition.

> instance mead from wine and honey, or electrum from gold and silver. Even if the blend occurs by chance and not by design, the same rule applies where materials are different and when they are the same. But suppose that corn owned by Titius is mixed with yours. If you both wanted the mixing done, you own the mass in common because every particle you each owned, i.e. every grain of corn, is by your agreement made common to you both. But if the mixture happens accidentally or is done by Titius against your will, the whole is not held in common, because the individual particles retain their own identity. The corn is not made common property here any more than flocks become common if the animals get mixed up. If one of you keeps the whole lot, a real action lies for the quantity of the other's individual contribution. The judge has power to allow for the quality of each contribution in assessing his award.

Thus the philosophy of the Roman system was that, in the case of granular mixtures, the retention of the integrity of the component parts of the mixture meant that there was no reason to conclude that any change in ownership had taken place. The only issue to resolve was the practical question of how to divide the mixture. By contrast, in the case of a fluid mixture there had been what has been described as an 'absolute interpenetration of their substance',[57] with the consequence that the whole passes into joint ownership.

Of course, with the benefit of a modern understanding of atomic activity, the distinction between granular and fluid mixtures can be said to be an artificial one. Nevertheless, it retains a certain intuitive appeal.

Granular Mixtures by Agreement in English Law

In *Re Stapylton Fletcher Ltd* [1994] 1 WLR 1181 the court considered a set of circumstances in which a wine merchant had become insolvent. While it was in business, the wine merchant both sold wine and also stored it pending demand from its customers. It had two physical warehouses, one (in essence) being its general stores (held in bond) and one being its client stores.

When a client purchased a case of wine, it was the merchant's practice to move the case from its general stores and place it in its client stores. The client stores therefore contained entirely wine that was the property of the clients. Detailed records were kept of which client was entitled to what wine from the client store, but the individual cases were not labelled with the name of a particular client. Every time a client required delivery of a case of wine, it was the merchant's practice to select the most conveniently accessible case of wine of the relevant type from the client stores and dispatch it. In other words, the case dispatched to the client was not necessarily the same physical case that was transferred into the client stores following order, although it was of the same type. This aspect of

[57] ibid.

the merchant's practice was known about and accepted by the clients. The client stores thus comprised a granular mixture created by consent.

Paul Baker QC, sitting as a High Court judge, found that the various clients were tenants in common of the wine in the client stores. This therefore confirms that the Justinian position as to granular mixtures by consent is true in English law: the original owners of the component chattels of such a mixture own the mixture as tenants in common.

It should perhaps be noted in passing that it was pivotal to Mr Barker QC's reasoning that there was the explicit appropriation of wine and its relocation from one store to the other when purchased by a client. This is the reason why *Re Stapylton* could be decided as it was. The position contrasts with the position in cases such as *Re Goldcorp Exchange Ltd* [1995] 1 AC 74 (PC), in which there was no clear appropriation of a particular share of a whole. In that case the court found that investors in gold, who had been given a certificate of entitlement to a certain amount of a share in gold but not an actual allocation of that gold, had no proprietary interest in the share. The point for present purposes is that nothing in *Re Goldcorp* undermines the finding as to tenancy in common in granular mixtures deriving from *Re Stapylton*.

An example of the law in action can be found in *Mercer v Craven Grain* [1994] CLC 328. In that case two owners of grain combined their grain in a hopper belonging to a third-party storage society. The terms of that storage were that the third party was permitted to deal with the grain on terms that it had to replace the grain with grain of the same kind and in the same quantity. The storage society contended that the grain owners had lost title in the grain by virtue of the fact that it had been not only mixed, but also removed and replaced and was therefore indistinguishable from the other grain. The House of Lords did not accept this analysis. Per Lord Templeman at 329:

> The storage society sought to defend the action on the grounds that despite cl. 8 of the storage agreement the plaintiffs lost title to their wheat. The plaintiffs' wheat was lawfully mixed with and became indistinguishable from wheat contributed by other persons. Wheat which included or may have included the whole or an unascertainable part of the plaintiffs' wheat was withdrawn from the mix from time to time. Therefore, it is said, by July 1991 the plaintiffs could not prove title to any wheat. Lord Mustill pointed out in the course of the argument that the storage society were bailees and could not question the title of their bailor. In any event, title to the wheat lawfully mixed could not be acquired by the storage society which by no stretch of the imagination had any right thereto. The title must have remained in the growers from time to time interested in the mix in proportion to their respective tonnages. The storage society was guilty of conversion if it allowed the mix to be so depleted by withdrawals that the balance remaining was not sufficient to satisfy the demands of the plaintiffs.

Mercer may also be authority for the proposition that a granular mixture which cannot, as a matter of practicality, be divided so as to return its components to their pre-mixture owners is to be treated as co-owned by the mixers. If that principle is correct, it represents a deviation from the Roman law, which, as discussed above, saw no need to recognise a change in ownership status as a result of a granular mixture, no matter how impossible it was to undo in practice.

Although *Mercer* does not grapple with this point in any detail, there are older authorities that tend to suggest the English law does recognise co-ownership. *Spence v Union Marine Insurance Company Ltd* (1868) LR 3 CP 427 was a case involving a ship carrying about 2,500 bales of cotton, all of which were marked for their intended recipients. Forty-three of those bales were marked as intended for the claimant.

The ship ran aground off Key West in Florida and 231 bales were lost altogether or were so badly damaged that they had to be sold at Key West. The remainder were placed on a chartered vessel and shipped to Liverpool for their intended consignees. Of the bales that arrived at Liverpool, the intended consignees of 641 of them were identifiable and so were sent to those consignees, albeit in a somewhat damaged state. Two of those identified bales went to the claimant. The remaining 1,645 bales that arrived at Liverpool could not be identified and were sold.

Due to a change in the price of cotton, it was financially advantageous for the claimant to claim for a dead loss of 41 bales from its insurer (the defendant) and so that is what it did. The defendant successfully maintained that the claimant could recover only its proportionate share of the value of the anonymous bales – a conclusion that proceeded on the basis that the claimant had co-ownership of the granular mixture in proportion to the amount it put in.

Bovill CJ applied two cases dealing with the mixture of fluids to the plainly granular mixture of the bales on board the ship. He appeared to reason that, where it was impracticable to reconstitute the granular components of the mixture to their original owners, the law imposed co-ownership in shares according to what was originally introduced to the mixture. In other words, he applied the established principles of fluid mixtures to granular mixtures that could not practically be unwound. At 438–39 he reasoned as follows:

> We need not discuss the distinction sometimes made between commixtio and confusion [ie granular and fluid mixtures], apparently upon the ground that it is possible to separate the individual solid particles, but not the liquid; because, in cases like the present, it is impracticable, and for all business purposes therefore impossible, to distinguish the particles, in respect of ownership.
>
> ...
>
> We are thus, by authorities in our own law, by the reason of the thing, and by the concurrence of foreign writers, justified in adopting the conclusion that, by our own law, the property in the cotton of which the marks were obliterated did not cease to belong the respective owners; and that, by the mixture of the bales, and their becoming undistinguishable by reason of the action of the sea, and without the fault of the respective owners, these parties became tenants in common of the cotton, in proportion to their respective interests. This result would follow only in those cases where,

> after the adoption of all reasonable means and exertions to identify or separate the goods, it was found impracticable to do so.
>
> We cannot assume that the whole of the plaintiffs' forty-one bales were amongst those that were destroyed, any more than we can assume that they all formed part of the 1645 which were brought home; and we see no means of determining the extent of the interest of the several owners, except by adopting a principle of proportion, and which would, we think, be equally applicable in determining the plaintiffs' portion of the 231 bales that were totally lost as of the 1645 which arrived in this country, though without the marks.

It therefore appears that the proper analysis of English law is that it differs from Roman law (at least Justinian law) in that co-ownership in proportion is imposed on a granular mixture where it is impractical to unwind the mixture and return the components to their original owners. The above interpretation of *Spence* seemed to receive approval by Lord Sumner in *Sinclair v Brougham* [1914] AC 398 at 459.

Fluid Mixtures in English Law

It is now tolerably clear that English law follows Roman law so far as fluid mixtures are concerned. That matter was addressed in *Indian Oil Corporation v Greenstone Shipping Company SA, The Ypatianna* [1988] QB 345. Before turning to an analysis of that case, it is helpful first to highlight Blackstone's description of the English law of fluid mixtures:[58]

> BUT in the case of confusion of goods, where those of two persons are so intermixed, that the several portions can be no longer distinguished, the English law partly agrees with, and partly differs from, the civil. If the intermixture be by consent, I apprehend that in both laws the proprietors have an interest in common, in proportion to their respective shares. But, if one willfully intermixes his money, corn, or hay, with that of another man, without his approbation or knowledge, or casts gold in like manner into another's melting-pot or crucible, the civil law, though it gives the sole property of the whole to him who has not interfered in the mixture, yet allows a satisfaction to the other for what he has so improvidently lost. But our law, to guard against fraud, allows no remedy in such a case; but gives the entire property, without any account, to him, whose original dominion is invaded, and endeavoured to be rendered uncertain, without his own consent.

Thus Blackstone identified the existence of a penal rule in which, where a person mixes another's property with his own dishonestly, the mixture belongs entirely to the person whose property was wrongly appropriated for the mixture. Although Blackstone refers to fraud, it is apparent that this rule has a wider application than merely fraud, and in fact had been held to be available in

[58] Book 2, 404.

various circumstances where a party wrongfully caused the mixture of chattels (albeit seemingly not where that mixture was accidental).[59]

In *The Ypatianna* the facts concerned an owner of a vessel that was chartered to take a cargo of crude oil from Russia to India. The claimant had loaded the vessel with oil, which had wrongfully been mixed with oil belonging to the vessel owner. The claimant therefore asserted ownership to the whole amount of the oil on the ship. In other words, the claimant was attempting to assert the penal rule identified by Blackstone.

Staughton J did not allow the penal rule to be imposed. At 368–69 he reasoned as follows:

> Two points of significance in my view emerge from the authorities. First, in some cases a decision had to be made 'not upon the notion, that strict justice was done, but upon this; that it was the only justice, that could be done,' *per* Lord Eldon L.C. in Lupton v. White, 15 Ves. Jun. 432, 440. Or as Lord Moulton put it, such cases 'have been little more than instances of cutting the Gordian knot – reasonable adjustments of the rights of the parties in cases where complete justice was **369* impracticable of attainment,' in Sandeman & Sons v. Tyzack and Branfoot Steamship Co. Ltd. [1913] A.C. 680, 695. Secondly, if the wrongdoer has destroyed or impaired the evidence by which the innocent party could show how much he has lost, the wrongdoer must suffer from the resulting uncertainty. Thus the jury in Armory v. Delamirie, 1 Str. 505 were directed by Pratt C.J. to award the plaintiff the value of the finest jewel which the socket would hold, not the finest jewel that had ever been known.
>
> The combined effect of those principles would justify and require that where it is totally unknown how much of the innocent party's goods went into the mixture, the whole should belong to him. But I do not see that they require or justify the same result where it is known how much was contributed by the innocent party, or even what the maximum quantity is that he can have contributed, being something less than the whole. That would not be the only justice that could be done; it would be injustice.
>
> As for the reason given by *Blackstone* – 'to guard against fraud – in my opinion that will be sufficiently achieved if the principle in Armory v. Delamirie, 1 Str. 505 is followed. I do not see that it is the function of civil justice to punish or discourage crime by awarding the victim more than he has lost, unless it be in the special case of an award of exemplary damages.

Thus the supposed penal rule exists only to resolve cases of the greatest evidential difficulty (and in fact the rule has no deliberate penal consequences). The position is simply described at page 370 of the judgment as follows:

> [W]here B wrongfully mixes the goods of A with goods of his own, which are substantially of the same nature and quality, and they cannot in practice be separated, the mixture is held in common and A is entitled to receive out of it a quantity equal to that of his goods which went into the mixture, any doubt as to that quantity

[59] See, for example, *Spence v Union Marine Insurance Co Ltd* (1868) LR 3 CP 427.

> being resolved in favour of A. He is also entitled to claim damages from B in respect of any loss he may have suffered, in respect of quality or otherwise, by reason of the admixture.

Thus, the rule as stated in its refined form deals with circumstances in which a fluid mixture comes into being as a result of the wrongdoing of one party. This leaves the question of what happens when a mixture comes into being by accident, or as a result of an agreement between the parties.

As to these circumstances, it is tolerably clear that an accidental mixture of chattels will lead to the mixture being co-owned as tenants in common by the original owners in shares equal to their contributions.[60] It seems extremely likely that the same position prevails where fluid mixtures are created by agreement; certainly that was Blackstone's position and there is no apparent reason to deviate from that (unless of course the parties have expressly agreed to hold the mixture in some other shares).

Thus the difference between ownership of a mixture where a mixture is created wrongfully and where it is created accidentally or by agreement is only a rule of evidence. That is to say the rule is simply that any doubt as to the proper shares in which the mixture is held is resolved in favour of the wronged party. Even though that is a rule of evidence only, it has the potential to have a profoundly significant impact.

This description of the rules of fluid mixtures leaves unresolved the position where there is a fluid mixture of two components that differ considerably in their value. In those circumstances, do the parties hold the resultant mixture in shares reflecting their input as to volume or value? There is no answer to that question in the English authorities but it is submitted that it must be the value rather than the volume that is the crucial factor. Certainly that is the view of Professor Birks,[61] who provides various support for the proposition from the civil tradition.

Limits of Co-ownership as a Way of Dealing with Mixtures

It is worth stating at this stage that, as discussed in greater detail above, a co-owner of chattels does have only restricted rights as against his co-owner. Unlike a co-owner of real property, a co-owner of personal property is not entitled as of right to any order for sale. Co-owners can by agreement partition their co-owned chattels, or a co-owner of more than 50 per cent can avail himself of the jurisdiction under s 188 Law of Property Act 1925 to force a petition. Other than those possibilities, however, a co-owner of a mixture risks being stuck with a joint tenancy that severely circumscribes how he can deal with his property.

[60] ibid 437.
[61] *Palmer and McKendrick, Interests in Goods*, 2nd edition, 248.

Thus in *Gill and Duffus (Liverpool) Ltd v Scruttons Ltd* [1953] 1 WLR 1407 bags of chestnuts burst in a ship's hold resulting in a mixture that all counsel at trial conceded (perhaps wrongly) was held in common between the parties. The defendant was the master porter, who had attempted a division of the mixed chestnuts to give effect to the parties' shares. The defendant was ultimately found liable for having failed to treat the mixers fairly because the master porter had no right to effect a partition of the mixture. Rather his obligation was to deliver the entire mixture to any co-owner who asked for it, consistent with the entitlements of a tenant in common of real property.

Divisions

The term 'division' is used to mean the opposite of a combination – that is to say a situation in which a single chattel is divided into parts, perhaps for the sale or onward transmission of one of the parts.

In many situations, this is a straightforward and uncontroversial process. When an apple is picked from a tree, or a portion of some store of liquid is decanted, the previous single entity has become two, and a new piece of personal property has come into being. This must be so even where a chattel is reduced to component parts that obviously belong together. If a vase is broken into a thousand fragments, it must be right that where there was once a single chattel there are now a thousand. Although there does not appear to be any authority for that proposition, it follows necessarily from the surely self-evident fact that, were the owner of one of those fragments to convey ownership of it to another person, the law would recognise that conveyance.

The situation is somewhat more difficult when considering proprietary rights in an unascertained part of a whole.

The first concept to introduce is that of *emptio generis*, which is to say a purchase by description only. In such circumstances no property right will be created. For example, in *Re Goldcorp Exchange Ltd* [1995] 1 AC 74 (PC) a purchaser contracted to purchase gold by description. Although a 'certificate of ownership' was provided to the purchaser, the purchased gold was not referable to any specific gold, or to a part of any specific stock of gold. Lord Mustill reasoned as follows at 89–90:

> It is common ground that the contracts in question were for the sale of unascertained goods. For present purposes, two species of unascertained goods may be distinguished. First, there are 'generic goods.' These are sold on terms which preserve the seller's freedom to decide for himself how and from what source he will obtain goods answering the contractual description. Secondly, there are 'goods sold ex-bulk.' By this expression their Lordships denote goods which are by express stipulation to be supplied from a fixed and a pre-determined source, from within which the seller may make his own choice (unless the contract requires it to be made in some other way)

> but outside which he may not go. For example, 'I sell you 60 of the 100 sheep now on my farm.'
>
> Approaching these situations a priori common sense dictates that the buyer cannot acquire title until it is known to what goods the title relates.

Thus no proprietary right will be created in circumstances where, for example, there is a contract for the sale of 'a horse'. No matter how many horses the vendor may own, nothing in the contract requires him to dispose of one of his present horses in order to satisfy his obligation under the contract.

The next question is to ascertain the position where a portion of a whole (or indeed a granular mixture as per Lord Mustill's example of sheep) is conveyed, without in some way specifying the precise part (or components of the mixture) that is to be conveyed.

In the case of a granular mixture, the position is, as discussed above in the context of *Re Stapylton*, that a person is conveyed a common ownership in the granular mixture in the appropriate share.

What, then, is the position where a portion of a single chattel is conveyed (for example, '10 gallons of a hogshead of wine')?

A substantial part of the answer is provided at ss 20A and 20B Sale of Goods Act 1979. Those provisions relate to the sale of part of a bulk (so a whole or mixture). Once a purchaser has made payment, s 20A operates to convey to him co-ownership in the bulk. Section 20B operates to circumscribe the effect of that co-ownership such that it does not operate as harshly on the vendor as would co-ownership subject to common law principles. For example, s 20B(1) provides that a co-owner created under s 20A cannot object to his co-owner dealing with parts of the bulk to the extent it does not impinge on his proportionate share.

The obvious question remaining is how the modern law deals with dispositions of part of a bulk that do not fall within the ambit of the Sale of Goods Act (for example gifts). The answer to that question is not entirely clear but there is a cautious inference to be drawn that the law would approach those situations in a way analogous to the regime in ss 20A and 20B Sale of Goods Act.

Authority for that inference is *Hunter v Moss* [1994] 1 WLR 452. In that case the court considered a declaration of trust in respect of 5 per cent of the settlor's shares in a company (shares being of course personal property), where the precise shares were not specified. The court held that, since the shares were indistinguishable from each other, it would be possible to satisfy the purpose of the trust without the need for the settlor to have determined precisely which shares should be held on trust.

Cases like *Hunter* and *Stapylton* establish that the courts wish to confer property rights in circumstances where a portion of a mixture has purportedly been conveyed. It is therefore to be inferred that the same approach would be adopted in the case of a portion of a whole.

2

Obtaining and Keeping Title to Property that is Bona Vacantia

PROPERTY THAT IS 'bona vacantia' is generally said to be property that has no owner. On reflection, this formula does pose problems. For example, does the very term 'property' imply an owner? Another word that has been used[1] is 'asset', but again, does not the word 'asset' imply an owner, or at least a value?

There is little of practical or even academic interest to be gained from wrangling of this kind. It is submitted that something that is bona vacantia is something that either is property or is capable of being reduced to property,[2] but at the present time has no owner. The term 'bona vacantia property' is used to describe things of this nature.

There is also a narrower sense in which the term 'bona vacantia' is used. That narrower sense is to refer to certain property that reverts to the ownership of the Crown in particular situations. As will become apparent, however, not all bona vacantia property belongs to the Crown.

It is important to bear in mind as a starting principle that title in a thing that is bona vacantia can, except insofar as it is owned by the Crown by prerogative, be acquired by a finder (*The Lusitania* [1986] QB 384). In practice it is rare for title to be acquired in this way because most property worth owning is either owned or, as we shall see, is passed by some operation of law into the ownership of the Crown or some other person.

ANIMALS

Animals present a particular complication. It is really only in the case of certain animals that one can say that there exist things that cannot be reduced to

[1] For example, by the authors of *Jowitt's Dictionary of English Law*, 4th edition.

[2] As to which the law likely remains as (presumably correctly) stated on page 427 of the 5th edition of *Crossley Vaines on Personal Property*: 'All material things affected by the hand of man are capable of ownership in English law and the *res nullius* in the sense of a chattel or premises incapable of acquisition does not exist; even water, gas, electricity and the like, can be reduced to ownership; we have no awful list, as the Romans had, in respect of *res sacrae*, *sanctae* and *religiosae* ... It is only in respect of wild animals that practical problems arise, for almost every other thing has at some time been the subject of ownership ...'.

property, or at least can only be reduced to property to a certain extent and by certain means.

Domestic Animals

There is no real difficulty with domestic animals. It has always been uncontroversial that domestic animals are capable of being owned in the same way as other chattels. In *Hamps v Darby* [1948] 2 KB 311 at 320–21 Evershed LJ approved Blackstone's categorisation of such animals: 'Our law apprehends the most obvious distinction to be between such animals as we generally see tame and are, therefore, seldom, if ever, found wandering at large …'.

As discussed above, the general position is that the offspring of a domestic animal belongs to the owner of the female parent.[3] This rule does not hold good when the female parent is in the possession (one may infer the lawful possession only) of a person other than the owner. Thus, where a person leases animals, the offspring of such animals belong to the lessee, unless the lease specifies to the contrary.[4]

Wild Animals

The default position in respect of wild animals, by contrast, is that they are owned by nobody (with the potential exception of 'royal' animals discussed below).

A form of proprietary entitlement can be asserted over wild animals, however. In *Hamps* the court approved Blackstone's analysis as follows:

> [I]t may happen that [wild animals] shall be sometimes tamed and confined by the art and industry of man. Such as are deer in a park, hares or rabbits in an enclosed warren, doves in a dovehouse, pheasants or partridges in a mew, hawks that are fed and commanded by their owner, and fish in a private pond or in trunks. These are no longer the property of a man than while they continue in his keeping or actual possession; but if at any time they regain their natural liberty his property instantly ceases, unless they have animum revertendi, which is only to be known by their usual custom of returning. … The law, therefore, extends this position farther than the mere manual occupation; for my tame hawk that is pursuing his quarry in my presence, though he is at liberty to go where he pleases, he is nevertheless my property; for he hath animum revertendi. So are my pigeons, that are flying at a distance from their home (especially those of the carrier kind) and likewise the deer that is chased out of my park or forest and is instantly pursued by the keeper or forester; all which remain still in my possession and I still preserve my qualified property in them, but

[3] See in addition to the matters discussed above the *Case of Swans* (1591) 7 Coke Reports 15b.
[4] *Tucker v Farm and General Investment Trust Ltd* [1966] 2 All ER 508.

> if they stray without my knowledge and do not return in the usual manner it is then lawful for any stranger to take them.

Then again a little later:

> In all these creatures reclaimed from the wildness of their nature the property is not absolute but defeasible; a property that may be destroyed if they resume their ancient wildness and are found at large. For if the pheasants escape from the mew, or the fishes from the trunk, and are seen wandering at large in their proper element, they become feræ naturæ again and are free and open to the first occupant that has ability to seize them. But while they thus continue my qualified or defeasible property they are as much under the protection of the law as if they were absolutely and indefeasibly mine: and an action will lie against any man that detains them from me or unlawfully destroys them.

Thus, it is possible to obtain a sort of ownership over wild animals by means of taming them, trapping them or containing them.[5] There is clearly ample scope for dispute and debate over whether a given animal has been tamed, contained or trapped, but ultimately that will be a matter for the facts of an individual case. For example, it seems unlikely to be controversial that a fish becomes the property of the person who catches it when it is caught. In *Hamp* itself the court was concerned with carrier pigeons, which were shot by a farmer defending his crop. The court found that the carrier pigeons were indeed the property of their keeper.

An extension to this rule arises in circumstances where the animal in question is wild but is found or killed on someone else's land. In *Blades v Higgs* (1865) 144 ER 1087 a poacher had entered onto the land of the Marquis of Exeter and killed 90 rabbits. The rabbits were taken from the land and sold to the plaintiff, who was a game dealer. The Marquis's servants took possession of the rabbits from the claimant when they were being delivered to him. The action was a dispute over the true ownership of the rabbits.

The court held that the rabbits belonged to the Marquis. The rationale was that, where an animal is killed by a trespasser, the ownership of the dead animal vests in the owner of the land. The House of Lords stated as follows:

> No property exists in wild and unreclaimed animals so long as they remain in a state of nature: but, when killed or reclaimed by the owner of the land on which they are found, or by his authority, they become at once his property absolutely when they are killed, and in a qualified manner when they are reclaimed. – Game found and killed by a trespasser under such circumstances as that it would be the property of the owner of the soil, or of the owner of the right of free-warren, if it had been found and killed by such owner instead of by the trespasser, in law becomes the absolute property of the owner of the soil or privilege immediately on its being so caught and killed by the trespasser.

[5] Or it seems by killing them – see below.

Another matter emerging from Blackstone's analysis quoted in *Hamp* is that the property created by owning, trapping or containing animals is qualified. The important qualification is that the property rights cease as and when the animal returns to its wild state. Again, one can see that it is highly likely that there would be a dispute as to exactly when this happened, but a principles-based approach is difficult to extrapolate from the authorities; in all likelihood it is a matter of fact for each case. In *Kearry v Pattinson* [1939] 1 All ER 65 the Court of Appeal considered circumstances in which a beekeeper's bees had swarmed onto his neighbour's land. The Court of Appeal's conclusion was that property in the bees had at one time belonged to the beekeeper but that property was lost at the point when the bees, having swarmed, left his land (thereby preventing further lawful pursuit). Per Slesser LJ at 479:

> Thus a qualified property may be had in bees in consideration of the property whereon they are found ... but there is no right to pursue a swarm of bees on to another man's land and such pursuit would amount to a trespass. I cannot help thinking that the power to pursue them which constitutes them chattels referred to in the old books means and can only mean that they may still be so regarded when the swarm is in such a place that their owner has still in law the right to pursue them in order to recapture them. They are ferae naturae before being hived, but they may be taken into the disposition of the owner per industriam by hiving and so become his property: see Pufendorf De Jure Naturae et Gentium, Book IV., ch. 6, s. 5, but may remain his property while they are swarming so long as they are in his sight and he has lawful power easily to pursue them.

The position of royal animals is particularly interesting. It is commonly said that all swans are owned by the Crown. This principle appears to be established by the *Case of Swans* (1591) 7 Coke Reports 15b (albeit upholding an ancient principle). Sir Edward Coke reasoned as follows:

> [A]ll white swans not marked, which having gained their natural liberty, and are swimming in an open and common river, might be seised to the King's use by his prerogative ... as a swan is a Royal fowl; and all those, the property whereof is not known, do belong to the King by his prerogative: and so whales and sturgeons are Royal fish, and belong to the King by his prerogative. And there hath been an ancient officer of the King's, called magister deductus cignorum, which continues to this day.[6] But it was resolved also, that the subject might have property in white swans not marked, as some may have swans not marked in his private waters, the property of which belongs to him, and not to the King; and if they escape out of his private waters into an open and common river, he may bring them back and take them again.

Thus it does not appear that the *Case of Swans* establishes the Crown's ownership of all swans, but rather only swans swimming in a common river or water; it was still possible for unmarked swans to be owned privately on private land.

[6] The ongoing annual practice of 'swan upping' on the Thames no doubt descends directly from the role of this officer and the significance of marking swans as explained in this dicta of Coke's.

Section 9 Wildlife and Countryside Act 1981 made the possession of and trade in swans (along with a great many other animals) a criminal offence. There is no definition of 'possession' under the statute, however, and it is not entirely clear that the combined effect of the *Case of Swans* and the Wildlife and Countryside Act 1981 is to vest all ownership of swans in the Crown. If a cygnet is born on private land, for example, and is contained there by the landowner (by gentle means of taming it rather than anything that might amount to 'possession'), it is far from clear that it would be the property of the Crown.

Also striking in the extract from Coke's judgment quoted above is the fact that sturgeon and whales are 'royal fish'. This is a rather less well-known aspect of the Crown's property in wild animals than the ownership of swans. It appears that the Crown's ownership of sturgeon and whales began with a statute called *De prærogativa regis* in the reign of Edward II. Blackstone explains the status of royal fish as being attributable to their 'superior excellence'.[7] Other commentators have named dolphin and porpoise as royal fish too (the latter at least having the support of the House of Lords in *Neill v Duke of Devonshire* (1882) 8 App Cas 135). The salmon, by contrast, although seemingly a royal fish in Scotland, and although a 'great fish' (Neill) is not a 'royal fish'.

Section 1 of the Wild Creatures and Forest Laws Act 1971 revokes the Crown's prerogative rights in wild animals, but expressly carves out prerogative rights in swans and royal fish. Thus there is no doubt that the Crown's ownership of these creatures remains good law.

The Receiver of Wreck appears to be empowered to process the capture of royal fish. In 2004 a fisherman caught a sturgeon in Swansea Bay and sold it in Plymouth. This created legal difficulties for him. Sections of the media reported the matter on the basis that he had infringed an ancient obligation to offer the sturgeon to the Queen prior to disposing of it himself (ie had infringed the Crown's ownership rights in royal fish). It is perhaps more likely that the unlucky fisherman's real difficulties related to the various offences committed by someone who kills and sells a sturgeon under the Wildlife and Countryside Act 1981.

PLANTS, NATURAL FEATURES AND THINGS ON LAND

The ownership of plants, natural features and things connected to land is relatively straightforward. So long as they are connected to the land they form part of the real estate and are not personal property.

As is well known, a chattel can be converted into a part of the real estate so long as there is a sufficient connection between the chattel and the real estate.

[7] Book 1, Chapter 8.

The question of whether an item has become sufficiently connected to become part of the real estate is one that depends on the degree of annexation and the purpose of annexation. Those subjects are dealt with in detail in specialist real estate works[8] and so will not be dealt with here.

It is perhaps worth noting in passing, however, that when a chattel becomes part of the real estate by sufficient annexation, the title to the chattel is extinguished and ownership passes to the owner of the real estate. This is so even where the chattels are affixed to the land by someone who does not have title to the chattels, and against the title holder's will. Per the Earl of Halsbury LC at 475 of *Reynolds v Ashby & Son* [1904] AC 466:

> The title to chattels may clearly be lost by being affixed to real property by a person who is not the owner of the chattels ... In effect, Holdway was authorized by the appellant to convert the chattels into fixtures, subject to the right of the appellant to enter and retake them if Holdway did not pay for them. But, apart from this knowledge and authority, the result would be the same, although not so obvious.

Of course, an item can be severed from land and in doing so a new chattel comes into being. It must be the case that such severance can occur naturally as well as by design. For example, an apple tree is obviously connected with the land in a sufficient way to constitute a part of it. When an apple falls from the tree, however, the apple on the ground clearly does not have that level of connection since it can simply be picked up off the ground. The apple must, therefore, be a piece of personal property – it can no longer be considered a part of the real estate.

The only philosophically sound analysis is that a chattel has come into being by operation of nature just as it would have done by man's agency if the apple was plucked.

Since the chattel severed from the land, by nature or by design, emerges from the real estate, the new chattel is naturally the property of the owner of the real estate. This must be so even where a chattel belonging to a third party has been attached to the real estate against the owner's will. Thus, if A steals a keystone from B and builds it into a house on C's land, by virtue of its attachment and the principle in *Reynolds* described above, that keystone will become part of C's real estate. If the house is then dismantled, the keystone will become personalty again, but having emerged from the real estate it will now belong to the owner of the real estate. The unfortunate original owner of the keystone would have to content himself with a remedy in damages against A.

The extent of a landowner's rights to personalty is highlighted by *Elwes v Brigg Gas Co* (1886) 22 Ch D 562. In that case land was demised to a gas

[8] See for example *Megarry and Wade, The Law of Real Property*, 8th edition, paragraph 23-005 onwards.

company and a prehistoric boat (being indisputably an item of personalty) was found buried beneath the soil. The boat was found to be the property not of the tenant finder, but of the land owner. Thus it is clear that undiscovered chattels belong to the owner of the land on which they are discovered. This is subject to the Crown's prerogative powers to reclaim treasure, as discussed further below.

An interesting feature of *Elwes* is that Chitty J found (at 566) that the boat had been abandoned by its original prehistoric owners. One must wonder whether it was in reality possible to make that finding on the facts. If that was not a safe finding, it opens the question of whether the boat ought in principle to have been found to be the property of its original owner, and being as that owner and his successors could not be identified, should have been held as bona vacantia for the Crown.

HUMAN TISSUE

For almost the entirety of English legal history, the question of property in human tissue has been confined to the very margins of legal activity. Only occasional, and often rather gruesome, cases had any cause to grapple with the issue. In recent decades, of course, the question has become of immense importance with the rise of *in vitro* fertilisation, organ transplants and other medical advancements.

It is beyond the scope of this general work on personal property to attempt a survey of the law as it governs these new and developing medical fields, much of which is regulated by specialist statute. A general sense of the principles of the common law as regards human tissue may be of interest, however.

Living Beings

At one time it was possible for living beings to be reduced to property at English law. The most obvious example is slavery, and unsettling authorities do indeed exist to support the proposition that slaves are personal property like any other. Thus, for example, in *Chambers v Warkhouse* (1692) 3 Lev 336: 'trover [a cause of action to protect goods] lies of musk-cats and of monkies, because they are merchandize; and for the same reason it has been adjudged, that trover lies of negroes'. Similarly in *Gregson v Gilbert* (1783) 3 Doug 232: 'It has been decided, whether wisely or unwisely is not now the question, that a portion of our fellow-creatures may become the subject of property'. Of course, early nineteenth-century legislation abolished slavery and thereafter there does not appear to be any suggestion it is possible to reduce living humans to personal property.

It is often said that women were at one time the chattels of their husbands. This is not quite a correct statement, however. The prevailing position appears to have been that the woman's separate legal identity was extinguished and merged with her husband's upon marriage. Baroness Hale described the position in *Jones v Garnett (Inspector of Taxes)* [2007] 1 WLR 2030 as follows:

> My Lords, income tax was invented only decades after Blackstone had given his classic definition of the relationship between husband and wife at common law (Blackstone's Commentaries (1765), Book 1, p 442):
>
> 'By marriage, the husband and wife are one person in law: that is, the very being or legal existence of the woman is suspended during the marriage, or at least is incorporated and consolidated into that of her husband: under whose wing, protection, and cover, she performs everything; and is therefore called in our law-French a *feme-covert* ...'
>
> At that date, a husband was absolutely entitled to his wife's earnings [and it might be added to all personal property]. He was not entitled to the income from property which had been settled to her separate use.'.

There is a clear forensic distinction between this arrangement, unpalatable though it appears to modern eyes, and a husband's actual ownership of his wife in the way a person at one time owned slaves. Thus in *Gregson* the court was concerned with an action for compensation as a result of slaves being thrown overboard a ship. The matter was approached in the same way as it would have been had corn or any other cargo of personalty been thrown overboard rather than human beings. There does not appear to be any authority in which a wife was treated as personalty in this way.

For completeness, it might be added that the legal status of women within marriage vis-à-vis property ownership was substantially overhauled by the Married Woman's Property Act 1882, which ended the old regime and created one that is more recognisable to modern eyes.

The law does not appear to have an answer to the question of whether a living person owns his body as property. The answer to the question hardly matters since laws exist to protect a person's body from harm caused by another; and there is no authority in law that a living person's body can become the property of another person (save in respect of the long-defunct case of slaves as discussed above). In *Williams v Williams* (1882) 29 Ch D 659 a person had attempted to direct the means of disposal of their body in a will, but the court found that this direction could not be enforced. This might imply that a person does not have property in his body (because he cannot determine how it is to be dealt with). On the other hand it may just be an application of the principle (discussed further below) that there is generally no property in a dead body.

Dead Bodies or Tissue

It is generally thought to be an ancient principle of English law that there is no property in a dead body (whether buried or unburied). The veracity of that notion as a general principle, however, is highly suspect.[9] The earliest reported authority cited in support of the proposition that a dead body cannot be property is *Haynes's Case* (1613) 12 Coke Reports 113. That case involved an individual called William Haynes, who dug up three bodies; took the winding sheets within which they were wrapped; and then re-interred the bodies. The court's reasoning (as discussed in Chapter 4 below) was that the winding sheets remained the property of the persons who owned them before they were used to wrap the corpses. Coke's report includes the following:

> [T]he property of the sheets remain in the owners, that is, in him who had property therein, when the dead body was wrapped therewith; *for the dead body is not capable of it* .... If apparel be put upon a boy, this is a gift in the law, for the boy hath capacity to take it; but a dead body being but a lump of earth hath no capacity' (emphasis added).

The italicised text above very obviously means, in the context of the quotation, that the corpse is not capable itself of owning the winding sheets. Nevertheless, *Haynes's Case* has been relied upon as authority for the proposition that a corpse cannot *itself* be property.[10]

Although *Haynes's Case* may not in reality be authority for the proposition that there is no property in a dead body, it nevertheless appears that it has been a generally accepted tenet of English law at least from around that time. Coke himself stated as follows:[11]

> It is to be observed that in every sepulchre, that hath a monument, two things are to be considered, viz. the monument, and the sepulture or burial of the dead; the burial of the cadaver is nullius in bonis, and belongs to ecclesiastical cognizance; but as to the monument, action is given at the common law for defacing thereof.

There are clear statements that a dead body cannot be property in, among others, *Foster v Dodd* (1867) LR 3 QB 67; *Williams v Williams* (above) and *R v Price* (1884) 12 QB 247. It can be argued persuasively that all of these remarks are obiter, but nevertheless (when coupled with a lack of authority to the contrary) they surely provide a clear indication of the law as it was understood to be at the beginning of the twentieth century. One further significant principle to emerge from *Williams* is that a person's executors have a right to possession of a corpse in order to arrange its burial.

The next significant development in this history of the common law was the decision of the High Court of Australia in *Doodeward v Spence* [1908] 6 CLR 40. On the unsavoury facts of that case, a two-headed foetus was

[9] In the following observations I am greatly indebted to Roger Magnusson's analysis within chapter 2 of the 2nd edition of *Palmer & McKendrick on Interests in Goods*, although I do differ from it in my view of the state of the English law prior to the 1990s.

[10] *Handyside's Case* (1749) 2 East PC 652.

[11] 3 Inst 203.

acquired by the claimant and exhibited by him as an oddity for commercial gain. He was prosecuted and the foetus was confiscated. The claimant then claimed for the recovery of the foetus on the basis that it was his property. The Australian High Court ruled that human tissue was in some circumstances capable of being reduced to property. Griffith CJ's reasoning appeared to be that there were plenty of examples of human remains that must sensibly be protected as personal property, for example mummies, prepared skeletons and anatomical and pathological collections of various kinds. His analysis of the law was therefore that there was an exception to the general position that there is no property in human tissue as follows:

> [W]hen a person has by the lawful exercise of work or skill so dealt with a human body or part of a human body in his lawful possession that it has acquired some attributes differentiating it from a mere corpse awaiting burial, he acquires a right to retain possession of it, at least as against any person not entitled to have it delivered to him for the purpose of burial [ie a reference to the right, as explained in *Williams* for executors to have possession of a body for the purposes of burial] …

In other words, the reasoning in *Doodeward* was that, where the implementation of human activity had led to the specimen of human tissue changing, for example by way of preservation, that sample of human tissue was capable of being reduced to personal property.

The impact of *Doodeward* on English law finally came to be considered in *Dobson v North Tyneside Health Authority and another* [1997] 1 WLR 597. A summary of the facts of that case will assist in understanding the court's reasoning and its implications.

A lady called Deborah Dobson collapsed while at work in October 1991. She was taken to North Tyneside General Hospital, which was a hospital operated by the first defendant. She was discharged a few days later. In December 1991 Ms Dobson again became very ill and, having been re-admitted to North Tyneside, was admitted to the Royal Victoria Infirmary, operated by the second defendant, and a different health authority. She died there of brain tumours a few days later. A doctor in that hospital removed Ms Dobson's brain and preserved it in paraffin, in case it should be needed for further examination in an inquest. In the event, the second defendant was not called upon to carry out any further examination of the brain and disposed of it. Some years later the claimant (Ms Dobson's administrator and the litigation friend of her children) sued the defendants. The case against the first defendant was that it had failed properly to diagnose Ms Dobson when she was admitted in October 1991. The case against the second defendant was that it had failed to keep the brain, thereby depriving the claimant of vital evidence in its case against the claimant.

Peter Gibson LJ distinguished *Doodeward*, noting that it was a case premised on property in a foetus, and that the court itself in *Doodeward* had expressed the view that the principle of reducing human tissue such as a foetus to property did not necessarily apply to a cadaver. Nevertheless, Gibson LJ did agree that the principle that the exercise of skill could reduce human tissue (including a cadaver) to personal property was properly arguable. In his view, however, the circumstances in *Dobson* were not such circumstances because preserving a brain in paraffin did not amount to a sufficient exercise of skill to create a piece of personal property, and even if it had done so there is no reason to think the property would have been that of the claimants:

> There is nothing in the pleading or evidence before us to suggest that the actual preservation of the brain after the post mortem was on a par with stuffing or embalming a corpse or preserving an anatomical or pathological specimen for a scientific collection or with preserving a human freak such as a double-headed foetus that had some value for exhibition purposes. There was no practical possibility of, nor any sensible purpose in, the brain being reunited with the body for burial purposes. Mr. Hone accepted that organs would not usually be preserved by the pathologist who carries out a post mortem and that if Dr. Perry had disposed of the brain without fixing it in paraffin, the plaintiffs would have no cause for complaint. I do not see how the fact that the brain was so fixed rendered it an item to possession of which the plaintiffs ever became entitled for the purpose of interment or any other purpose, still less that the plaintiffs ever acquired the property in it.

As to the right of administrators and others to possession of a body, the court accepted that there was such a right vested in people charged by law with the duty of burying a body (ie no such right was available to next of kin generally, and any right of possession was restricted purely to being a right for the purposes of burial). Such a right was of no relevance to the *Dobson* case, however, because the claimant administrator had not been appointed until some years after Ms Dobson's death.

The Court of Appeal again considered the *Doodeward* exemption to the general common law position on property in a corpse in *R v Kelly* [1999] 2 WLR 384. In that case two defendants had been convicted of theft for stealing body parts from the Royal College of Surgeons. They appealed on the basis that the body parts were incapable of constituting property, and therefore the offence of theft could not be made out. The Court of Appeal disagreed; approved *Doodeward* as applicable to English law; and interpreted Gibson LJ's decision in *Dobson* as also upholding *Doodeward*:

> [I]n our judgment, parts of a corpse are capable of being property within section 4 of the Theft Act 1968 if they have acquired different attributes by virtue of the application of skill, such as dissection or preservation techniques, for exhibition or teaching purposes: see Doodeward v. Spence, 6 C.L.R. 406, 413, 414 in the judgment of Griffith C.J. to which we have already referred and Dobson v. North Tyneside Health Authority [1997] 1 W.L.R. 596, 601 where this proposition is not dissented from and appears, in the judgment of this court, to have been accepted by Peter Gibson L.J.; otherwise, his analysis of the facts of Dobson's case, which appears at that page in the judgment, would have been, as it seems to us, otiose.

It is not entirely clear why the Court of Appeal in *Dobson* considered the removal and preservation of the brain was insufficient to engage the *Doodeward* exemption, but the Court of Appeal in *Kelly* felt that preserving anatomical specimens in the Royal College of Surgeons *was* sufficient to engage the exemption. Whether the exemption is engaged, however, will inevitably turn on the facts of any given case.

In *Re Organ Retention Group Ltd* [2005] QB 506, Gage J considered the *Doodeward* exemption to be well settled in English law and applicable more widely than simply in the context of theft (paragraph 147). The *Organ Retention Group* case involved post mortems that had been carried out with the permission of next of kin, but contrary to their knowledge organs had been removed, retained and subsequently disposed of by the hospital. The court said as follows about the property in organs after such a procedure at paragraph 156:

> [O]nce the post mortem examinations have been completed the law as to what rights are vested in the parents or the pathologists is far from clear. For myself, I prefer the view expressed by the authors of Clerk & Lindsell that on the assumption that the Doodeward exception applies the pathologists became entitled to possess the organs, the blocks and slides at least until a better right is asserted.

Moreover, Gage J held (paragraphs 156–58) that the right to possess a body to arrange its burial did not extend to an entitlement to recover organs in circumstances where a post mortem had lawfully been carried out with consent.

Living Tissue

Throughout most of the history of the English common law, there was no meaningful possibility of owning living tissue (as distinct from a human being). Clearly, as of the second half of the twentieth century in particular, that position changed substantially.

As noted above, legislation exists that closely regulates the use of human tissue whether extracted from a living or dead body. In particular, the Human Tissue Act 2004, the Human Fertilisation and Embryology Act 1990, and the manifold statutory instruments made under those Acts provide a largely complete legal regime dealing with tissue samples taken from living and in many cases dead persons. It is beyond the scope of this work to examine that complex regulatory regime.

It may perhaps be noted, however, that the common law might have a role in protecting the bodily tissue of a living person on its way to destruction. Following the *Organ Retention Group* case described above, it seems likely that tissue extracted during any medical procedure would properly be regarded as the personal property of the extractor. Ordinary common law principles provide that, even where an item of personal property is placed in a dustbin as refuse, it has not been abandoned by its owner – merely placed in refuse for disposal.[12]

[12] *Williams v Phillips* (1957) Cr App R 5.

Thus it appears likely that the common law would protect property rights in human tissue placed in the appropriate facilities for disposal. This point would appear to apply equally to human tissue extracted from dead bodies as from living.

WRECK, SALVAGE AND TREASURE

Wreck

'Wreck' has at least two different meanings at law. Part IX of the Merchant Shipping Act 1995 does not offer a comprehensive definition of 'wreck' but does state that 'wreck' 'includes jetsam, flotsam, lagan and derelict found in or on the shores of the sea or any tidal water'. This definition appears wide enough in scope to include items still in the sea, as opposed to washed up on the shore.[13]

By contrast, the common law, when dealing with wreck, appears to have confined itself only to those items that have washed onto the shores. Thus in *R v Forty-Nine Casks of Brandy* (1836) 166 ER 401 Sir John Nicholl stated as follows at 408–09:

> It may here be necessary to refer to some authorities, in order to ascertain what is legally meant by 'wreck of the sea,' or 'shipwreck.' 'It is to be observed,' says Blackstone, 'that in order to constitute a legal wreck, the goods must come to land; if they continue at sea, the law distinguishes them by the uncouth appellations of jetsam, flotsam, and ligan. These three are, therefore, accounted so far a distinct thing from the former, that by the King's grant to a man of wrecks, things jetsam, flotsam, and ligan will not pass'.

Further illumination of the terms 'flotsam', 'jetsam' and 'ligan' (also called 'lagan'), and a basis for the principle stated in *Forty-Nine Casks of Brandy* is found in *Att Gen v Sir Henry Constable* (1600) 77 ER 218, in which the court stated as follows:

> *flotsam* is when a ship is sunk, or otherwise perished, and the goods float on the sea; *jetsam* is when the ship is in danger of being sunk, and to lighten the ship the goods are cast into the sea, and afterwards notwithstanding the ship perish. *Lagan (rel potius ligan)* is when the goods which are so cast into the sea, and afterwards the ship perishes, and such goods cast are so heavy that they sink to the bottom, and the mariners, to the intent to have them again, tie to them a buoy, or cork, or such other thing that will not sink, so that they may find them again, *& dicitur lig. a ligando*: and none of these goods which are called *jetsam, flotsam* or *ligan*, are called wreck so long as they remain in or upon the sea; but if any of them by the sea be put upon the land, then they shall be said wreck.

[13] Additionally, it is considerably wider in its scope than the common law definition of wreck, in that it includes jetsam, flotsam and lagan (see further below).

Thus, so far as the common law that deals with personal property is concerned, an item is only wreck if it washes up on the shores of England.

Of course, that definition excludes from present consideration questions arising from the loss of English ships (or ships containing English cargo) in waters that are not English territorial waters (whether the items wash up on shore or not). Those questions are outside the scope of the English common law of real property, and relate instead to the conflict of laws. Clearly, those questions have the potential to be immensely complex and are beyond the scope of this work. It is perhaps worth saying as a matter of practical reality, however, that insofar as a vessel sinks in the territorial waters of another country, the laws of that other country will likely hold sway over any access to the wreck. Certainly in the UK the Protection of Wrecks Act 1973 affords the government powers to deal with wreck in such a way as to preclude its owner, whether a UK national or otherwise, from dealing with wreck that might be his property.

With the question of definition resolved, it is possible to turn to the question of proprietary rights in wreck. First, however, something must be said of the role of the Receiver of Wreck in handling wreck.

The Receiver of Wreck was initially established by the Merchant Shipping Act 1894. Its role was and remains the administration and disposal of wreck. Presumably, when it was first constituted, this was a necessary step to prevent people living in coastal areas from looting wrecked ships and pillaging cargo washed up on the shore. The Receiver of Wreck subsequently became regulated by the Merchant Shipping Act 1995 and remains regulated by that Act, as amended until now. As noted above, the Merchant Shipping Act 1995 adopts a wider definition of 'wreck' than does the common law, such that its regime applies to flotsam, jetsam and ligan.

Of the essence of the regime is that a person who finds or takes possession of wreck within UK limits, whether the owner or otherwise, is required to report the wreck to the Receiver of Wreck. The Receiver of Wreck will then advertise the find and any person with a claim to its ownership will have to satisfy the Receiver of Wreck of that ownership before it can be passed to him.

If the Receiver of Wreck is satisfied that a person other than the finder has good title to the wreck (for which a one-year period is allowed), that person will be granted title to the wreck. Deductions will be made, however, for 'salvage, fees and expenses due'. Similarly, in the event that no satisfactory claimant is found for the wreck and it goes unclaimed, the wreck is sold and the proceeds belong to the Crown bona vacantia. Again, however, deductions are made (per s 243(3)–(5) Merchant Shipping Act 1995) for expenses and 'salvage' (in the latter case in such amount as the Secretary of State thinks fit).

Salvage

The reference to 'salvage' in the Merchant Shipping Act 1995 referred to above is a reference to a reward payable to a finder of wreck. The entitlement to an award for salvage is a self-contained principle of maritime law; it is not replicated in any principle of property on land. Whereas on land there is no right to a reward or remuneration for saving property from destruction, the position is not the same in a maritime context. In maritime law, the salver of property is entitled to a reward; the origins of this entitlement appear to lie in the public policy desirability of encouraging a person to take steps (often at risk to himself) to protect the person or property of others on the sea. In *Five Steel Barges* (1890) 15 PD 142 the court described the right as follows:

> The jurisdiction which the Court exercises in salvage cases is of a peculiarly equitable character. The right to salvage may arise out of an actual contract; but it does not necessarily do so. It is a legal liability arising out of the fact that property has been saved, that the owner of the property who has had the benefit of it shall make remuneration to those who have conferred the benefit upon him, notwithstanding that he has not entered into any contract on the subject. I think that proposition equally applies to the man who has had a benefit arising out of the saving of the property.'

Salvage rights and their enforcement are complex matters beyond the scope of this work. It should be sufficient for present purposes to observe that a salvor has an action *in personam* against the owner of the salved property. In order to enforce that remedy the salvor is entitled to a lien over the salved property, which is perfected by an action *in rem* in the Admiralty Court (under s 20(2)(j) Supreme Court Act 1981). Such a lien is normally given priority over other types of lien, including pre-existing liens.[14]

Treasure and Other Finds

'Treasure' has a specific meaning within s 1 Treasure Act 1996 but there are many potential finds which, while in a more conversational sense would constitute 'treasure', do not fall within the statutory definition. There are thus two parallel regimes governing finds: the statutory regime for 'treasure' and the common law regime governing other kinds of find. These two will be examined in turn.

The statutory definition of 'treasure' in the Treasure Act 1996 is somewhat involved. In essence, the following things count as 'treasure':

1. per s 1(1)(a):

> any object at least 300 years old when found which—
>
> (i) is not a coin but has metallic content of which at least 10 per cent by weight is precious metal;
>
> (ii) when found, is one of at least two coins in the same find which are at least 300 years old at that time and have that percentage of precious metal; or

[14] See, for example, *The Russland* [1924] P 55 and *The Veritas* [1901] P 304.

(iii) when found, is one of at least ten coins in the same find which are at least 300 years old at that time';

2. items that are at least 200 years old and have been designated by the Secretary of State by regulation as being treasure for these purposes (ss 1(b) and 2(1) Treasure Act 1996);
3. items that would have been classed as 'treasure trove' before s 4 Treasure Act 1996 came into being. 'Treasure trove' is a common law concept meaning items made of gold or silver[15] that were found hidden in the ground or in a secret place and whose owner was unknown. The element of being hidden for later recovery (as distinct from merely being lost or abandoned) is essential to the definition of 'treasure trove'.[16]

By s 4(1) of the Treasure Act 1996, ownership of any 'treasure', as defined by the Act, vests with the Crown (or its franchisee, which is to say any person on whom the Crown has conferred a right to treasure trove, such as the Duke of Cornwall). This, however, is subject to any 'prior interests and rights'. These 'interests and rights' (per s 4(2) Treasure Act 1996) are essentially those interests and rights held at the time the treasure was left where it was found, or rights derivative of such rights. In practice, these 'interests and rights' are therefore overwhelmingly likely to be rights of an owner or possessor that have not been abandoned (as discussed further below), and the rights of such a person's successor in title or legatees.

Section 10 Treasure Act 1996 provides for a discretionary reward to be paid in circumstances where the Crown decides that such treasure should be passed to a museum. The Secretary of State must decide whether the museum should pay a reward to obtain the treasure. Such a reward may be paid to the finder of the treasure and/or to the occupier of the land on which it was found, or any other person with an interest in such land. The value of the reward must not exceed the market value of the treasure and is subject to certain other circumscriptions provided in statute and a related code of conduct.

It is now possible to examine the common law regime that applies to finds that are not 'treasure' within the meaning of the Treasure Act 1996.

As described above, English law does not recognise a concept of absolute ownership per se. Instead, ownership amounts to a bundle of rights conferred on a person. It is therefore possible for a person to acquire rights in personal (or real) property by taking possession of the property. Such rights are capable of being enforced against any person who does not have a better title than the possessor.[17]

[15] *Attorney-General of the Duchy of Lancaster v GE Overton (Farms) Ltd* [1980] 3 All ER 503.
[16] *Attorney-General v Trustees of the British Museum* [1903] 2 Ch 598.
[17] *Parker v British Airways Board* [1982] QB 1004 (CA) 1017.

Consistent with that approach, the starting point is that a person who finds personalty that is lost or has been abandoned can confer rights on himself by taking possession of that personalty (a more detailed discussion of the law as to finding is below). Where the previous owner has abandoned his ownership of the property (as to which see below) the finder may acquire ownership rights enforceable against the entire world (subject to any claim the Crown may have in *bona vacantia*). Where the chattel has merely been lost, the finder can acquire possessory rights enforceable against everyone but the true owner.

Given the rarity of abandonment of ownership (discussed further below) it is the latter situation that is more common, and complex. It is tolerably clear that, when a person takes possession of another person's goods, he becomes a bailee of those goods, with all of the responsibilities that entails.[18] In particular, in the case of lost chattels, it appears that the finder owes a duty to take steps to return the chattel to the true owner insofar as that is possible. In *Parker v British Airways Board* [1982] QB 1004 (CA) a bracelet was found in the departure lounge of an airport. The main part of the court's reasoning (discussed further below) concerned the tension between the possessory rights of a finder as against a land owner. Donaldson LJ did, however, take the opportunity to set out a number of principles governing the rights and duties of finders of chattels, including the following:

> A person having a finder's rights has an obligation to take such measures as in all the circumstances are reasonable to acquaint the true owner of the finding and present whereabouts of the chattel and to care for it meanwhile.

It is by the convenient device of bailment and the duty to take reasonable steps to acquaint the true owner with the find that the law protects the true owner from an unscrupulous finder. However, there does not appear to be any analytical reason why a breach of the duty of bailment would interfere with the finder's possessory title, rather it simply confers further and specific rights of action on the true owner.

As noted above, one of the primary sources of dispute in the law concerning the finding of chattels is the tension between the rights of the land owner (or occupant) and the finder. Thus in *Parker* the dispute was between, on the one hand, the person who had found the bracelet in the lounge at Heathrow and, on the other hand, the airport authority, both of which asserted title to the bracelet when the true owner could not be found.

The Court of Appeal in *Parker* (at 1017–18) endorsed the following principles on the subject of finders' rights versus land occupants' rights in the case of found chattels:

> 1. An occupier of land has rights superior to those of a finder over chattels in or attached to that land and an occupier of a building has similar rights in respect

[18] *Gilchrist Watt & Sanderson Pty Ltd v York Products Pty Ltd* [1970] 1 WLR 1262 (PC).

of chattels attached to that building, whether in either case the occupier is aware of the presence of the chattel.

2. An occupier of a building has rights superior to those of a finder over chattels upon or in, but not attached to, that building if, but only if, before the chattel is found, he has manifested an intention to exercise control over the building and the things which may be upon it or in it.
3. An occupier who manifests an intention to exercise control over a building and the things which may be upon or in it so as to acquire rights superior to those of a finder is under an obligation to take such measures as in all the circumstances are reasonable to ensure that lost chattels are found and, upon their being found, whether by him or by a third party, to acquaint the true owner of the finding and to care for the chattels meanwhile. The manifestation of intention may be express or implied from the circumstances including, in particular, the circumstance that the occupier manifestly accepts or is obliged by law to accept liability for chattels lost upon his 'premises,' e.g. an innkeeper or carrier's liability.
4. An 'occupier' of a chattel, e.g. a ship, motor car, caravan or aircraft, is to be treated as if he were the occupier of a building for the purposes of the foregoing rules.

In *Parker* the court decided that the airport authority had not manifested sufficient intention to exercise control over chattels left on its land to have a better right than the finder. Other authority shows, however, that the courts are readily persuaded to apply the law in favour of the occupant. In *Waverley Borough Council v Fletcher* [1996] QB 334 (CA) the claimant was a local authority that occupied a park. The park had been made available to the public for the purposes of recreation. The defendant was a member of the public who was using a metal detector in the park (lawfully, since a bye-law prohibiting such activity had been torn down at the relevant time). In the course of his activities the defendant found a medieval brooch, which he recovered from the ground by excavating to a depth of nine inches. The Court of Appeal found that, because the brooch had been found *in* rather than on the land, it properly belonged to the local authority.

It is also tolerably clear that, when a person finds a chattel in the course of his employment, he must account for that chattel to his employee and cannot keep it for himself.[19]

BONA VACANTIA IN THE NARROW SENSE – SPECIAL CIRCUMSTANCES IN WHICH OWNERSHIP REVERTS TO THE CROWN

As noted above, there are certain special circumstances in which ownership of personalty reverts to the Crown. These are discussed below.

[19] *City of London Corporation v Appleyard* [1963] 2 All ER 843 at 988.

Intestacy

The Crown is the recipient of last resort of the estate of a person who dies intestate. In other words, insofar as a deceased's estate does not pass by will, under the Intestacy Rules or under the Administration of Estates Act 1925, or under the Inheritance (Provision for Family and Dependents) Act 1975, the Crown will become the owner of the estate.

Insofar as the Crown does receive such property, it is entitled to make ex gratia payments to such persons as it may deem fit (whether family of the deceased or otherwise) under s 46(1)(vi) Administration of Estates Act 1925.

Property of a Dissolved Company

Broadly speaking there are two circumstances that lead to a company being dissolved: when it has been wound up or if it has been engaged in a prolonged period of inactivity and is therefore removed from the register by the Registrar.

In either case, any property the company owns at the time of its dissolution vests in the Crown bona vacantia (pursuant to s 1012 Companies Act 2006). Ordinarily a dissolved company will not have any property because it will either have been passed to shareholders, in the case of a solvent dissolution, or to creditors, in the case of dissolution following insolvent winding up. Nevertheless, situations can arise when a company has property after its dissolution, in particular where the property was unknown at the time of the dissolution (a cause of action being a common example).

Chapter 3 of Part 31 of the Companies Act 2006 therefore provides a regime by which a dissolved company can be restored to the register (to which the Crown must consent). On the restoration of a company under that regime it is deemed to have continued to exist instead of being dissolved, thereby allowing its property to be dealt with in the normal way.

Failure of a Trust

In certain circumstances it is possible for property unsuccessfully settled into a trust to pass to the Crown bona vacantia. This is not the ordinary position when a trust fails; ordinarily the property is held on a resulting trust for the settlor. Such a resulting trust is imposed automatically as a matter of law to deal with the otherwise problematic question of beneficial ownership of the property.

For example, in *Re Gillingham Bus Disaster Fund* [1958] Ch 300 charitable donations were obtained to defray the funeral expenses and care costs of certain Royal Marines killed and injured in a bus accident. The collection raised so much money that all the relevant expenses were met and there was a very large surplus of funds. No express term of the trust existed to deal with such a situation, and so the question arose of whether the surplus was held on a resulting trust for the settlors, or whether the Crown could take the surplus bona vacantia. Harman, J concluded that a resulting trust would be imposed.

> The general principle must be that where money is held upon trust and the trusts declared do not exhaust the fund it will revert to the donor or settlor under what is called a resulting trust. The reasoning behind this is that the settlor or donor did not part with his money absolutely out and out but only sub modo to the intent that his wishes as declared by the declaration of trust should be carried into effect. When, therefore, this has been done any surplus still belongs to him. This doctrine does not, in my judgment, rest on any evidence of the state of mind of the settlor, for in the vast majority of cases no doubt he does not expect to see his money back: he has created a trust which so far as he can see will absorb the whole of it. The resulting trust arises where that expectation is for some unforeseen reason cheated of fruition, and is an inference of law based on after-knowledge of the event.

As will be apparent from the above extract, it is nevertheless still possible in certain circumstances for assets to pass to the Crown bona vacantia. What is required is for funds to be parted with by a settlor 'out and out'. This encompasses circumstances in which a resulting trust would be unworkable because donations have been made anonymously, for example in the case of collecting tins on the street, or in the case of raffles, sweepstakes and similar.[20] Additionally, it is presumably the case that if a settlor expressly agreed that no resulting trust should come into being, or it was the essence of the gift that beneficial ownership would be parted with forever, a resulting trust would not come into being, in which case the trust's property would pass to the Crown bona vacantia.

[20] *Re West Sussex Constabulary's Widows, Children and Benevolent (1930) Fund Trusts* [1971] Ch 1.

3

Obtaining Title to a Chattel from a Third Party

THE LAW GOVERNING the conveyance of title to a chattel differs depending on whether the chattel is gifted or whether it passes under a contract of sale. In the latter case the operation of statute greatly supplements, perhaps it might more properly be said replaces, the common law position.

SALE

Substantial specialist works exist dealing with the sale of goods. No attempt will be made to duplicate those works, and this section is restricted to making a few observations that are of importance when considering the transfer of title to chattels generally.

Terms as to Good Title Passing

Clearly, and in contrast to the position with gifts, a buyer is not achieving a windfall, and has a particular and legitimate interest in ensuring what he receives is what he has paid for. The *nemo dat quod non habet*[1] rule is discussed elsewhere in this work. It is highly relevant to any sale of goods too, in that the buyer will not receive a better title to the goods than the seller is able to provide.

As has been mentioned elsewhere, the English law does not have a theory of absolute ownership as such (in contrast to, say Roman law). Rather it has a system of relative title, in which the quality of a person's title is judged relative only to another's.[2] In this relative title, the 'owner' is really the person with the best possessory title in the world (and even that may not involve a right to immediate possession, in the sense that a temporary bailee may enjoy a right to exclude the 'owner' from possession for a time).

It is therefore a matter of concern to the buyer to ensure the quality of the seller's title. Section 12 Sale of Goods Act 1979 sets out the following terms as

[1] ie the rule that nobody can give a better title than they themselves have.
[2] See, for example, Auld LJ in *Waverley Borough Council v Fletcher* [1996] QB 334.

to title that are ordinarily implied into a sale of goods contract, including the following at sub-s 2:

> (a) [T]he goods are free, and will remain free until the time when the property is to pass, from any charge or encumbrance not disclosed or known to the buyer before the contract is made, and
> (b) the buyer will enjoy quiet possession of the goods except so far as it may be disturbed by the owner or other person entitled to the benefit of any charge or encumbrance so disclosed or known.

The above provisions do not apply where there is

> a contract of sale in the case of which there appears from the contract or is to be inferred from its circumstances an intention that the seller should transfer only such title as he or a third person may have.

Even in those circumstances, however, there is still an implied term to the effect that 'all charges or encumbrances known to the seller and not known to the buyer have been disclosed to the buyer before the contract is made'.

The Sale of Goods Act 1979 does not endeavour to describe what amounts to 'quiet enjoyment' for the purposes of s 12(2)(b), and it will also be noted that on a literal reading it purports to have limitless future effect. There have been cases in which the meaning of that term has been tested, and in particular a seller has been found liable for a third party's interference with a buyer's enjoyment of the goods by virtue of that implied term.

For example, in *Microbeads v Vinhurst* [1975] 1 WLR 218 an English company had bought various road-marking machines from a Swiss seller in 1970. Although this dispute took place before the passage of the Sale of Goods Act 1979, a term on the lines of the term now at s 12(2)(b) was implied into the contract by operation of the Sale of Goods Act 1893. The buyers were dissatisfied with the performance of the machines and so did not pay the last instalment of the purchase price. The sellers sued to recover the balance, issuing proceedings in late 1970. Meanwhile, in late 1967 another English company called Prismo had filed specifications and an application for a patent in respect of such a machine. In 1972 the patent was granted (and it was at this point that Prismo was able to take steps to enforce its patent; prior to that point nobody (including in particular the Swiss seller) had known the design of Prismo's machine.

The buyer's primary position was that the machines were not fit for purpose but it latterly amended its defence to run the point that the fact that the machines infringed Prismo's patent meant that the seller had infringed the warranty implied by the predecessor of s 12(2)(b) Sale of Goods Act 1979. The seller opposed this argument on the basis that the defect in title complained of (ie Prismo's ability to interfere with the use of the machines) was not in existence and could not be known about at the time of the sale. The Court of Appeal disagreed, per Denning, MR:

> It seems to me that when a buyer has bought goods quite innocently and later on he is disturbed in his possession because the goods are found to be infringing a patent,

> then he can recover damages for breach of warranty against the seller. It may be the seller is innocent himself, but when one or other must suffer, the loss should fall on the seller: because, after all, he sold the goods and if it turns out that they infringe a patent, he should bear the loss. In the present case the Prismo company can sue for infringement now and stop the buyer using the machines. That is a clear disturbance of possession. The buyer is not able to enjoy the quiet possession which the seller impliedly warranted that he shall have.

Logically, the principle that a seller is bound to a term as to the absence of interference with future enjoyment of goods must have some major limitations. In *The Playa Larga* [1983] 2 Lloyd's Rep 171 Ackner LJ appeared to accept at 178 that 'the seller would not be liable where the buyer's possession was disturbed by the wrongful act of a third party totally unconnected with the seller'.

Section 6 Unfair Contract Terms Act 1977 provides an absolute prohibition on excluding or restricting the operation of s 12 Sale of Goods Act 1979. This prohibition applies in both consumer and business contracts and is not subject to any kind of qualification allowing restrictions on s 12 as long as such restrictions are reasonable. This is therefore an unusually onerous prohibition by the standards of the Unfair Contract Terms Act.

As a slight aside, the absolute bar on restricting the operation of s 12 is somewhat inconsistent with the relative reluctance of the common law to imply terms as to title historically. Although it is clear that the courts have long been willing to enforce warranties as to title,[3] it was settled law that no term would be implied.[4] The reason seems to have been a preference for the old principle of *caveat emptor* – buyer beware – and the court's view seems to have been that buyers were at liberty to bargain for such a warranty of good title, and the court would not intervene if they had failed to do so.

What, then, is the position as to whether a buyer who has made appreciable use of the goods is entitled to make use of the s 12 warranties? This was the type of matter before the court in the leading authority of *Rowland v Divall* [1923] 2 KB 500. In that case the defendant had bought a car from a third party and sold it on to the plaintiff for £334. The plaintiff, who was a car dealer, drove the car from Brighton where he had bought it to his show room in Bedford, where he put it on display. The car was then sold on to a buyer called Colonel Railsdon for £400. After a time Colonel Railsdon was stopped by the police, who took possession of the car as it had been reported stolen – it transpired that the person who had sold it to the defendant had himself stolen it. The plaintiff refunded Colonel Railsdon the £400 paid and brought a claim against the defendant. The claim was framed as one seeking the recovery of the £334 on the basis of total failure of consideration.

[3] See, for example, *Crosse v Gardner* (1688) 90 ER 656.
[4] *Morley v Attenborough* (1849) 154 ER 943.

At first instance the judge dismissed the claim on the basis that the plaintiff had had intermediate possession of the car for four months, and it could not be said in those circumstances that there had been a total failure of consideration. The Court of Appeal disagreed, awarding the plaintiff the cost of buying the car from the defendant on the basis that 'the buyer has not received any part of that which he contracted to receive – namely, the property and right to possession – and, that being so, there has been a total failure of consideration'.

The Court of Appeal's reasoning is somewhat opaque, however, and has attracted a degree of criticism.[5] On the one hand, it could be explained as reasoning founded on restitutionary principles, ie that the benefit conferred on the plaintiff was insufficient to give rise to any valid consideration, allowing him to succeed in a claim for money had and received/restitution. On the other hand, it could be explained as a decision founded in the law of sale of goods contracts, namely that (notwithstanding the passage of time and the plaintiff's inability to return the car) he had exercised a right to terminate the contract.

Neither analysis is entirely satisfactory, however. On the particular facts of the case it was not unreasonable for the plaintiff to recover the amount he had paid to the defendant (given that he had refunded Colonel Railsdon). On principle, however, the conclusion is dubious because the defendant did not provide *no* property in the car – he provided such title as he had, which was a possessory title good against everyone apart from the true owner. That is a title that often will be of considerable benefit.

The application of the principles in *Rowland* could therefore give rise to the over-compensation of claimants. An example of such over-compensation was to be found in *Butterworth v Kingsway Motors Ltd* [1954] 1 WLR 1286. A Miss Rudolph had acquired a car under a hire purchase agreement, pursuant to which title remained in the hire purchase company. Miss Rudolph nevertheless sold the car to a motor dealer. The motor dealer in turn sold the car to a produce merchant, which sold the car to another motor dealer called Kingsway Motors, which was the defendant.

Kingsway Motors sold the car to Mr Butterworth, the plaintiff, for £1,275. Mr Butterworth used the car without incident for about ten and a half months. After that time, Mr Butterworth received correspondence from the hire purchase company to the effect that it was the true owner of the car. He was offered the opportunity to acquire ownership by settling Miss Rudolph's outstanding liabilities under the hire purchase agreement but declined to do so. Instead Mr Butterworth sued Kingsway Motors for the full amount of the purchase price, relying on *Rowland*. By that point, the value of the car had diminished to about £800 (it further diminished to £450 by the date of trial) and of course Mr Butterworth had had the use of it for nearly a year. Nevertheless, the court

[5] See, for example, *Benjamin's Sale of Goods*, 10th edition, 4-006.

expressly followed *Rowland* and compensated Mr Butterworth in full – a clear windfall recovery for Mr Butterworth. Per Pearson J at 1294:

> I hold that, on the authority of Rowland v. Divall, the plaintiff was on that date entitled to rescind that contract of sale. The possible contention for the defendants that such rescission was precluded by the plaintiff's use of the car for a substantial period and the deterioration in its condition and/or depreciation in its market value during that period is answered by the reasoning of Bankes L.J. in that case.

In 1966 the Law Reform Committee criticised the decision in *Rowland* on the basis that a buyer ought to give credit for such enjoyment of the goods as he has had. The Law Commission subsequently recommended in 1968 that this issue be addressed by a reform of (what is now) s 12 Sale of Goods Act 1979. Numerous working papers followed, however, and in 1987 the Law Commission decided to make no such recommendation for the reform of s 12. The only principled reason for this position appears to have been that the Law Commission did not see why a buyer should have to pay a seller for the use of someone else's goods. This reasoning is plainly unsatisfactory, however, because it fails to take account of the relativity of title in the English system of property law.

Thus the decision in *Rowland* remains good law, even though it has been subject to trenchant criticism for over five decades. As the authors of *Benjamin's Sale of Goods* observe,[6] it is clearly a rule that deserves reconsideration, such that the maximum recovery allowed by a buyer is restricted to compensation for the actual loss the buyer has suffered as a result of the defect in title.

The rule in *Rowland* is subject to a slightly ameliorating statutory provision at s 6(3) Torts (Interference with Goods) Act 1977. As discussed elsewhere in the context of improvements to chattels, where proceedings are brought by a buyer against a seller for the recovery of the purchase price by reason of total failure of consideration, so long as the seller acted in good faith an allowance will be made for any improvements the seller has made to the goods.

The Mechanics of Title Passing

In many disputes arising from sales of goods it can be critical to determine precisely when title in the goods passes from the seller to the buyer. This is a complex issue and the reader is referred to the relevant specialist works for detailed commentary.[7]

The starting point for a general survey of the position is that the question of the passage of title will depend on the question of what sort of goods are being sold, and in the first instance on whether the goods are specific or unascertained goods.

[6] ibid.
[7] See especially ibid, chapter 5.

'Unascertained goods' are not defined in the Sale of Goods Act 1979, but a tolerably clear sense of what is meant can be found at s 18, rule 5 Sale of Goods Act 1979. 'Unascertained' goods appear to be goods that cannot presently be produced and are capable of being identified only by description. This includes, for example, goods identified by reference to a generic description (for example 'a ton of flour'); 'future goods' within the meaning given in s 61 of the Act (ie 'goods to be manufactured or acquired by the seller after the making of the contract of sale'); and an unspecified part of a known bulk (for example 'two tonnes of the wheat presently on board the ship X').

So far as specific goods are concerned, s 17 Sale of Goods Act 1979 provides that title to the goods passes when the parties to the contract intend title to pass.

As to unascertained goods, notwithstanding the fact that s 17 refers only to specific goods, it is also the starting point that title to unascertained goods passes when the parties intend it to pass.[8] This is subject to an important qualification at s 16 Sale of Goods Act 1979, which provides that no title can pass unless the goods have been ascertained. In other words, regardless of the intention of the parties, the absolute earliest point at which title to the goods may pass is once they have been ascertained. That s 16 qualification is itself subject to an exception provided at s 20A. Section 20A deals with purchases from a bulk and provides, broadly speaking, that where the parties to a contract for the purchase from a bulk have identified the bulk, and the purchaser has made payment, the purchaser will own part of the bulk as a tenant in common in proportion with the payment he has made. These issues are discussed elsewhere in this work in the context of mixtures.

With the exception of s 20A, however, it is worth stressing that a purchaser of unascertained goods does not, by virtue of the fact that he has paid for them, acquire any equitable title to, or interest in, those goods. Per Lord Brandon of Oakbrook in *Leigh and Sillavan Ltd v Aliakmon Shipping Co Ltd* [1986] AC 785 at 812–13:

> I do not doubt that it is possible, in accordance with established equitable principles, for equitable interests in goods to be created and to exist. It seems to me, however, extremely doubtful whether equitable interests in goods can be created or exist within the confines of an ordinary contract of sale. The *Sale of Goods Act 1893*, which must be taken to apply to the c. and f. contract of sale in the present case, is a complete code of law in respect of contracts for the sale of goods. The passing of the property in goods the subject matter of such a contract is fully dealt with in sections 16 to 19 of the Act. Those sections draw no distinction between the legal and the equitable property in goods, but appear to have been framed on the basis that the expression 'property', as used in them, is intended to comprise both the legal and the equitable title. In this connection I consider that there is much force in the observations

[8] *Karlshamns Oljefabriker v East Port Navigation Corp (The Elafi)* [1981] 2 Lloyd's Rep 679 at 683.

of Atkin L.J. in *In re Wait [1927] 1 Ch. 606*, 635–636, from which I quote only this short passage:

> 'It would have been futile in a code intended for commercial men to have created an elaborate structure of rules dealing with rights at law, if at the same time it was intended to leave, subsisting with the legal rights, equitable rights inconsistent with, more extensive, and coming into existence earlier than the rights so carefully set out in the various sections of the code.'

As is apparent from the above, the intention of the parties is of critical importance to determining the point at which title passes. How, then, does the court deal with the often-occurring situation of the intention of the parties being uncertain? The answer is with reference to various rebuttable presumptions that are set out at s 18 of the Act. Section 18 contains five rules to cover different scenarios, which do not lend themselves to a worthwhile summary – it will be necessary in practice to examine the rules individually to determine their applicability to the particular situation.

It may be useful, however to make one point as to the first of the rules. The first rule is one of the most important and, superficially, the simplest, but it does present a difficulty of interpretation. It states as follows:

> Where there is an unconditional contract for the sale of specific goods in a deliverable state the property in the goods passes to the buyer when the contract is made, and it is immaterial whether the time of payment or the time of delivery, or both, be postponed.

The complexity in this rule arises from the phrase 'unconditional contract', which is not a readily comprehensible term. In one sense, no contract is 'unconditional', in that consideration is a prerequisite of there being any contract at all. What appears to be meant by this phrase is not a contract in which there is no obligation on the buyer at all, but rather a contract in which there is no condition that must be fulfilled in order for the transfer of goods to take place.[9]

GIFTS

The starting point is that there appear to be two requirements for an effective gift of chattels:

1. an intention on the part of the donor to give; and
2. delivery of the chattel (and that delivery not being repudiated).

In *Cochrane v Moore* (1890) 2 QBD 57, Fry LJ provided the following detailed reasoning as to those two preconditions being an essential component of a gift:

> Upon long consideration, I have come to the conclusion that actual delivery in the case of a 'gift' is more than evidence of the existence of the proposition of law which

[9] See *Benjamin's Sale of Goods*, 10th edition, paragraph 5-019.

> constitutes a gift, and I have come to the conclusion that it is a part of the proposition itself. It is one of the facts which constitute the proposition that a gift has been made. It is not a piece of evidence to prove the existence of the proposition; it is a necessary part of the proposition, and, as such, is one of the facts to be proved by evidence. The proposition is not – that the one party has agreed or promised to give, and that the other party has agreed or promised to accept. In that case, it is not doubted but that the ownership is not changed until a subsequent actual delivery. The proposition before the Court on a question of gift or not is – that the one gave and the other accepted. The transaction described in the proposition is a transaction begun and completed at once. It is a transaction consisting of two contemporaneous acts, which at once complete the transaction, so that there is nothing more to be done by either party. The act done by the one is that he gives; the act done by the other is that he accepts. These contemporaneous acts being done, neither party has anything more to do. The one cannot give, according to the ordinary meaning of the word, without giving; the other cannot accept then and there such a giving without then and there receiving the thing given. After these two things done, the donor could not get possession of the chattel without bringing an action to force the donee to give it back. Short of these things being done, the donee could not get possession without bringing an action against the donor to force him to give him the thing. But if we are to force him to give, it cannot be said that he has given. Suppose the proposing donor offers the thing saying, 'I give you this thing – take it'; and the other says, 'No, I will not take it now; I will take it tomorrow.' I think the proposing donor could not in the meantime say correctly to a third person, 'I gave this just now to my son or my friend.' The answer of the third person would (I think rightly) be: 'You cannot say you gave it him just now; you have it now in your hand.' All you can say is: 'That you are going to give it him to-morrow, if then he will take it.' I have come to the conclusion that in ordinary English language, and in legal effect, there cannot be a 'gift' without a giving and taking. The giving and taking are the two contemporaneous reciprocal acts which constitute a 'gift.' They are a necessary part of the proposition that there has been a 'gift.' They are not evidence to prove that there has been a gift, but facts to be proved to constitute the proposition that there has been a gift.

When considering whether a chattel has been 'delivered', it is necessary to consider also whether it has been accepted by the recipient. As Lord Halsbury has observed,[10] it is certainly not possible for a donor to compel a donee to accept a gift of a chattel. By the same token, it appears clear (per Cotton LJ at 288 of *Standing v Bowring*) that a person can be vested with a gift without being aware of the gift. Thus there is no need for active acceptance of a chattel by the donee in order for a gift to be completed. The law appears therefore to be that the donee of a chattel has the right to repudiate the gift, but until he exercises that right (even if he does not yet know it is his to exercise) the gift is effective.

It should also be noted that, if the recipient of a gift accepts the gift on terms that he considers it a loan, it will nevertheless be effective as a gift unless the

[10] *Standing v Bowring* (1885) 31 Ch D 282.

donor agrees that it will indeed be a loan. Thus in *Dewar v Dewar* [1975] 1 WLR 1532 the court reasoned as follows:

> [W]here a person intends to make a gift and the donee receives the thing given, knows that he has got it and takes it, the fact that he says: 'Well, I will only accept it as a loan, and you can have it back when you want it' does not prevent it from being an effective gift. Of course, it does not turn it into a loan unless the donor says: 'Very well, let it be a loan.' He could not force the donor to take it back, but the donor, having transferred it to him effectively and completely, intending to make a gift, and he – so far from repudiating it – having kept it, it seems to me that that is an effective gift.

The mechanics of the act of delivery in the context of a gift also require a degree of consideration. The first point to note is that it is entirely possible for a gift of a chattel to be effected by deed (see, for example, *Day v Royal Collage of Music* [2014] Ch 211 at 67). While in practice this is no doubt a comparatively rare means of gift, it is clearly the prudent course, especially where gifts are made of intangible personalty or personalty that is bulky or otherwise difficult to deliver in a physical sense. Similarly, as the existence of a deed is likely to preclude all argument about the fact of a gift or whether any conditions attach (see further below) a deed is the prudent course where a valuable chattel is being gifted.

Where there is no deed, it is generally essential for there to be a physical act of delivery of possession of a chattel. Words of gift alone, no matter how explicit, are generally not enough.

This principle was powerfully illustrated in *Re Cole* [1964] Ch 175, 185 (CA). In that case the donor was a businessman who had bought a house in London in which he lived for a time away from his wife and children, who resided in Lancashire. The businessman furnished the house at great expense and in due course his wife moved down to London to live in the property as their matrimonial home.

On her arrival, the businessman took his wife around the rooms of the house and showed her the furnishings – in some cases she handled the items. The businessman used words to the effect of, 'all this is yours'. Some years later the businessman became bankrupt and a dispute arose as between his wife and his trustee in bankruptcy as to the ownership of the valuable furnishings.

At first instance the court agreed that the circumstances coupled with the businessman's choice of wording were sufficient to perfect a gift to his wife (bearing in mind in particular that it was not possible physically to deliver to his wife an entire household's worth of furnishings). The Court of Appeal disagreed, however. Its reasoning is based on the premise that an act of delivery entails passing possession into the recipient's hands – where the recipient is already in possession there is no need for any further act of delivery. The Court of Appeal's reasoning was founded on various authorities establishing that the shared use of furnishings within a shared establishment does not confer any entitlement to possession.

It is respectfully submitted that *Re Cole* might have been decided differently were it before the Court of Appeal today. First, the judgment's reliance on historic authorities dealing with rights of possession within marriage makes it appear anachronistic. For example, per Harman LJ at page 190:

> I cannot find that there was any change of possession here. It is argued that a wife living in her husband's house, and therefore having control to some extent of the furniture in it, is in possession of it, but this, I think, does not follow. In the ordinary case where a wife lives with her husband in a house owned and furnished by him, she has the use of the furniture by virtue of her position as wife, but that gives her no more possession of it than a servant has who uses the furniture. As to this, see Goddard L.J. in *Youngs v. Youngs*. It is true that it may be doubtful who is in possession of the furniture and that you must look to the title, as in *Ramsay v. Margrett*, but in the absence of delivery there is no title in her, as was pointed out by Lord Evershed M.R. in *Hislop v. Hislop*.

Secondly, the Court of Appeal's judgment is conspicuous by its failure to explain quite what the businessman could have done to effect delivery of an entire household full of items to his wife. In some circumstances the law allows for the possibility that symbolic delivery is possible in the case of items that it is impractical too deliver (see further below). It is not at all clear why it should not be equally possible symbolically to gift an entire household of possessions, so long as the requisite intention is found.

Although the court's reasoning in *Re Cole* may prove to be suspect if ever tested again, it does illustrate an important point: namely that a donor must always be very careful to ensure an element of physical deliverance is achieved in order for a gift to be perfected. In circumstances where simple physical delivery is impossible, it is hard to be sure that the court will accept that any steps that are taken (no matter how clearly they evince an intention to make a gift) will be adequate to amount to delivery.

Having said that, there are circumstances in which the law seems content to accept a step short of physical delivery as adequate delivery for the purposes of a gift. *Re Cole* is to be contrasted with *Lock v Heath* (1892) 8 TLR 295. In the latter case, a husband sought to give all his furniture to his wife. He physically delivered a chair along with an inventory of the rest of the furniture, and said, 'I give you all the goods mentioned in this inventory'. The court was content to accept that a gift had been perfected in *Lock*.

The difference between *Lock* and *Re Cole* appears to be that in *Lock* the delivery of the chair and the inventory amounted to a representative delivery of the class of goods as a whole, generally referred to as 'symbolic' delivery.

The courts have adopted a similar approach in circumstances in which physical delivery of a chattel is impossible. In *Rawlinson v Mort* (1905) 93 LT 555 a parishioner bought an organ, which he lent to a church. The organ was erected in the church and the vicar provided the parishioner with a letter confirming that it was held under a loan. The parishioner subsequently befriended the church organist and formed a desire to gift the organ to him. The parishioner gave the organist the vicar's letter, and on a subsequent occasion he placed the organist's hand on the organ and said to a third party in the organist's presence that he was effecting the gift. A dispute subsequently arose between the organist and the original vicar's successor as to the correct owner of the organ. The court found that the gift to the organist had been validly completed, because the parishioner had done everything that could have been done in the circumstances to perfect the gift.

As has already been noted, delivery is the act of transfer of possession, and so where possession already vests in the donee, as under a bailment, there is no formality for completing a gift other than an expression of the intention to make it. The same principle applies where an item has been lost and is gifted to a donee in the event it is ever found.

That is demonstrated by *Thomas v Times Book Co* [1966] 1 WLR 911. The poet Dylan Thomas delivered his original manuscript for *Under Milk Wood* to his producer at the BBC on 15 October 1953. Copies were hastily arranged to enable Thomas to take the original to the USA for a reading tour. On 17 October 1953 the original was returned to Thomas, who subsequently lost it, believing himself to have left it in a taxi or one of a number of pubs in Soho he had visited that day.

Thomas notified his producer of the loss, and the latter arranged to attend the airport at the time of Thomas's departure with copies of the manuscript. In gratitude, Thomas said that the producer could keep the original manuscript if he could find it, and offered the name of the pubs he had visited in case the producer wanted to look.

In due course the producer found the manuscript, which he kept for some years and then sold. Thomas's widow Caitlin brought a claim against the producer and subsequent purchasers of the manuscript on the basis that the manuscript was never properly gifted to the producer and therefore remained part of Thomas's estate. Plowman J rejected the widow's argument, reasoning as follows:

> It is then said on behalf of the plaintiff that even if Dylan Thomas intended to give this manuscript to Cleverdon, he did not succeed in giving effect to that intention because there was no delivery of the subject-matter of it to Cleverdon by Dylan Thomas. I feel bound to reject that argument. The fact is that Cleverdon got possession of this manuscript from the Soho public-house in which it had been left by Dylan Thomas and that he got that possession with the consent of Dylan Thomas. That, in my judgment, is sufficient delivery to perfect a gift in Cleverdon's favour. I can see nothing in In re Cole, A Bankrupt which was relied upon by Mr. Sparrow, which precludes me from taking what appears to me to be the common-sense view of the matter, and concluding that when Cleverdon got possession of the manuscript with the consent of Dylan Thomas, the gift was perfected.

It is also a settled principle that, where a gift fails for want of delivery, and the donee comes into possession of the chattel at a later stage, the gift can be perfected. This is the so-called rule in *Strong v Bird* (1874) LR 18 Eq 315 (in which case the donee had been forgiven a debt by the donor, and the forgiveness was completed when the done was appointed as the donor's executor and so gained possession of her estate).

It is perhaps worth noting at this stage that certain pieces of intangible personalty cannot be transferred without formalities, usually prescribed by statute. For example, s 53(1)(c) Law of Property Act 1925 provides that an equitable interest in a trust can only be conveyed in writing. It is beyond the scope of this work to examine the various different formalities.

FAILED GIFTS

Vitiating Factors

As is well known, contracts are capable of vitiation if one of certain factors are present, for example mistake. Although authorities on the subject are comparatively rare, similar vitiating factors operate in the case of gifts, although different principles apply.

Mistake

In the case of mistake, there is of course a substantial body of law describing the possibility of contracts being void for mistake at common law. No equivalent doctrine exists in respect of gifts.[11]

The principles of equity, however, do step in to offset the possibility of injustice. The position was set out by Morgan J in *Merwe v Goldman* [2016] EWHC 790 (Ch), [2016] 4 WLR 71 (summarising the principles given by the Supreme Court in *Pitt v Holt* [2013] UKSC 26, [2013] 2 AC 108) in the following way:

> For present purposes, the principles can be summarised as follows: (1) a donor can rescind a gift by showing that he acted under some mistake of so serious a character as to render it unjust on the part of the donee to retain the gift: para 101, quoting *Ogilvie v Littleboy (1897) 13 TLR* 399 at 400; (2) a mistake is to be distinguished from mere inadvertence or misprediction: para 104; (3) forgetfulness, inadvertence or ignorance are not, as such, a mistake but can lead to a false belief or assumption which the law will recognise as a mistake: para 105; (4) it does not matter that the mistake was due to carelessness on the part of the person making the voluntary disposition unless the circumstances are such as to show that he deliberately ran the risk, or must be taken to have run the risk, of being wrong: para 114; (5) equity requires the gravity of

[11] See *Chitty on Contracts*, 32nd edition, 1-139.

the mistake to be assessed in terms of injustice or unconscionability: para 124; (6) the evaluation of unconscionability is objective: para 125; (7) the gravity of the mistake must be assessed by a close examination of the facts which include the circumstances of the mistake and its consequences for the party making the mistaken disposition: para 126; (8) the court needs to focus intensely on the facts of the particular case: para 126; (9) a mistake about the tax consequences of a transaction can be a relevant mistake: paras 129–132; (10) where the relevant mistake is a mistake about the tax consequences of a transaction, then:

> 'in some cases of artificial tax avoidance, the court might think it right to refuse relief, either on the ground that such claimants, acting on supposedly expert advice, must be taken to have accepted the risk that the scheme would prove ineffective, or on the ground that discretionary relief should be refused on grounds of public policy': para 135;
>
> (11) it is not pointless, nor is it acting in vain, to set aside a transaction and to remove a liability to pay tax, even where that is the principal, or the only, effect of the setting aside: paras 136–141.'

Undue Influence

The doctrine of undue influence is dealt with extensively in other works. For present purposes, it is sufficient to note that it exists as a primarily equitable doctrine that is capable of setting aside gifts in circumstances where:

1. a relationship of trust and confidence exists between the donor and donee; and
2. the gift amounted to an abuse of that relationship.

The unconscionability or otherwise of the transaction is critical to make out undue influence; the authenticity of the consent is not relevant.

Duress

In the realm of contract law the concept of duress is closely related to that of undue influence. As the name suggests, the principle of duress arises where a party enters into a contract having had his consent induced by some illegitimate threat, giving him no practical choice but to enter into the contract.

It is not clear whether the principle of duress applies to a gift as it does to a contract. It is submitted that it probably does since the justification underpinning the contractual concept of duress applies equally well to gifts. Alternatively, since the element of intention to make a gift is without exact parallel in contract law, it is perhaps open to a donor under duress to say that the requisite element of intention was lacking.

Want of Formality

As has been described above, it is possible for a gift to fail for want of formality. This could arise, for example, because some statutorily or contractually imposed formality has not been honoured, or it could be, as in *Re Cole*, because physical delivery has not been achieved.

In such circumstances of a failed gift, the law generally presumes that there was *not* an intention on the part of the transferor to make a gift, and the transferee will hold the property on a resulting trust for the benefit of the transferor.[12]

In some circumstances, however, the opposite presumption prevails, namely that a transfer is intended to be a gift. The principal circumstance in which this presumption (called the 'presumption of advancement') exists is where a father makes a gift to his son. The presumption was described as follows by Lord Denning in the Privy Council in *Chettiar v Chettiar* [1962] AC 294:

> [W]henever a father transfers property to his son, there is a presumption that he intended it as a gift to his son; and if he wishes to rebut that presumption and to say that his son took as trustee for him, he must prove the trust clearly and distinctly, by evidence properly admissible for the purpose, and not leave it to be inferred from slight circumstances.

Although the presumption of advancement may ostensibly have an air of obsolescence, it appears to have been accepted as recently as 2002 in *Collier v Collier* [2002] EWCA Civ 1095, albeit applied without question to a daughter as well as a son.

Historically, another instance of the presumption of advancement was a transfer from a husband to a wife, but not vice versa. As long ago as the late 1960s the Court of Appeal cast doubt on the validity of this presumption (*Pettitt v Pettitt* [1970] AC 777). It is doubtful whether this presumption of advancement carries any real weight in the modern era, and if it does from husband to wife it almost certainly does from wife to husband too.

There is some support for other presumptions of advancement between family members (see, for example, *Tinsley v Milligan* [1993] 3 WLR 126).

In the case of both presumptions of advancement and presumptions of resulting trust, it is possible to rebut the presumption with evidence to the contrary. In the case of rebutting a presumption of resulting trust, a successful rebuttal does not lead to the gift being perfected in spite of want of formality; all that can be achieved is proof that the donor did indeed intend to make the gift.

Indeed, it has historically been a cornerstone of equity that a trust will not be imposed to perfect an imperfect gift. In *Milroy v Lord* (1862) 45 ER 1185 a

[12] *Standing v Bowring* (1885) 31 Ch D 282 (CA).

settlor intended to convey some shares in a bank to the defendant trustee to be held on trust for the benefit of the plaintiffs. It was a condition of the effective transfer of shares that the new owner should be registered in the bank's books, but this never happened. Consequently the legal transfer of the shares was never effected.

The court's conclusion was that the attempted settlement was defective. Had the settlor decided to hold the shares on trust himself, the trust would have been effective because there would have been no need for a disposition of the legal interest and the gift would not have failed for want of formalities. As it stood, however, the gift did not succeed. Crucially for present purposes, the Court of Appeal declined to find the existence of an implied trust to effect the gift by other means. *Milroy v Lord* is authority usually cited in support of the equitable maxim 'equity will not assist a volunteer'.

In practice, the rule in *Milroy v Lord* has not been as rigorously and harshly enforced as the judgment may imply. The courts have tended to temper the impact of the rule and over the years have watered it down somewhat. In *Pennington v Waine* [2002] 1 WLR 2075 Arden LJ explained the position. The following quotation is lengthy but it is worth reproducing in full as a succinct judicial exposition of the important issue of the ways in which the court may deviate from the strict rule in *Milroy v Lord*:

> … the principle that equity will not assist a volunteer at first sight looks like a hard-edged rule of law not permitting much argument or exception. Historically the emergence of the principle may have been due to the need for equity to follow the law rather than an intuitive development of equity. The principle against imperfectly constituted gifts led to harsh and seemingly paradoxical results. Before long, equity had tempered the wind to the shorn lamb (i e the donee). It did so on more than one occasion and in more than one way.
>
> 55 First it was held that an incompletely constituted gift could be upheld if the gift had been completed to such an extent that the donee could enforce his right to the shares as against third parties without forcing the donor to take any further step. Accordingly, if a share transfer has been executed by the donor and duly presented to the company for registration, the donee would be entitled, if necessary, to apply to the court for an order for rectification of the share register under *section 359 of the Companies Act 1985*. Such an order would not, of course, be granted if for example the directors had a discretion to refuse to register the transfer and had timeously passed a valid resolution to decline to register the transfer: see *Buckley on the Companies Acts* (looseleaf ed), para 359.277.
>
> 56 That exception was extended in Rose v Inland Revenue Comrs [1952] Ch 499 and other cases by holding that for this exception to apply it was not necessary that the donor should have done all that it was necessary to be done to complete the gift, short of registration of the transfer. On the contrary it was sufficient if the donor had done all that it was necessary for him or her to do.
>
> …
>
> 59 Secondly equity has tempered the wind (of the principle that equity will not assist a volunteer) to the shorn lamb (the donee) by utilising the constructive trust. This

does not constitute a declaration of trust and thus does not fall foul of the principle (see *Milroy v Lord 4 De GF & J 264* and *Jones v Lock LR 1 Ch App 25*) that an imperfectly constituted gift is not saved by being treated as a declaration of trust. Thus, for example, in *T Choithram International SA v Pagarini [2001] 1 WLR 1 the Privy Council* held that the assets which the donor gave to the foundation of which he was one of the trustees were held upon trust to vest the same in all the trustees of the foundation on the terms of the trusts of the foundation. This particular trust obligation was not a term of the express trust constituting the foundation but a constructive trust adjunct to it. So, too, in *Rose v Inland Revenue Comrs [1952] Ch 499, the Court of Appeal* held that the beneficial interest in the shares passed when the share transfers were delivered to the transferee, and that consequently the transferor was a trustee of the legal estate in the shares from that date. At one stage in his judgment Sir Raymond Evershed MR went further and held that an equitable interest passed when the document declaring a gift was executed. Sir Raymond Evershed MR said, at pp 510–511:

> 'If a man executes a document transferring all his equitable interest, say, in shares, that document, operating, and intended to operate, as a transfer, will give rise to and take effect as a trust; for the assignor will then be a trustee of the legal estate in the shares for the person in whose favour he has made an assignment of his beneficial interest. And, for my part, I do not think that the case *Milroy v Lord* is an authority which compels this court to hold that in this case – where, in the terms of Turner LJ's judgment, the settlor did everything which, according to the nature of the property comprised in the settlement, was necessary to be done by him in order to transfer the property – the result necessarily negatives the conclusion that, pending registration, the settlor was a trustee of the legal interest for the transferee'

…

60 Thirdly equity has tempered the wind to the shorn lamb by applying a benevolent construction to words of gift. As explained above an imperfect gift is not saved by being treated as a declaration of trust. But where a court of equity is satisfied that the donor had an intention to make an immediate gift, the court will construe the words which the donor used as words effecting a gift or declaring a trust if they can fairly bear that meaning and otherwise the gift will fail. This point can also be illustrated by reference to *T Choithram International SA v Pagarini [2001] 1 WLR 1*. In that case the donor signed the trust deed setting up the foundation and then simply made an oral declaration of gift of all his wealth to the foundation. The Privy Council held that the gift to 'the foundation' could only properly be construed as a gift to the purposes declared by the trust deed and administered by the trustees. Lord Browne-Wilkinson giving the judgment of the Privy Council referred, at p 11, to the arguments that the courts below had accepted, namely that:

> 'the court will not give a benevolent construction so as to treat ineffective words of outright gift as taking effect as if the donor had declared himself a trustee for the donee: *Milroy v Lord 4 De GF & J 264*. So, it is said, in this case TCP [the donor] used words of gift to the foundation (not words declaring himself a trustee): unless he transferred the shares and deposits so as to vest title in all the trustees, he had not done all that he could in order to effect the gift. It therefore fails. Further it is said that it is not possible to treat TCP's words of gift as a declaration of trust because they make no reference to trusts. Therefore the case does not fall within either of the possible methods by which a complete gift can be made and the gift fails'

Lord Browne-Wilkinson disagreed with this conclusion, at pp 11–12:

> '*Although equity will not aid a volunteer, it will not strive officiously to defeat a gift*. This case falls between the two common form situations mentioned above. Although the words used by TCP [the donor] are those normally appropriate to an outright gift – 'I give to X' – in the present context there is no breach of the principle in *Milroy v Lord* if the words of TCP's gift (i e to the foundation) are given their only possible meaning in this context. The foundation has no legal existence apart from the trust declared by the foundation trust deed. Therefore the words 'I give to the foundation' can only mean 'I give to the trustees of the foundation trust deed to be held by them on the trusts of the foundation trust deed'. Although the words are apparently words of outright gift they are essentially words of gift on trust.

CONDITIONAL GIFTS

The possibility of conditional gifts is alluded to above and examined in more detail in this section.

The concept of a gift being subject to some form of reservation or condition may seem as odds with the normal conversational use of the word 'gift', which perhaps implies a total renunciation of control and influence on the part of the donor. Nevertheless, the possibility of gifts that are subject to conditions has long been recognised in English law, albeit it is an arcane area that is rarely considered.

Conditional Gifts of Chattels as Distinct from Gifts of Realty

Prior to the Law of Property Act 1925 (and as discussed further in Chapter 1 above) the various possible estates in land were easily capable of giving effect to conditional gifts of land. For example, a gift of an estate in fee tail was subject to the condition that it could only pass to the donee's heir (as determined by law) and not to any person the donee may nominate.

Section 1 Law of Property Act 1925 dispensed with all possible legal estates in land, except for fee simple absolute in possession and legal lease. All other estates and the conditional interests they carried with them therefore became available only in equity. That remains the position.

The position with chattels is less clear. The concept of estates in land is underpinned by the principle that all land belongs to the Crown. Any other person is capable of holding only an estate in land – ie certain rights in land in respect of which the Crown retains residual ownership (albeit in the modern era the rights attendant on an estate are very substantial, and the Crown's residual rights have shrunk to very limited rights of reversion – see Part 1 above). By contrast, there is no equivalent concept of estates governing ownership of chattels because ownership of chattels does not ultimately vest in the Crown.

In consequence there is a school of thought that the common law is and has always been incapable of recognising conditional ownership of chattels, and that at law ownership is either absolute or nil. It would follow from that proposition that conditional gifts are impossible in law, and any kind of conditional gift could only be recognised in equity. This is apparently what was meant in the sixteenth-century authority *Devise* (1580) Brook New Cases 59:

> Agreed for good Law, that the occupation of a Chattel may be devised by way of Remainder, but if the thing it self were devised to use, the Remainder is void; for *a gift or devise of* a *Chattel for an hour*, is for ever; and the donee, or devisee may give, sel, and dispose it, & the remainder depending upon it, is void.

On the other hand, it is plain that the common law *does* recognised contingent rights of ownership in chattels, for example the rights of a possessor against all but a person with better title. Indeed, as has been observed on several occasions elsewhere in this book, the English law does not recognise an absolute right of ownership as such. Instead 'ownership' really amounts to a bundle of rights, some or all of which may vest in a person who can realistically be called an 'owner'. Thus, in the case of *Armory v Delamirie* (1721) 93 ER 664, which is discussed in detail elsewhere, the rights of a finder of a jewel were vindicated against a silversmith who had taken possession from him. The finder could to an extent therefore be described as the 'owner' of the jewel, in that he was entitled to enforce his rights to it against the world, but his rights were not absolute, because he would not have been able to enforce them against the person who had lost the jewel.

As Robert Chambers has argued[13] there are three mechanisms that the common law might deploy to give effect to elements of conditionality in a gift. It is to be stressed that this is purely a consideration of the common law mechanisms available. As stated above, there is considerable scope to make conditional gifts in equity, and in practice this is probably how most conditional gifts would take effect.

Conditional Ownership

First, the common law might recognise a concept of conditional ownership. In other words, a type of proprietary interest in the chattel that is subject to the possibility of reverting to the donor. This notion is rarely encountered and may perhaps not even exist. Still, it received at least some support in *Kwei Tek Chao v British Traders and Shippers Ltd* [1954] 2 QB 459.

[13] Chapter 18 of the 2nd edition of *Palmer and McKendrick, Interests in Goods*, to which I am indebted in this section.

In that case, sellers of goods had arranged for shipment to Hong Kong under a 'c.i.f. contract', which was a contract under which the seller paid the costs of transport and insurance, and title to the goods passed to the buyer when the goods were unloaded at the receiving port. Devlin J analysed the position as to ownership in the following way at 487:

> I think that the true view is that what the buyer obtains, when the title under the documents is given to him, is the property in the goods, subject to the condition that they revest if upon examination he finds them to be not in accordance with the contract. That means that he gets only conditional property in the goods, the condition being a condition subsequent. All his dealings with the documents are dealings only with that conditional property in the goods. It follows, therefore, that there can be no dealing which is inconsistent with the seller's ownership unless he deals with something more than the conditional property. If the property passes altogether, not being subject to any condition, there is no ownership left in the seller with which any inconsistent act under section 35 could be committed. If the property passes conditionally the only ownership left in the seller is the reversionary interest in the property in the event of the condition subsequent operating to restore it to him. It is that reversionary interest with which the buyer must not, save with the penalty of accepting the goods, commit an inconsistent act.

Of course, *Chao* was a case involving a contract rather than a gift, and as such the concept of a condition subsequent is a more familiar mechanism for reversing the transfer of title. Still, it appears tolerably clear that the donee of a gift is entitled to disclaim ownership and thereby return ownership to the donor, and that pending that disclaimer the donee is the owner of the gift.[14] It may be, therefore, that the conditional ownership contemplated by Devlin J, where a party receives title to goods they are entitled to reject, also exists where a donee receives a gift that he is entitled to reject. If so, it may well be that a gift of a chattel can be impressed with a condition subsequent by the donor, which creates a similar conditional ownership pending it being triggered.

Bailment

Bailment is considered in relative detail elsewhere in this book. For present purposes, it can be noted that bailment is a mechanism by which a conditional gift may be effected. *Clough Mill Ltd v Martin* [1985] 1 WLR 111 is another case in a contractual context with possible relevance to the law of gift. The facts involved a vendor of yarn to a fabric manufacturer, which was subject to a contractual retention of title clause. The clause provided that title to the yarn would not pass to the buyer until the seller had been paid in full or the yarn had been sold to a third party. That poses the question of whether the buyer,

[14] See for example *Standing v Bowring* (1885) 31 Ch D 282.

in arranging an onward sale to a third party, had title to do so. Robert Goff LJ stated as follows at 116:

> I for my part can see nothing objectionable in an agreement between parties under which A, the owner of goods, gives possession of those goods to B, at the same time conferring on B. a power of sale and a power to consume the goods in manufacture, though A will remain the owner of the goods until they are either sold or consumed. I do not see why the relationship between A and B, pending sale or consumption, should not be the relationship of bailor and bailee, even though A has no right to trace the property in his goods into the proceeds of sale. If that is what the parties have agreed should happen, I can see no reason why the law should not give effect to that intention.

The earlier case of *Re Stoneham* [1918] 1 Ch 149 supports the proposition that it is perfectly possible for a bailee to become an owner of goods pursuant to a gift. In that case a testator, during his life, had divided his time between a property in Brighton and one in Essex called Beredens. In 1910 he encouraged his grandson, Robert, to move to Beredens and live there permanently, thereby making him bailee of various chattels at the property, including, in particular, oak furniture and suits of armour. The court found that in 1913 the testator had orally gifted the chattels in question to Robert. A dispute arose about whether Robert's oral gift was effective, or whether the chattels passed pursuant to the terms of his will.[15] The court concluded that, in circumstances where an intended donee is already in possession of the goods, an oral gift is sufficient for a gift to be effective. That is in contrast with the position (as discussed elsewhere) where an intended donee is not in possession of goods, in which case some specific act of delivery is required.

The possibility of a bailee acquiring ownership on the satisfaction of a condition is available to address a gift that is subject to a condition. If that condition is not met then the bailee/potential donor is liable to produce the chattel to the bailor/donee under ordinary bailment principles. This seems to underpin the approach the courts have taken to disputes over the return of engagement rings and the like, which are dealt with further below.

Money Had and Received

The action of 'money had and received' is most familiar in the context of contractual disputes, but in fact is available in all circumstances where payments have been made by mistake or otherwise where consideration has failed. It seems likely that a similar approach would be available in the case of a gift of

[15] As an aside, and as the court also noted, it is rather curious that the point came to be argued since the terms of the testator's will *also* provided for Robert to receive the chattels in question.

money made subject to a condition, especially given the court's present general tendency to increase the role of restitution in English law.

Certainly it is well established that deposits paid in advance of a contract are to be refunded when the contract is never concluded on a money had and received basis.[16] More recently, the courts have confirmed that this basis for recovery of money is available even in circumstances where the agreement concluded or to be concluded between parties stopped short of being a contract.[17] In fact, as noted in *Chitty on Contracts*,[18] the courts are so keen to distance the law of money had and received from a purely contractual principle, the phrase 'failure of basis' has been coined as opposed to the more traditional 'failure of consideration'. It appears to follow that any gift of money subject to a condition is highly likely to be amenable to the principles of money had and received.

The Nature of a Condition Imposed

Insofar as a condition is imposed on a gift, the court will have to decide whether it is a condition precedent or a condition subsequent. A condition precedent is a condition that must be fulfilled before the donee can receive the gift. A condition subsequent involves the gift being effective at the outset, but also being capable of being vitiated on the happening of certain events.

Both conditions precedent and subsequent can be imposed on gifts. In *Sifton v Sifton* [1938] AC 656 the Privy Council made clear that, in cases where it is difficult to establish whether a condition is meant to be precedent or subsequent, the court will presume that it was intended to be subsequent.

The question of whether a condition is precedent or subsequent may not always be easy to determine. *Sifton* was a case in point: a bequest was made to the testator's daughter, 'so long as she continues to reside in Canada'.

The question of whether a condition is precedent or subsequent is critical, however. For one thing, a donee of a gift subject to a condition subsequent will have a vested interest, which, among other things, can be passed in a will.[19]

Perhaps even more importantly, where a condition is invalid, for example by virtue of being uncertain, impossible or illegal, there will be dramatically different consequences depending on whether the condition imposed was precedent or subsequent.

The position with conditions subsequent is comparatively straightforward. Where a condition subsequent is invalid, the condition will drop off the gift and the donee will take the gift free of any condition. An example was *Clayton v Ramsden* [1943] AC 320. In that case a testator left a bequest that was, in general

[16] See, for example, *Chillingworth v Esche* [1924] 1 Ch 97.
[17] *Spaul v Spaul* [2014] EWCA Civ 679.
[18] 33rd edition, 29-057.
[19] See *Re Greenwood* [1903] 1 Ch 749.

terms, conditional upon the donee not marrying someone who was not Jewish. The House of Lords formed the view that this was a condition subsequent that was void for uncertainty, and accordingly the bequest should take effect without being subject to any condition.

In *Re Allen* [1953] Ch 810 the Court of Appeal considered a bequest conditional on the donee '[being] a member of the Church of England and an adherent to the doctrine of that Church'. The Court of Appeal concluded that this was a condition subsequent rather than a condition precedent. As such it was not subject to the same strictures of certainty as a condition precedent, but the court affirmed that an uncertain condition subsequent would drop off with the effect that the donee would take the property without that condition having effect:

> A condition subsequent operates to divest or determine a gift or estate previously or otherwise vested; so that if the condition be void the gift or estate remains. It has been long established that the courts (which are inclined against the divesting of gifts or estates already vested) will hold a condition subsequent void if its terms are such that (apart from mere difficulties of construction of the language or of the ascertainment of the facts) it cannot be clearly known in advance or from the beginning what are the circumstances the happening of which will cause the divesting or determination of the gift or estate.

This case is therefore also authority for the proposition that conditions subsequent in gifts are much more apt to be invalid for reasons of uncertainty than conditions precedent. It should also be noted that the onus is on the donee to demonstrate that a condition precedent has been met.

What, then, is the position where a condition precedent is invalid? In the case of real property, the position is the opposite as it is with a condition subsequent, namely that the gift will fail.[20]

The situation is rather more complex in the case of personalty, however. In *Re Piper* [1946] 2 All ER 503 the court affirmed the following proposition:

> [T]he civil law, which in this respect has been adopted by the courts of equity, differs in some respects from the common law in its treatment of conditions precedent; the rule in civil law being that where a condition precedent is originally impossible, or is illegal as involving *malum prohibitium*, the bequest is absolute, just as if the condition had been subsequent. But where the performance of the condition is the sole motive of the bequest, or its impossibility was unknown to the testator, or the condition which was possible in its creation has since become impossible by the act of God, or where it is illegal as involving *malum in se*, in these cases the civil agrees with the common law in holding both gifts and condition void.

As may be apparent from the above, the prohibition against the enforcement of conditions *mulum in se* (ie 'evil in intent') operates to ameliorate much of the

[20] *Re Elliott* [1952] Ch 217.

harshness that would be caused by donors attaching interfering conditions to gifts. In *Clayton* the court complained of the testator seeking to 'direct the lives of his children from beyond the grave'. In *Re Gape's Will Trusts* [1952] Ch 743 a testatrix had imposed a condition precedent on various bequests to the effect that the donee must take up permanent residence in England within six months of the bequest. Evershed MR observed as follows at 746–47:

> It is well established that the courts are always adverse to conditions which may affect a free choice in matters relating to a marriage or in matters relating to conscience. These considerations of public policy have obviously no application in the present case. I assume, however – and I think it is right to assume – that the test in all conditions subsequent of this character is the same, whether the condition relates to such a matter as religion or to such a matter as residence.

Another type of condition attached to a gift that is generally invalid is a condition designed to persuade a person to separate from his or her spouse. In *Brown v Peck* (1758) 1 Eden 140 a testator made a particular bequest to his niece, who had married without the niece's mother's consent. The bequest was £2 a month if the niece continued to live with her husband, or £5 a month if the niece left her husband and returned to live with the niece's mother. The court found that the niece was entitled to £5 per month even if she stayed with her husband because the condition was impossible at the time it was imposed and was in any event contrary to the public good.

This principle has given rise to some complications in circumstances where a person has wanted to benefit a married person who was without the support of a spouse. In *Sparks v Southall* [1920] 1 Ch 122 a testator was, at the time of his death, living with a married woman who had been abandoned by her husband. The testator bequeathed to her the sum of £750, 'provided and so long as she shall not return to live with her husband and provided and so long as she shall not remarry and subject to her leading a clean moral and respectable life in the opinion of my executors and trustees'. Prima facie this condition might have failed as tending to prevent the married woman from returning to her husband. Lawrence J found, however, that the proper purpose to impute to the condition was that the testator intended to maintain the donee insofar as she did not have the protection of a husband to look after her and the condition was accordingly valid:

> I think that it would be altogether unreasonable to hold that because of this proviso the Court ought to impute to the testator an intention that the gift should operate so as to prevent her returning to her husband or remarrying rather than an intention to provide her with maintenance until she should again live under the protection of a husband who would undertake the duty of maintaining her. Further, the condition that she should live a clean, moral and respectable life in my opinion tends to negative the contention that the real object was to prevent her from returning to her husband.

On the other hand, and rather more recently, the court in *Re Johnson's Will Trusts* [1967] Ch 387 had to consider a bequest of income to a testator's daughter that was subject to a condition precedent that the income would not be paid, 'during such time as my said daughter is married to and living with her present husband'. Buckley J considered evidence showing, perhaps unsurprisingly, that the testator did not much like his daughter's husband and feared that the husband would waste the money bequeathed. Buckley J held, however, that evidence of motivation was of no real assistance in deciding whether a condition was valid. Rather he reasoned:

> It seems to me that one must look at the provision itself and attempt to assess whether it is a provision of such a kind as will have results of a sort which should be regarded as undesirable. It may be that regarding the matter in that way one may come to the conclusion, as Lawrence J. did in *In re Lovell*, that there is nothing objectionable in the disposition or one may come to the conclusion, as did Simonds J. in In re Caborne,[21] that the tendency of the disposition is such as to encourage the breaking up of a subsisting marriage, in which case that is something to which this court will not give effect, upon the ground that it is undesirable from the point of view of public policy.

It should also be added that any gift attaching a condition requiring the gift to be used for an illegal purpose will, it is submitted, be dealt with on the same principles that make a sum passing under an illegal contract void. Indeed, it is submitted that a sum passing under a contract that is found to be void for illegality and a sum passing by way of a gift with a void condition that it be used in an illegal way are in substance the same thing, and are unlikely to be considered separately by the courts.

The law in this area, and in particular on the question of what happens to the money passed, has undergone considerable change in recent times as a result of the Supreme Court's decision in *Patel v Mirza* [2017] AC 467. That case was concerned with a payment made by the claimant to the defendant with the mutual intention that it should be invested in shares pursuant to inside information that the defendant expected to receive. Investment pursuant to inside information was of course illegal. In the event, however, the inside information never materialised and the claimant sought the return of his money.

Before explaining the Supreme Court's reasoning in *Patel*, it is appropriate to refer to the previous leading authority on the question, which was *Tinsley v Milligan* [1994] 1 AC 340. In *Tinsley*, Ms Tinsley and Ms Milligan had contributed equally to the purchase price of a house. The property was purchased in Ms Tinsley's sole name but it was understood between the parties that they owned it in equal shares. The reason the property was placed in Ms Tinsley's sole name was so that Ms Milligan could fraudulently claim benefits from the Department of Social Security.

[21] [1943] Ch 224; [1943] 2 All ER 7 in which the court found that the effect of a condition was to encourage the 'violation of the sanctity of marriage' and accordingly that it should not be upheld.

In due course, Ms Milligan and Ms Tinsley fell out and Ms Tinsley sought possession from Ms Milligan on the basis that she was the sole owner. Ms Milligan counterclaimed for an order vindicating her 50 per cent equitable ownership of the property, which Ms Tinsley opposed on the basis that the entire transaction had been entered into for illegal purposes and ought therefore to be void.

In *Tinsley* the House of Lords favoured Ms Milligan and found that she was entitled to a 50 per cent interest in the property. Its reasoning was that Ms Milligan did not need to rely in her claim on any matter of wrongdoing. She could vindicate her 50 per cent beneficial ownership simply by appealing to the principles of resulting trusts: namely that as a person who had contributed 50 per cent of the purchase price she was deemed to be entitled to 50 per cent of the equity under a resulting trust.

The decision in *Tinsley* was subject to a high level of criticism for many years, not for its result but for its reasoning. In particular, the reliance on a resulting trust analysis produced consequences that seemed highly arbitrary, especially that under the 'presumption of advancement', had a parent contributed money to the purchase of the property, as had Ms Milligan, the parent would have been deemed to intend to make a gift of the money such that he or she would have had no entitlement to recover the funds under a resulting trust.

In *Patel*, therefore, the Supreme Court did not follow *Tinsley*. Instead it took the view that Mr Patel was entitled to recover his money (as presumably would Ms Milligan) on a restitutionary analysis. Per Lord Toulson at paragraph 121:

> A claimant, such as Mr Patel, who satisfies the ordinary requirements of a claim for unjust enrichment, should not be debarred from enforcing his claim by reason only of the fact that the money which he seeks to recover was paid for an unlawful purpose. There may be rare cases where for some particular reason the enforcement of such a claim might be regarded as undermining the integrity of the justice system, but there are no such circumstances in this case.

The decision in *Patel*, therefore, supports the proposition that, where a gift is made on the condition that it is used for an illegal purpose, the donor will generally be able to recover on the gift. It also supports the proposition referred to above that a claim for money had and received is a mechanism available to the common law to give effect to the conditional nature of a gift.

On the other hand, it is to be stressed that if conditions are imposed on a gift that are not invalid for reasons of public policy or for some other reason, the condition will be enforced even if unusual. Thus in *Re Neeld* [1962] Ch 643 the testator had made a bequest on the condition that any beneficiary who should come into possession of the bequest should adopt a particular surname. Lord Evershed MR made it plain that he considered such a condition to be rather outmoded, but nevertheless was prepared to enforce it:

> The question of public policy I can deal with more shortly. It is no doubt true that in this day and age it may by some be thought old-fashioned to impose an obligation

> as to change of name upon the husband to whom a woman is or may thereafter be married. I confess, however, that it does not seem to me fair or sensible to say that the obligation, in any true or real sense, can interfere with the ordinary sanctity in which marriage is held. It is possible that on occasion some embarrassment might be occasioned. On the other hand, we are here concerned with one who is, by settlement or will, conferring a substantial benefit on others, and it does not seem to me that there is anything in our law which would justify the view that such a donor is not entitled, if he wishes, to attach conditions of this kind to his benefaction. Lord Mansfield, nearly 200 years ago, thought clauses of this kind 'silly,' and I do not doubt that there may be many today who hold a similar view. In my judgment, however (as I stated in *In re Gape*), if clauses of this kind, which have been part of the conveyancing system in our country for very many years, ought now to be treated as contrary to public policy, that is a matter for Parliament rather than for the courts.

Conditions Governing the Use of the Gift

It is often the case that a donor (typically a testator) makes a gift to a person purportedly subject to a condition that certain payments are made to a third party. In such circumstances the law treats the gift as a trust. That is because, where the donee is the donor's heir, as is often the case, then the donee will otherwise benefit from breaching the condition.

Thus, in *Re Frame* [1939] Ch 700 a testator made a bequest on terms that the legatee should adopt his daughter and make certain payments to other children. The legatee endeavoured to adopt the daughter but the attempt failed due to opposition. Simonds J stated as follows at 703–04:

> A devise, or bequest, on condition that the devisee or legatee makes certain payments does not import a condition in the strict sense of the word, but a trust, so that, though the devisee or legatee dies before the testator and the gift does not take effect, yet the payments must be made; for it is a trust, and no trust fails for want of trustees.

'Quistclose' trusts are a well-known example of equity intervening to ensure that something passed from A to B is used in accordance with A's specific intended purpose. The Quistclose principle is available in the context of a conditional gift was well as property that passes for a commercial purpose.

In *Barclays Bank Ltd v Quistclose Investments Ltd* [1970] AC 567 a company was in great financial difficulty and in particular was gravely overdrawn with its bankers, Barclays. It had arranged a bail-out package with a financier but the financier was only prepared to proceed if the company could find the money to pay a dividend it had previously declared. The company accordingly arranged a loan from Quistclose Investments for the specific purpose of paying the dividend (and Barclays knew that fact). A cheque was provided and paid into a purpose-opened bank account with Barclays. The company went into liquidation, however, before the dividend was paid.

Quistclose accordingly brought a claim asserting an equitable entitlement to the money on the basis that it was impressed with a particular purpose, and that purpose having failed the money should properly considered to be held on a resulting trust for the benefit of Quistclose. Lord Wilberforce agreed, saying as follows at 581–82:

> There is surely no difficulty in recognising the co-existence in one transaction of legal and equitable rights and remedies: when the money is advanced, the lender acquires an equitable right to see that it is applied for the primary designated purpose ... when the purpose has been carried out (i.e., the debt paid) the lender has his remedy against the borrower in debt: if the primary purpose cannot be carried out, the question arises if a secondary purpose (i.e., repayment to the lender) has been agreed, expressly or by implication: if it has, the remedies of equity may be invoked to give effect to it, if it has not (and the money is intended to fall within the general fund of the debtor's assets) then there is the appropriate remedy for recovery of a loan. I can appreciate no reason why the flexible interplay of law and equity cannot let in these practical arrangements, and other variations if desired: it would be to the discredit of both systems if they could not.

If Lord Wilberforce was able to find that the lender's available remedy in common law did not preclude an additional remedy in equity, it may follow a fortiori that in the case of a gift, where there is no legal remedy to consider, a Quistclose trust will apply to the gift.

The courts appear never to have been called upon to decide precisely that question but it would appear logical as a matter of analysis, and derives strong support from *Conservative and Unionist Party v Burrell* [1982] 1 WLR 522. In *Burell* the court was called upon to consider whether the Conservative Party was an unincorporated association, which was significant for tax purposes. Although making no express reference to Quistclose trusts, Brightman LJ stated as follows at 529–30, while reflecting on the rights of a donor of funds for a particular but non-charitable purpose:

> [S]uppose that the recipient is the treasurer of an organisation which receives and applies funds from multifarious sources for certain political purposes. If the contributor pays money to that treasurer, the treasurer has clear authority to add the contribution to the mixed fund (as I will call it) that he holds. At that stage I think the mandate becomes irrevocable. That is to say, the contributor has no right to demand his contribution back, once it has been mixed with other money under the authority of the contributor. The contributor has no legal right to require the mixed fund to be unscrambled for his benefit. This does not mean, however, that all contributors lose all rights once their cheques are cashed, with the absurd result that the treasurer or other officers can run off with the mixed fund with impunity. I have no doubt that any contributor has a remedy against the recipient (i.e. the treasurer, or the officials at whose direction the treasurer acts) to restrain or make good a mis-application of the mixed fund.

The courts have periodically had to consider a situation in which a donor has made a gift that is subject to a condition that particular action is taken within a specified term. Where the condition is met within the time provided for, there is no difficulty in the gift being made. Where the condition is not met at all, again it is clear that the gift will not be made, subject to what is said above about conditions precedent and (more often) subsequent dropping off in certain circumstances so as to enable the donee to take free.

What is slightly more problematic is the scenario in which an intended donee attempts to comply with the condition, but does so out of time. Here the case law is not entirely consistent.

In *Taylor v Popham* (1782) 28 ER 1059 a testator had granted his son annuities during his lifetime. In his will the testator made a gift of £600 to his son Robert on the proviso that Robert executed a release in respect of any entitlement to the annuities within three months of the testator's death. It appears that Robert executed such a release but not in the time limit given and the release was therefore rejected by the executors. Thereafter, Robert appears to have asserted his full entitlement under the annuities, which he contended was over £23,000. His position was that the release was ineffective and therefore he was entitled to seek the full amount from the estate. The testator's other beneficiaries contested this analysis and took the position that the release was effective, and accordingly Robert had no further entitlement from the estate, except to the £600 gift. The court agreed with the other beneficiaries and concluded that the release was effective even though given out of time. Unfortunately the court's reasoning, indeed the judgment as a whole, is rather opaque, and no basis appears to be given for the court's conclusion.

Notwithstanding *Taylor*, which may be said to militate in favour of a general tolerance to non-compliance with the exact terms of conditions attached to gifts, the better position is surely that the court will excuse a failure of strict compliance with a time limit if compliance with the time limit was not of the essence of the gift. This would mirror the way the court approaches whether a failure to comply with a contractual time limit gives rise to a right to terminate for repudiatory breach.

This approach has support from the authorities. For example, in *Re Goodwin* [1924] 2 Ch 26 the court was faced with somewhat similar facts as in *Taylor*. A testator had bequeathed his wife an annuity of £500. This was intended to be a substitute for and replace an annuity of £70, which she was already receiving. Accordingly, the £500 annuity was to be available to her only if she relinquished within six months the £70 annuity. The testator's estate appeared unable to meet the annuity of £500, so the wife took no steps to relinquish the £70 annuity. Fifteen years later she died but the trustees of the testator's estate were in a position to pay the £500 annuity. Accordingly, the wife's beneficiaries sought that payment, which was opposed on the basis that she had not satisfied the condition within the appropriate time. Romer J allowed the full £500 annuity payment and reasoned as follows:

> It is well settled by authority that where a gift in a will is made subject to a condition, even a condition precedent, to be performed within a specified time, but the condition is not in fact performed within that time, then, at any rate in the absence of an express gift over, it is always a question for the Court to determine whether the time

> so specified was of the essence of the matter. In determining that question the Court must have regard to what was presumably the intention of the testator in inserting the condition, what it was that he desired to bring about or to guard against; and if the Court finds that a performance of the condition at a time subsequent to the expiration of the period fixed by the testator in substance provides for the very thing that the testator intended to provide for, so that all parties can be put in substantially the same position as they would have been in had the condition been performed within the proper time, time is not regarded as of the essence, and such performance is treated as a sufficient compliance with the condition.

This approach allows the court sufficient flexibility to do justice in the various possible circumstances involving gifts subject to a time-limited condition. It is clearly to be preferred to any inflexible approach in which conditions are uniformly either strictly imposed or ignored.

Engagement Presents

A particular body of law exists that governs the position when a present is given during an engagement in the expectation of marriage.

Historically, from at least the Middle Ages, the law had sought to protect women (men did not generally enjoy such protection for obvious societal reasons) from a man agreeing to marry them but then reneging on that agreement. Initially this was a matter purely for the ecclesiastical courts but in the reign of Charles I was put within the jurisdiction of the temporal courts. This action was known as 'breach of promise' and was in effect the enforcement of a contract (albeit with certain features particular to that cause of action that developed over time). As the Law Commission put the position in its 1969 report (referred to below):

> The action for breach of promise, as it has evolved, reflects the refusal of the common law to draw any distinction between commercial and other types of agreement. Hence mutual promises to marry fulfil all the conditions of a legally binding contract and can be enforced in much the same way as, for example, a contract of employment.

By the late nineteenth century there appears to have been a significant climate of opinion to the effect that breach of promise was an obsolete or at least problematic action. Section 2 Evidence Further Amendment Act 1869 provided that no action for breach of promise could succeed unless the evidence of the plaintiff was corroborated by some other source. This was a means of tackling a risk perceived by the legislators that spurious suits may be brought by fortune-hunting young women, who were perhaps felt likely to charm a jury in their favour. That is certainly the position depicted in Gilbert and Sullivan's comic operetta *Trial by Jury*, in which a breach of promise suit is ultimately settled by the judge agreeing to marry the plaintiff.

In any event, the action for breach of promise endured until the late 1960s; the footballer George Best was one of the last defendants to such a suit.

On 14 October 1969 the Law Commission produced a report into actions for breach of promise, considering whether it was an obsolete action and if so whether some alternative arrangements should replace it.

The Law Commission's conclusion was that breach of promise should be abolished. This was partly because the existence of the cause of action encouraged claims of 'a "gold-digging" nature', and partly because as a matter of public policy it was not desirable to discourage engaged persons from breaking their engagement if they wished (the expected result being a reduction in the stability of marriages). The effect of the abolition of a claim in breach of promise was to be that damages would no longer be available for the breach. It was recognised by the Law Commission, however, that specific provision needed to be made dealing with gifts of property that had been made in the expectation of the future marriage.

The result of the Law Commission's report was certain provisions of the Law of Property (Miscellaneous Provisions) Act 1970. Section 1 of the Act prevented an agreement to marry being a contract capable of enforcement.[22] Section 2 of the Act deals with the property of engaged couples and applies to engaged couples the same principles as are applied to married couples.

Section 3 of the Act deals with gifts made by the parties to the engagement and states as follows:

> (1) A party to an agreement to marry who makes a gift of property to the other party to the agreement on the condition (express or implied) that it shall be returned if the agreement is terminated shall not be prevented from recovering the property by reason only of his having terminated the agreement.
> (2) The gift of an engagement ring shall be presumed to be an absolute gift; this presumption may be rebutted by proving that the ring was given on the condition, express or implied, that it should be returned if the marriage did not take place for any reason.

The effect of sub-s 1 is to place gifts made during the course of an engagement and conditional on marriage on the same footing as all other gifts made conditional on the happening of a future event. In other words, the sub-section removes any presupposition that terminating the engagement should preclude a party from recovering a gift made during the engagement on the condition that the marriage would take place.

Sub-section 2, clearly enough, raises a rebuttable presumption that an engagement ring has been given as an absolute gift, and accordingly that it does not have to be returned if the marriage does not take place. This sub-section appears to have attracted some controversy, with some expressing the view that an engagement ring is clearly a gift that is intended to be conditional on

[22] In passing, s 5 of the Act also removed some even more obsolete torts: those of enticement (enticing a person away from their spouse); seduction (an action available to parents whose child was seduced, raped or enticed away); and harbouring another's spouse.

marriage. Ultimately, however, this is not a view that has been taken by Parliament, and the only advice can be that, where a party wishes to recover the ring in the event that the engagement breaks down, he or she must make that condition explicit.

'Death Bed Gifts'

A different and discrete area of law applies to gifts made in contemplation of the donor's death. These tend to be known as 'death bed gifts' for shorthand (albeit they are not always made literally on a death bed), or more technically by the Latin term *donationes mortis causa*. A definition of that term was given by Nourse LJ in *Sen v Headley* [1991] Ch 425 at 431–32 as follows:

> [T]he three general requirements for such a gift may be stated very much as they are stated in *Snell's Equity*, 29th ed. (1990), pp. 380–383. First, the gift must be made in contemplation, although not necessarily in expectation, of impending death. Secondly, the gift must be made upon the condition that it is to be absolute and perfected only on the donor's death, being revocable until that event occurs and ineffective if it does not. Thirdly, there must be a delivery of the subject matter of the gift, or the essential indicia of title thereto, which amounts to a parting with dominion and not mere physical possession over the subject matter of the gift.

The death bed gift has received a good deal of attention from the courts. It will be apparent that its main feature, as distinct from any other gift made during life, is that the donor delivers the gift, but on terms that the gift will not actually be perfected until the donor's death.

This gives rise to an obvious factual problem in many cases: how the court is to determine whether a gift is indeed conditional on death, or was intended to take effect in any event. The court's approach seems to be to assume that a gift made when death is imminent is to be presumed to be conditional on death. Thus in *Gardner v Parker* (1818) 56 ER 478 a gravely ill man gave an intimate a bond for £1,800 saying, 'You take that and keep it'. The court found that it was a death bed gift in view of the donor's grave ill health at the time.

So long as the gift has been made in contemplation of death, it does not matter if the donor subsequently dies of a different ailment. In *Wilkes v Allington* [1931] 2 Ch 104 the donor had been suffering from a chronic and fatal condition for five years and made his gift on the basis that he did not have long to live as a result of that condition. In the event he died of pneumonia following a chill, but the court was still content to treat the gift as a death bed gift. *Wilkes* is also further authority for the presumption that a gift made in circumstances of extreme ill health is to be treated as a death bed gift.

There is authority to suggest that it is a condition of a death bed gift not only that the donor should die, but also that the donor should predecease the donee. That appeared to be considered trite by Luxmore LJ in *Delgoffe v Fader* [1939]

Ch 922 at 927. If this is the correct position it has the potentially significant consequence that the estate of the donee will not benefit from the death bed gift. This is an interesting question and not one on which the law can confidently be said to be settled, given the lack of discussion of the point in *Delgoffe*.

A death bed gift differs from a testamentary gift only in the fact that a donee enjoys control of a death bed gift during the donor's lifetime. A death bed gift can be revoked by the donor during his lifetime, however,[23] and so the donee enjoys little in respect of the subject matter of the gift that would not be enjoyed by an intended legatee who had received the chattel as a bailee.

There is a curious feature of death bed gifts that merits particular attention. As stated above, the ordinary position is that a gift will fail for want of formality, and the courts will not step in to perfect it – the equitable maxim is that equity will not assist a volunteer.

In the case of death bed gifts, however, the courts adopt a more lenient approach. This approach seems to have begun with the decision in *Duffield v Elwes* (1827) 4 ER 959. In *Duffield*, an individual, incapacitated and quite literally on his death bed, wished to make a gift to his daughter of an entitlement to be paid a debt secured by a mortgage. With the assistance of a friend, he placed the physical mortgage deeds close to his daughter on the bed, then took her hand and placed it on the deeds. It was common ground that this was insufficient to comply with the requisite formalities for transferring the entitlement to be repaid the secured sums. Nevertheless the court concluded that there was a valid death bed gift, which took effect on the basis that the executors of the donor's estate held the entitlement to be paid the money on trust for the daughter.

The fact that equity interferes in this way is undoubtedly an oddity. Cotton LJ made that point in *Re Dillon* (1890) 44 Ch D 76, which was a case involving an attempted gift of a banker's deposit note, which was lacking formality:

> The delivery gives no legal title to the donee, nor did the delivery of the security in Duffield v. Elwes; but the House of Lords there laid it down that the executors were trustees for the donee and must do what was necessary to perfect the transfer. This would not be so in the case of an incomplete voluntary gift inter vivos the Court would not interfere to compel either the donor or his executors to perfect it; the doctrine is an anomalous one peculiar to the case of a *donatio mortis causâ*, but it is established by the decision of the House of Lords.

There have been cases in which the donor of a death bed gift placed legal ownership of the gift with the donee. One such case was *Staniland v Willott* (1852) 42 ER 416. In that case a gravely ill donor transferred shares to the donee but then recovered from the condition. It was successfully argued that the donee was to be treated as trustee of the shares for the benefit of the donor because the

[23] See *Delgoffe* at 927.

donor having survived the original sickness, the transfer could not be treated as a death bed gift.

REJECTING A GIFT

As has been stated above, it is open to a donee to reject a gift, and if the donee is not aware that the gift has been made he has a reasonable time on becoming aware to reject the gift. The leading authority in this area is *Re Paradise Motor Co* [1968] 1 WLR 1125. The facts of that case deserve consideration.

Paradise concerned an individual called Albert Watson who held shares in the Paradise Motor Company, along with his co-owner Mr Dean. Mr Dean owned 350 shares, which Mr Watson bought out in 1948. The company's articles of association provided that any transfer of shares had to be in writing signed by both the transferor and the transferee. On buying out Mr Dean, Mr Watson caused a transfer of Mr Dean's 350 shares in the company to be made to Mr Watson's stepson Mr Johns. The transfer bore what appeared to be Mr Johns's signature, but was in fact a forgery (probably forged by Mr Watson himself).

By 1954 Mr Watson had fallen out with Mr Johns and was minded to take back 300 of the 350 shares. He therefore caused another share transfer to be executed transferring 300 of the shares back to Mr Watson. Again Mr Johns's signature appeared on the transfer and again it was a forgery.

The company subsequently went into receivership and the receivers contacted Mr Johns to notify him that, as a holder of 50 shares, he may be entitled to a distribution in the receivership. Knowing nothing of any shares, Mr Johns wrote back to the official receiver robustly denying that he was a shareholder. Perhaps significantly to the final reasoning, Mr Johns's solicitor had also had a long telephone conversation with the official receiver.

Subsequently, when Mr Watson attempted to contact Mr Johns about the shares via Mr Johns's half-brother, the half-brother reported back to Mr Watson, 'All he has to say is, "I have no shares, I want no shares, and if I had any money to come off the bastard I would not even take it"'.

Mr Johns subsequently changed his mind and asserted ownership of the 350 shares. This was opposed on the basis, among other things, that Mr Johns had disclaimed the gift in the message he had sent back to Mr Watson via his half-brother, and that once disclaimed Mr Johns could not withdraw the disclaimer.

The Court of Appeal agreed, and in doing so differed with the first instance judge, who had concluded that Mr Johns could not be considered properly to have rejected the gift since he did not have reasonably full information about the nature and amount of the gift. The Court of Appeal's reasoning was based on the fact of the communications from the official receiver, and perhaps particularly the long telephone conversation between Mr Johns's solicitor and the official receiver. These communications, the Court of Appeal considered, comprised sufficient knowledge of Mr Johns's potential interest in the shares to make the disclaimer effective.

Two other significant findings emerge from *Paradise*.

First, the Court of Appeal found that rejecting a gift operated by way of a disclaimer rather than a disposition. The significance of this point is that there was no need for the rejection to be in writing so as to comply with s 53(2) Law of Property Act 1925.

Secondly, the Court of Appeal found that, once a gift is rejected, it cannot then be reclaimed. It appears that a disclaimed testamentary gift can be recovered (ie the disclaimer can be withdrawn) but the position is not the same with a lifetime gift. Thus at 1143 of the judgment:

> The second argument was based on decisions that, in the case of disclaimer of a benefit under a will, a disclaimer may be withdrawn if no one has changed his position on the faith of it. We do not decide whether these decisions or dicta are correct; they are *In re Young, Fraser v. Young*, and *In re Cranstoun, decd., Gibbs v. Home of Rest for Horses and Others*. It seems to us, however, that disclaimer of an attempt inter vivos to make a gift cannot be withdrawn. Maybe a will remains an outstanding offer of a gift. Surely, however, this is not so when the proposing donor, rebuffed, is still alive.

This is a finding that may be of the utmost significance in appropriate cases; it appears that a gift, once disclaimed, even if in the heat of the moment, cannot afterwards be recovered. This decision may seem harsh to a donee, but the Court of Appeal preferred the view that there is no reason why a would-be donor, if initially rebuffed by the proposed donee, should be held to his original benevolence. In the Court of Appeal's view this was to be contrasted with the position of a testamentary donor since a testamentary donor was no longer conscious of the rebuff 'in worldly terms'.

FAILURE OF TRANSFER OF GOODS OBTAINED BY FRAUD

In *Shogun v Hudson* [2004] 1 AC 919, the House of Lords considered the following circumstances:

1. A fraudster had entered a car dealership with a stolen driving licence posing as the party whose driving licence he had taken.
2. The fraudster applied to purchase a car on hire purchase terms – the claimant was the hire purchase company.
3. Having credit-checked the individual whose driving licence the fraudster had stolen, the fraudster was granted a hire purchase agreement over the car, and took the car away from the dealer.
4. The fraudster subsequently sold the car to a third party, who was the defendant in the *Shogun* case. The third party had purchased the car in good faith and for value from the fraudster. The case was a dispute about

which of the hire purchase company on one hand and the third party on the other had title to the car.

The House of Lords held that the agreement between the claimant and the fraudster was vitiated by the fraud and the claimant's mistake about the fraudster's identity. Consequently, the statutory exemption[24] permitting a hire purchaser to pass good title to a buyer in good faith did not apply. Therefore, the matter was within the normal operation of the *nemo dat* principle discussed in detail above. In other words, since the claimant and not the fraudster had title to the car and at the time of the purported sale to the defendant, the sale was ineffective and title could not pass to the defendant.

Shogun is generally cited as an authority of importance to the circumstances in which a contract will be vitiated for fraud or mistake. For present purposes, however, it also emphasises the effect of the *nemo dat* rule to prevent title passing in a sale of goods transaction, even to a purchaser in good faith for value without notice.

EQUITABLE INTERESTS IN PERSONALTY

The interplay of trust principles with the disposition of personalty is touched on above. It is beyond the scope of this short work to give a comprehensive analysis of the operation of trusts within the context of personalty; such an analysis can be found in the well-known specialist trust works. For present purposes it is sufficient to say that personalty is capable of being held on trust. In that capacity it is amenable to the various permutations of equitable interests and ownership that apply to all trust property.

SECURITY OVER PERSONALTY

Pledge

A pledge is a simple form of possessory security of ancient standing. It was described by Holt CJ in *Coggs v Bernard* (1703) 2 Lord Raymond 909 as arising 'when goods or chattels are delivered to another as a pawn, to be a security to him for money borrowed of him by the bailor; and this is called in Latin vadium, and in English a pawn or a pledge'.

It is in the context of a 'pawn' that the pledge is perhaps most familiar. Pawning personalty as security for a short-term loan has a long history and as a form of consumer borrowing has been regulated for centuries. The present regulation

[24] Section 27 Hire Purchase Act 1964.

is contained in ss 114–25 Consumer Credit Act 1974. The broad key components of those regulations are as follows:

1. A pledgee must almost always give a pledgor a receipt for the pledge.
2. A pledge can be redeemed for six months, or such other period as the parties may agree. If such a period has expired, the pledge nevertheless can be redeemed until the pledged item has been sold by the pledgee.
3. Delivery of the pledge receipt and payment of an amount owing triggers an obligation on the part of the pledgee to deliver the pledged item (except in circumstances where the pledgee reasonably believes the person presenting the receipt is not the pledgor). It is an offence to unreasonably refuse to allow a pledge to be redeemed.
4. If a pledge receipt has been lost, the pledgor can execute a statutory declaration in a prescribed form, which can stand in place of the pledge receipt.
5. At the end of the pledge's redemption period, in the case of some low-value pledges the pledgee takes title to the pledged item. In other cases the pledge becomes realisable by the sale by the pledgee of the pledged item, although notice of sale must first be given to the pledgor.
6. A negotiable instrument cannot be accepted in satisfaction of a pledge.

It is also worth noting that, by common law principles, a pledgee is entitled to transfer his interest under the pledge to third party.[25]

Pledges are also possible in the context of commercial relationships, although they appear to have little usefulness in most commercial loan transactions. That is presumably for two reasons:

1. Intangible property makes up much of the personalty held by commercial entities, but intangible property is often not amenable to pledging, since transfer of possession is an essential component of a pledge.
2. Such tangible personalty as businesses do tend to have, for example computer hardware and plant, can rarely be spared from the business's ordinary trading activities to enable possession to be transferred to a pledgee.

Liens

Like a pledge, a common law lien[26] is a form of security based largely on possession (or perhaps more accurately the ability to deprive the owner of possession). Unlike a pledge, a lien is non-consensual in nature. Broadly speaking, a common law lien is a situation in which a person has possession of another's chattel and is entitled to refuse to hand the chattel over to the owner unless he is paid.

[25] *Donald v Suckling* (1866) LR 1 QB 585.
[26] The comparatively rare phenomenon of equitable liens is considered further below.

Common law liens exist in two types: general and special (or particular). General liens enable the lienee to require the discharge of all sums owed to them before relinquishing the property in question. A particular lien entitles the lienee to retain an item until all sums relating to those particular items are settled. General liens are available only in certain established relationships. Probably the most well-known such relationship is that between a solicitor and his client over the client's papers; other professionals such as bankers and stockbrokers have similar rights. The courts are reluctant to extend the range of circumstances in which a general lien will come into being[27] and they are therefore rarer than particular liens.

Although not strictly a question of the law of liens, this is nevertheless a convenient point to mention the particular question of a client's ownership of the papers on his solicitor's file. It tends to be widely assumed that a client owns all the papers on his solicitor's file. On that analysis it follows that, so long as the client does not have any outstanding fees such that a lien could be asserted, a solicitor is required to hand over the entirety of the papers on his file to the client on demand, or (as is more usual) transfer those papers to a new solicitor.

This widely held belief, however, does not appear to be correct, and in fact a large portion of the papers likely to be found on a solicitor's file are likely to belong to a solicitor, and thus not to be the subject of a lien and not papers that a solicitor has to produce to his client or transfer to a new solicitor.

On 21 March 2017 the Law Society issued a practice note called 'Who Owns the File?'. Clearly this practice note is not of legal force per se but it cites good authority in support of its propositions[28] and has been drafted with the assistance of several well-respected practitioners. The practice note has also been expressly approved by Soole J in *Hanley v J C & A Solicitors* [2018] EWHC 2592 (QB). The practice note is therefore very likely to be an accurate statement of the law and will probably be treated by the court as highly persuasive.

The practice note is a relatively lengthy document that is worth considering in full if an issue of a solicitor's ownership of documents has to be considered in practice. Perhaps the most significant observation is at paragraph 2 of the practice note, which states that a solicitor's work is divided into work done as an agent and work done as a professional advisor. Although unusual features of a retainer may cause a different result, in general a solicitor retains property in the papers generated in the course of his conduct as a professional advisor, such as, for example, and as illustrated by the Law Society Note:

- Documents prepared for the firm's own benefit or protection, or prepared as the means by which the firm discharges its function belong to the firm (for example, file copies of letters written to the client, notes regarding time taken, or made

[27] See the distillation of the law in *Snell's Equity*, 33rd edition, paragraph 44-003.

[28] *Leicestershire CC v Michael Faraday & Partners* [1941] 2 KB 205; *Chantrey Martin v Martin* [1953] 2 QB 286; and *Gamba Holdings v Minories Finance* [1989] BCLC 115.

for protective purposes regarding advice to the client, drafts and working papers generally).

- Copies of internal emails and correspondence during the course of the retainer, and all emails and correspondence written by the client to the firm belong to the firm.

It is apparent from the above extract that a great many documents on a solicitor's file, which perhaps in practice are often assumed to be the property of the client, are in fact the property of the solicitor, who is entitled to retain them.

The Court of Appeal also signalled that the correct law as to the ownership of documents on a solicitor's file differs from the generally assumed position that a client owns all the documents in *Avonwick Holdings Ltd v Shlosberg* [2017] Ch 210. In *Avonwick* an individual had gone bankrupt, prior to which he had been represented by Messrs Fladgate, a solicitors' firm. The bankrupt's trustee in bankruptcy sought and obtained privileged information from Fladgate pursuant to s 311 Insolvency Act 1986, which provides as follows:

> The trustee shall take possession of all books, papers and other records which relate to the bankrupt's estate or affairs *and which belong to him or are in his possession or under his control* (including any which would be privileged from disclosure in any proceedings) (emphasis added).

The litigation arose because the trustee in bankruptcy was represented by the same firm of solicitors as the bankrupt's principal creditor. The bankrupt sought an injunction precluding the solicitors from acting for both parties on the basis that his privileged information was known to the solicitors and ought not to be revealed to his creditor even with his trustee's consent. For present purposes, the important observation is that of Arnold J at paragraph 50:

> It should be noted before proceeding further that there is no evidence as to the extent to which … (ii) Fladgate, as distinct from their former clients, may have a claim to ownership of some of the documents (at least qua pieces of paper). Both counsel addressed me upon the assumptions that (a) all of the documents had been printed or written on paper prior to the bankruptcy and (b) Mr Shlosberg owned all of the pieces of paper prior to the bankruptcy (even though it is quite possible that Fladgate owned some of them: see *Halsbury's Laws of England*, 5th ed, vol 66 (2015), para 583 and the authorities cited). I shall do likewise (emphasis added).

In other words, counsel in the case appear to have assumed that everything on the Fladgate file belonged to the bankrupt (and ergo fell within the scope of s 311 such that it could be inspected by the trustee in bankruptcy). The judgment of the Court of Appeal, however, hints heavily that there would have been an argument available that certain of the key papers belonged to Fladgate and therefore were properly outside the scope of s 311.

Overall, it is suggested that the question of the ownership of the papers on a solicitor's file is one that should be given more detailed consideration when it arises in practice. In the context of persuading a client who has instructed a new firm to pay fees, it may even be that an offer to provide copies of papers that are the property of the solicitor is more persuasive than the threat of exercising a lien over those papers that do belong to the client.

Particular liens are the more frequently occurring example of a common law lien. They were described by Diplock LJ (as he then was) in *Tappenden v Artus* [1964] 2 QB 185 (CA) at 195 in the following way:

> The common law remedy of a possessory lien, like other primitive remedies such as abatement of nuisance, self-defence or ejection of trespassers to land, is one of self-help. It is a remedy in rem exercisable upon the goods, and its exercise requires no intervention by the courts, for it is exercisable only by an artificer who has actual possession of the goods subject to the lien. Since, however, the remedy is the exercise of a right to continue an existing actual possession of the goods, it necessarily involves a right of possession adverse to the right of the person who, but for the lien, would be entitled to immediate possession of the goods. A common law lien, although not enforceable by action, thus affords a defence to an action for recovery of the goods by a person who, but for the lien, would be entitled to immediate possession.

Therefore common law liens are capable of taking effect in a wide variety of circumstances. Two of the most well recognised by the law are:

1. The 'artificer's lien' or 'mechanic's lien'. This is a lien that comes into being when a craftsman (often in the reported cases this has been a motor mechanic) carries out work on a chattel. To establish an artificer's lien, the person in possession of goods must actually improve them in some way; it is not enough to give them routine maintenance and prevent their deterioration. Thus in *Hatton v Car Maintenance Company* [1915] 1 Ch 621, the court did not allow a car maintenance company to assert the artificer's lien. The distinction between the position in *Hatton* and *Tappenden* (referred to above) appears to be that in the former case the alleged lienee merely attended to ongoing maintenance of the car, whereas in the latter case the alleged lienee was asked to repair a broken car and did so. This distinction between maintenance and improvement has an air of artificiality to it, and it is easy to imagine fierce dispute about where to draw the line.
2. The 'common calling lien'. These liens arose during the Middle Ages for the benefit of certain service providers who were obliged by law for public policy reasons to offer their services to all comers. These 'common callings' included being a ferryman and particularly an innkeeper. As to the latter, the innkeeper's lien has been highly enduring and remains as good law now. It applies to all luggage that is brought by a guest to an inn,[29] though not it appears to chattels sent to a guest after his arrival.[30] An innkeeper has a specific right to sell goods left or deposited with him, subject only to a requirement to retain the goods for six weeks in case payment of the debt is made.[31]

[29] *Mulliner v Florence* (1878) 3 QBD 484 (CA).
[30] *Broadwood v Granara* (1854) 10 Ex 417.
[31] Innkeepers Act 1878.

Common law liens require possession (or, as exemplified by the inkeeper's lien, an entitlement to withhold possession)[32] and an entitlement to a debt to vest in the same person. They cannot therefore be transferred to a third party (in contrast to a pledge).[33] By that same principle, if the property that is subject to a lien is returned to the owner, the lien ceases to apply unless there is express agreement to the contrary.[34]

It is also an essential feature of particular common law liens that possession was lawfully in the hands of the lienee at the time when the debt became due.[35] Accordingly, a creditor cannot 'create' a lien by receiving a chattel after the debt fell due.

At common law, a lien carries with it no power of sale (hence the need to create an express statutory power in the case of an innkeeper's lien). The absence of a power of sale could, in the case of certain property which is onerous to maintain, create difficulties for a lienee, who will remain (in common with any bailee – as to which see further below) under a duty to take reasonable care to preserve the chattel.

The difficulty of the absence of a right to sell property subject to lien is compounded by the fact that authority exists to the effect that a lienee is not permitted to recover from the lienor costs incurred in exercising the lien. That authority is *Somes v British Empire Shipping Co* (1860) 8 HLC 338, although the principle has had startlingly little judicial attention since that time. The breadth of the applicability of *Somes* was greatly restricted by the Court of Appeal in *Metall Market OOO v Vitorio Shipping Co Ltd* [2014] QB 760. It is apparent from that case that the *Somes* principle does not apply in the context of shipping, and probably not in any context other than an artificer's lien. It is worth setting out the following extract from Sir Bernard Rix's judgment in *Mettall* in order to understand what residual force the *Somes* principle may have:

> … In my judgment, the Somes principle is a narrow one, applicable to an artificer's lien but of doubtful status outside that context. It appears to be founded in the technical doctrine that a right of lien does not carry with it any cause of action to recover an indemnity for the expenses of exercising it in the absence of some other basis for recovery, such as in contract or bailment or tort. It also appears to be founded in a pragmatic concern that an artificer may act purely for his own benefit in retaining the chattel, in circumstances where there is no breach involved on the part of the lienor other than the failure to pay the price of the artificer's labour, which is the failure which gives rise to the lien, and where there is no benefit to the lienor. It is not clear, for there was no discussion in the Somes case, why that breach (of non-payment) does not by itself give rise to a claim in damages, where the natural and reasonable consequence is that the chattel is retained to secure performance of the obligation

[32] *Re Cosslett (Contractors) Ltd* [1998] Ch 495 at 509.
[33] *Legg v Evans* (1840) 6 M & W 36.
[34] *Albermarle Supply Co v Hind* [1928] 1 KB 307 CA.
[35] *Tappenden* at 196.

> to pay. It may be, but I speculate, it is on the ground that no damages are ordinarily payable for breach of an obligation to pay money. Of particular importance for these purposes, however, is that in the ordinary case of an artificer's lien contemplated in the Somes case there is no breach of contract involved in the lienor's failure to remove his chattel from the artificer at the time due for payment (see Lord Wensleydale's example of the tailor) and no contemplation let alone contract that the lienee will be inconvenienced or incur expense as a result of the exercise of his lien or that the lienor will be expected to pay accordingly.
>
> 123 Such a doctrine may work more or less satisfactorily in the typical case of an artificer's lien, but in a highly commercial setting such as shipbuilding or ship-repairing the Somes case itself illustrates the harshness and uncommerciality of the limitations of the doctrine. Where the lienor cannot pay, the lien is worthless, because it does not bring with it a right of either expenses or sale; and where the lienor will not pay, he can blackmail the lienee with the expense of retention: even though he could choose, if he wished, to obtain the release of his chattel by giving adequate security for the lienee's claim (and nowadays by a payment into court).
>
> 124 Fortunately, there is no sign that the Somes principle was of wide application. It was subject to any express or implied contract for the payment of the expenses of retention, as the Somes case itself recognised.

Although, as stated above, there is no automatic right for a lienee to sell property that is subject to a lien, it may be that a lienee can trigger an entitlement to sell the property under s 12(1)(a) Torts (Interference with Goods) Act 1977. That provision allows a bailee to sell a bailor's goods (subject to the regime for such sale at Schedule 1) where a bailor is in breach of an obligation to take possession of his goods. For example, it could perhaps be argued in the context of an artificer's lien that the lienor is under a contractual obligation to pay for the lienee's services and remove his goods, and that the failure to do so triggers the right at s 12.

A further consideration that has engaged the courts in the context of common law liens is the rights of a lienee against the owner of a chattel when the owner is not the person who has placed the chattel into the lienee's possession. Thus, in *Albermarle Supply Co v Hind and Company* [1928] 1 KB 307 the facts were as follows:

1. The plaintiff had leased three taxis to a Mr Botfield. The terms of that lease required Mr Botfield to keep the taxis in good repair. The terms also required him not to create any lien over the taxis.
2. Mr Botfield engaged the defendant to maintain the taxis. The defendant was a mechanics business and it stored the taxis at its garages, cleaned them, replaced tyres and otherwise maintained them and carried out those repairs that were necessary.
3. Mr Botfield fell behind with the defendant's bills. He subsequently fell behind with the plaintiff's lease charges and the plaintiff sought to take possession of the taxis. The defendant opposed the plaintiff taking possession of the taxis on the basis that it asserted a lien.

The question before the court was whether the defendant was entitled to assert a lien against Mr Botfield in such a way as to defy the wishes of the taxis' owners. The court concluded that the lien could be asserted in this way. Its reasoning (see especially page 318) was that the act of leaving the taxis in the hands of Mr Botfield created an implied authority to have the taxis maintained in circumstances that gave rise to a lien. The court considered it to be irrelevant that a term of the contract existed prohibiting Mr Botfield from allowing a lien to come into place. Its view was that, since the defendant was entirely unaware of that restriction, it could not have the effect of limiting the scope of Mr Botfield's implied authority. It should be noted when considering this judgment that the court appears to have used the phrase 'implied authority' to mean what would now be described as 'apparent authority' (that latter phrase appears at page 318 seemingly interchangeably with 'implied authority').

Equitable Liens

The above observations deal with common law liens. As mentioned above, there is also a species of interest called an equitable lien. Equitable liens differ considerably from common law liens. The principal difference is that there is no requirement for possession of the property that is subject of the lien. Thus, rather than affording a defence against a claim for possession as does a common law lien, equitable liens afford the lienee rights to seek an order for sale from the court.[36] Equitable liens are therefore similar in nature to equitable charges, except that equitable liens come into being as a matter of equity in the context of certain relationships and (unlike equitable charges) do not depend on the agreement or actions of the parties themselves.

Overwhelmingly the most common examples of an equitable lien in practice are the liens available to an unpaid vendor for the purchase price, and a purchaser for his deposit. These equitable liens are available in respect of real as well as personal property (including in circumstances where a purchaser of real property has already taken possession). Equitable liens also arise for a solicitor over property he has recovered for his client, and for a trustee or personal representative over trust property for their own expenses.

As may be apparent from the two examples given above, equitable liens are lacking in an obvious unifying concept. In *Whitebread & Co v Watt* [1902] 1 Ch 835 at 835 it was said that 'it [ie an equitable lien] is a right which may be said to be invented for the purpose of doing justice'. There are at least some common features of equitable liens, one being, as noted above, that they give rise to a right to apply to the court for an order for sale. This is a reflection of the fact that an equitable lien is a right *in rem* and accordingly – an important and

[36] *Swiss Bank Corp v Lloyds Bank Ltd* [1982] A.C. 584 at 595.

perhaps under-appreciated fact – gives a holder the status of a secured creditor in any insolvency proceedings.[37]

Notwithstanding some characteristics, the list of equitable liens is sufficiently varied that it is difficult to identify any common basis. Some equitable liens arise as a consequence of a particular legal relationship. For example, trustees have an equitable lien over trust property in respect of the legitimate expenses incurred by the trustee in the discharge of his function. Thus in *Re Pumfrey* (1882) 22 Ch D 255 a trustee was permitted to sell real estate held on trust to repay money the trustee had borrowed to complete a purchase on the beneficiaries' behalf. This lien has been said to arise as a matter of equity as part of the 'price' that a beneficiary must pay for a trustee's services.[38] It is entirely consistent with the well-known indemnity a trustee enjoys from trust assets.[39]

Another example of an equitable lien apparently (from Commonwealth authority) arising from a legal relationship is the equitable lien held by a receiver over the property he is administering.[40]

Other equitable liens have been found to arise outside the context of specific legal relationships. One such equitable lien, perhaps a useful one in practice, is a lien held by a person who has spent money on property under the mistaken belief that he is entitled to it. The operation of this type of lien and its characteristics were examined in the somewhat opaque case of *Falcke v Scottish Imperial Insurance Co* (1886) 34 Ch D 234. In that case the facts and reasoning were as follows:

1. A person known as 'E Emanuel' took out a life insurance policy, which he subsequently mortgaged to a Mr Falcke.
2. Emanuel then went into what is described as 'liquidation', even though he appears to have been an individual, but in any event some form of insolvency process.
3. Various friends of Emanuel offered his creditors a deal, whereby the friends would pay a certain portion of his debts in exchange for an assignment of all his property, except for the equity of redemption of his various secured debts. This arrangement was carried out, leading to Emanuel being discharged.
4. Emanuel then entered into discussions with a solicitor called Mr Davis. Davis purported to act for Falcke. The outcome of those discussions was, so far as Emanuel was concerned, an agreement that he would pay £50 for Falcke's interest in the policy. This appears to have meant in effect that Emanuel understood himself to be redeeming the mortgage.
5. In reliance on the agreement he had reached with Davis, Emanuel paid the £50. Davis later informed Emanuel, however, that the purchase could not

[37] *R & H Tresize v Bilato Nominees Pty Ltd* (1986) 83 FLR 44.
[38] *Re Beddoe* [1893] 1 Ch 547 at 558.
[39] See *Lewin on Trusts*, 19th edition, chapter 21.
[40] *Shirlaw v Taylor* (1991) 102 ALR 551.

be completed immediately because other charge holders in respect of the policy had first to consent to the transaction. Emanuel accordingly paid two premiums on the policy in the expectation that he would be redeeming the mortgage, or at least in some way benefitting from the agreement to purchase that he had reached with Davis.

6. Falcke subsequently died and Davis disappeared – it appears that he had not in fact been engaged by Falcke to conclude the agreement after all.
7. Falcke's executor brought proceedings to enforce the security over the policy. In the course of those proceedings the policy was sold, and those chargees that ranked above Falcke's were paid off. That left a residual sum of just under £1,733. Emanuel contended that this sum should be paid over to him in its entirety because he had purchased Falcke's interest, or, more importantly for present purposes, that at the least he should be able to recover the sums he had paid over by way of the premium in the belief that he had acquired Falcke's interest under the policy.
8. Emanuel's position was rejected on the basis that it was the unauthorised Davis, rather than Falcke or some genuine agent of his, who had concluded the proposed agreement and prompted Emanuel to make the payment.

At 241 Cotton LJ explained the working of this kind of equitable lien in the following way:

> Now let us see what the general law is. It is not disputed that if a stranger pays a premium on a policy that payment gives him no lien on the policy. A man by making a payment in respect of property belonging to another, if he does so without request, is not entitled to any lien or charge on that property for such payment. If he does work upon a house without request he gets no lien on the house for the work done. If the money has been paid or the work done at the request of the person entitled to the property, the person paying the money or doing the work has a right of action against the owner for the money paid or for the work done at his request. If here there had been circumstances to lead to the conclusion that there was a request by *Falcke* that this premium should be paid by *Emanuel*, then there would be a claim against *Falcke* or his representative for the money, and I do not say that there might not be a lien on the policy. But in my opinion there is no evidence upon which we should be justified in coming to the conclusion that there was any request expressed or implied by *Falcke* to *Emanuel* to pay this money. An express request is not suggested. Was there an implied request? I think that in a case of this sort, when money is paid in order to keep alive property which belongs to another, a request to make that payment might be implied from slight circumstances, but in my opinion there is no circumstance here in evidence from which such a request can be implied.

It should be stressed, however, that the courts have stated that a constructive trust is an alternative to this kind of equitable lien. Thus, Lord Denning MR in *Hussey v Palmer* [1972] 1 WLR 1286 at 1290 reviewed various authorities and stated as follows:

> In those cases it was emphasised that the court must look at the circumstances of each case to decide in what way the equity can be satisfied. In some by an equitable

> lien. In others by a constructive trust. But in either case it is because justice and good conscience so require.

Undeniably, the constructive trust has gained a great deal of judicial attention in more recent decades, and so it appears to follow that the equitable lien of the kind contemplated in *Falcke* has likely fallen out of fashion. The truth is that the availability of both remedies is so flexible that the court can decide which is more naturally appropriate to the circumstances. At one time this was presumably somewhat unsatisfactory, in that a litigant could never be sure what remedy he would have. Since the passage of the Trust of Land and Appointment of Trustees Act 1996, however, the distinction has presumably become far less important, in that a beneficiary of a trust of land can now apply to the court to ask it to exercise the powers of a trustee, including making an order for sale, which is the primary remedy of an equitable lienee.

Mortgages Over Chattels

The concept of a mortgage of property is of course extremely familiar in the context of real property. Properly considered, however, the kind of security taken by lenders over real property in the modern era is not a 'mortgage', at least not in the traditional sense.

Traditionally a mortgage entailed the conveyance of a property by a mortgagor to a mortgagee in exchange for a sum of money. Usually the mortgagor remained in possession of the property throughout the term of the mortgage. The mortgagor was entitled, after a specified given period, to redeem the mortgage and recover the property if he repaid the sum of money (usually plus interest). In equity, the mortgagee was not allowed to impose any conditions that prevented the mortgagor from redeeming so long as he could pay off the appropriate sum. That right in equity to redeem the mortgage is referred to as the 'equity of redemption', and any attempt to impose a condition precluding the mortgagor from redeeming is referred to as a 'clog' on the equity of redemption.

Since the Law of Property Act 1925,[41] a mortgage of real property (both freehold and leasehold) cannot be effected in law in the way described in the paragraph above. Instead legal security is permitted by a term of years with a right of redemption or (the method invariably used in practice) a 'charge by deed expressed by way of legal mortgage'. Thus, the distinction between a legal charge and a legal mortgage ceased to exist. 'Mortgages' in general parlance refer to legal charges protected by deed and (in the case of registered land) by entry at HM Land Registry. It should perhaps be mentioned that the 'traditional' form of mortgage is still possible in equity, where the mortgagor's equitable interest is transferred to the mortgagee.

[41] Sections 85–86.

No equivalent provisions in the Law of Property Act 1925 exist in respect of personalty, however. Therefore, the traditional form of mortgage can still exist in respect of chattels. This is so both in law and equity. A mortgagee of real property will have the various rights and obligations set out in the Law of Property Act 1925 (except insofar as any such provisions of that act are expressed as particular to freehold or leasehold land). In particular, so long as such a mortgage is created by deed, a mortgagee of personalty should enjoy the powers set out at s 101 Law of Property Act 1925.

It is also possible to have legal and equitable charges over personalty. As will be apparent from the discussion above, the principal difference between a charge and a mortgage is that a mortgage entails the transfer of the property (whether legal or equitable) whereas a charge does not.

FUTURE GOODS

Issues have occasionally arisen in connection with attempts to deal with chattels which do not as yet have independent existence. Typically these issues have arisen in the context of extracting a part from a mixture, and in this context are dealt with above. Broadly, in the context of the sale of goods, historic difficulties were caused by the inability to identify a purchaser's share of a bulk, but these difficulties have generally been alleviated by ss 20A and 20B Sale of Goods Act 1979 (as inserted in 1995). Outside the context of sale of goods separate principles apply and are discussed in more detail above.

The court has only rarely had to deal (at least in remotely modern times) with questions of law concerning chattels that do not yet exist outside the context of mixtures. One case dealing with the point was *Lunn v Thornton* (1845) 1 Common Bench Reports 379. In that case a baker had contracted to sell all his goods, 'then remaining and being, or which [380] should at any time thereafter remain and be in, upon, or about his dwelling-house, and also all other [of] his effects elsewhere'.

The purchaser contended, somewhat unattractively it might be said, that this wording gave him the right to take possession of any of the seller's goods that he might acquire at any time in the future. The Court of Common pleas disagreed, and gave the following survey of the relevant ancient authorities:

> On the part of the plaintiff, the authorities were strong to shew that no personal property could pass by grant, other than that which belonged to the grantor at the time of the execution of the deed. Perkins (tit. Grants, § 65) says, 'It is a common learning in the law, that a man cannot grant or charge that which he hath not.' So, in Hobart's Reports (page 132), it is laid down, that 'a man cannot grant all the wool that shall grow upon his sheep that he shall buy hereafter; for, there he hath it neither actually nor potentially' – a distinction which seems to be adopted by Perkins (tit. Grants, § 90) 'that, if a man grants unto me all the wool of his sheep for seven years, the grant is good.' By which is evidently intended, the wool of sheep which the grantor at that

> time has. And, still further, the plaintiff relied on the authority of Bacon's Maxims (reg. 14): 'Licet dispositio de interesse futuro sit inutilis, tamen potest fieri declaratio præcedens, quæ sortiatur effectum, interveniente novo actu.' Upon which it is to be observed, that Lord Bacon takes the first branch of the maxim, namely, that a disposition of after-acquired property is altogether inoperative, as a proposition of law that is to be considered as beyond dispute; and only labours to establish the second branch of the maxim, namely, that such disposition may be considered as a declaration precedent, which derives its effect from some new act of the party after the property is acquired; for, he says, 'The law doth not allow of grants, except there be a foundation of interest in the grantor; for, the law will not accept of grants of titles, or of things in action, which are imperfect interests, much less will it allow a man to grant or incumber that which is no interest at all, but merely future.'

In equity, however, the position is somewhat more flexible. In *Holroyd v Marshall* (1862) 10 HOLC 191 a mill owner had charged mill machinery in its mill, and also any future mill machinery that would arrive at the mill in substitution for the existing machinery. Although acknowledging this attempt to deal with future property could not succeed in law, the House of Lords found that it could succeed in equity. Per Lord Chelmsford at [220]:

> [I]t appears to me that sufficient attention has not been paid to the different effect and operation of agreements relating to future property at law and in equity. At law property, non-existing, but to be acquired at a future time, is not assignable; in equity it is so. At law (as we have seen), although a power is given in the deed of assignment to take possession of after-acquired property, no interest is transferred, even as between the parties themselves, unless possession is actually taken; in equity it is not disputed that the moment the property comes into existence the agreement operates upon it.

Indeed, it is this reasoning that makes it possible for businesses to offer floating charges over money and other assets from time to time owned by chargor. Were it not for the modifying effect of equity on dealing with future property, this commonplace commercial activity would not be possible.

MONEY

There are occasionally allusions to the law of personalty as applied to money elsewhere in this work. As it is such a factually important part of the law of personalty, however, and as it presents particular features, it is considered specifically here.

Defining Money

The first and most obvious issue presenting itself in the context of money is one of definition. In anything approaching an ordinary conversational use of the word, money refers both to currency and to entitlement to at least some forms of credit (for example money held to a depositor's credit in a current account – see further below).

One of the earliest reasoned explanations of the meaning of money was in *Shelmer's case* (1725) Gilb 200. In that case a wealthy testatrix had made a general bequest of residual 'money' to her servants. Among her assets were a considerable amount of cash and the entitlement to be paid various sums pursuant to mortgages and rent arrears on her tenanted properties. She also owned South Sea stock and entitlement to annuities. The court was prepared to give the word 'money' a fairly wide meaning:

> [T]he Word (*Money*) mentioned in the Bequest to the Servants in her Will, is a general Word, but yet not so large and comprehensive as the Word *Pecunia* in the *Roman* Tongue; for such Word in that Language, *All the Testatrix's Substance, both Real and Personal, that can be converted into Money*; but the Word *Money* in our Language answers to the *Barbarians Latin* Word *Moneta*, and is a Genus that comprehends two Species, *viz.* ready Money and Money due, that is to say, the Money in her own Hands, or her Money in the Hands of any Body else; and therefore in this Case the Bequests to her Servants will comprehend Mr. *Wood's* Mortgage, and the Arrears of Rent, since these must be looked upon by all the Rules of Construction to be Mrs. *Shelmer's* Money at the Time of her Death; but the Word *Money* will not comprehend *South-Sea* Stock or *Annuity* Stock, because that is an Interest arising out of Funds, settled by publick Laws; and though it be redeemable by Money, or saleable for Money, yet it can be no more looked upon as Money at the Time of Mrs. *Shelmer's* Decease than a Term of Years, a Coach and Horses, or any other Real or Personal Chattel whatsoever can.

Thus in the eighteenth century the courts were receptive to the idea that money meant both physical cash and also choses in action. As discussed further below, it is unsurprising that choses in action are generally considered to be 'money', since the entire post-medieval banking system is predicated on a depositor exchanging legal title to money for a debt owed by a bank. On the other hand, other personalty was not money, even including highly liquid investments such as shares, and right to money such as annuities.

In the mid-twentieth century the House of Lords had to consider the definition of 'money', again in the context of a will, in *Perrin v Morgan* [1943] AC 399. Lord Russell of Killowen's view was essentially that 'money' was a protean concept, and the definition had to depend on the circumstances (but was in any event quite wide):

> [T]he word 'money' has not got one natural or usual meaning. It has several meanings, each of which in appropriate circumstances may be regarded as natural. In its original sense, which is also its narrowest sense, the word means 'coin.' Moneta was an appellation of Juno, and the Temple of Moneta at Rome was the mint. Phrases like 'false money' or 'clipped money' show the original use in English, but the conception very quickly broadens into the equivalent of 'cash' of any sort. The question: 'Have you any money in your purse?' refers presumably to bank notes or Treasury notes, as well as to shillings and pence. A further extension would include not only

> coin and currency in the possession of an individual, but debts owing to him, and cheques which he could pay into his banking account, or postal orders, or the like. Again, going further, it is a matter of common speech to refer to one's 'money at the bank,' although in a stricter sense the bank is not holding one's own money and what one possesses is a chose in action which represents the right to require the bank to pay out sums held at the call of its customer. Sums on deposit, whether with a bank or otherwise, may be included by a further extension, but this is by no means the limit to the senses in which the word 'money' is frequently and quite naturally used in English speech. The statement: 'I have my money invested on mortgage, or in debentures, or in stocks and shares, or in savings certificates,' is not an illegitimate use of the word 'money' on which the courts are bound to frown, though it is a great extension from its original meaning to interpret it as covering securities, and, in considering the various meanings of the word 'money' in common speech, one must go even further, as any dictionary will show. The word may be used to cover the whole of an individual's personal property – sometimes, indeed, all of a person's property, whether real or personal. 'What has he done with his money?' may well be an inquiry as to the general contents of a rich man's will. Horace's satire at the expense of the fortune-hunter who attached himself to childless Roman matrons, has its modern equivalent in the saying: 'It's her money he's after.' When St. Paul wrote to Timothy that the love of money is the root of all evil, he was not warning him of the risks attaching to one particular kind of wealth, but was pointing to the dangers of avarice in general. When Tennyson's Northern Farmer counselled his son not to marry for money, but to go where money is, he was not excluding the attractiveness of private property in land. These wider meanings of 'money' are referred to in some of the reported cases as 'popular' meanings, in contrast to the 'legal' meaning of the term.

An important statute relevant to the construction of the term, 'money' is the Bills of Exchange Act 1882. Section 3 of that statute provides a definition of 'bill of exchange', of which the most important part for present purposes is sub-s 1:

> (1) A bill of exchange is an unconditional order in writing, addressed by one person to another, signed by the person giving it, requiring the person to whom it is addressed to pay on demand or at a fixed or determinable future time a sum certain in money to or to the order of a specified person, or to bearer.

A 'cheque' is the archetypal bill of exchange, and following the reasoning in *Perrin* is almost certainly 'money'. It therefore seems well arguable that any other bill of exchange is likely also to qualify as 'money'.

Section 83 Bills of Exchange Act 1882 also defines the concept of a 'promissory note'. Whereas a 'bill of exchange' is broadly an order by A requiring to B to pay C, a 'promissory note' is an enforceable[42] promise by A to pay B. Per s 83(1):

> A promissory note is an unconditional promise in writing made by one person to another signed by the maker, engaging to pay, on demand or at a fixed or determinable future time, a sum certain in money, to, or to the order of, a specified person or to bearer.

[42] By virtue of s 88 Bills of Exchange Act 1882.

Historically it was the case that a bank note was the archetypal promissory note, as discussed further below. It follows that it is highly likely that a promissory note is likely to qualify as 'money'.

The many statutory uses of the word 'money' tend to have their own definitions, albeit these can be inclusive rather than comprehensive. For example, the Representation of the People Act 1983 has a definition including within its scope, '(a) any office, place or employment, and (b) any valuable security or other equivalent of money, and (c) any valuable consideration' but does not purport to fully define everything that could constitute money.

So far as general principles as to the definition of 'money' are concerned, its protean character makes it difficult to venture much with certainty. The following seem to be fairly reliable principles of definition:

1. Physical currency is money.
2. An entitlement to be paid money is also money.
3. Depending on context, other assets may also be money.

A powerful illustration of the protean nature of money, and the importance of context, is the rise of virtual currencies such as 'Bitcoin'. One can imagine that virtual currencies may be properly construed as money in some contexts but not others. For example, various revenue statutes require a 'payment of money'. For those purposes, it is hard to imagine a 'payment' of virtual currency would be deemed acceptable.

On the other hand, it is abundantly clear that virtual currency has been designed by its creators to have the characteristics of money and is explicitly self-described in that way. Virtual currency may be somewhat suspect as a 'store of value' (ie one of the traditional purposes of currency), but then traditional money in the modern era is also somewhat suspect for those purposes since it is affected by inflation and based purely on fiat. On any view, virtual currencies operate as a medium for exchange – ie a means of enabling transactions to take place without it being a prerequisite that both parties have something to trade for the goods or services that are the subject of the transaction. That is a traditional purpose of money and what would probably be said to be its main enduring purpose today.

Consequently, it is hard to escape the conclusion that virtual currencies have money-like qualities that go beyond those of most examples of personalty. It may very well be, therefore, that if confronted with, for example, a bequest of 'money', a court may find that a testator's Bitcoin holdings fell within the scope of that bequest. A counter-argument might be that nobody is bound as a matter of the law of any jurisdiction to accept Bitcoin as payment, and it cannot properly be considered as money for that purpose. On the other hand, nor is there an obligation for contracting parties to make Sterling, or the currency of any nation state, a permissible means of settling a contractual liability; if a party wishes to be paid in gold, for example, that is a perfectly permissible contractual arrangement to make.

Money 'in the Bank'

Any consideration of the practical reality of 'money' in the context of law must be considered with reference to the fundamental relationship between a bank and its depositor client. Since at least Roman times, it has been a fundamental of the system of banking that bankers make money by accepting deposits (on which interest is usually paid) and then applying those deposited monies profitably elsewhere, for example by lending.

Initially money deposited in banks was coin physically held on the premises (typically in the early instances in temples, whose sacred status and constant occupation made the money secure). Quickly, however, the retention of the depositor's physical coin by banks ceased to have a role in the deposit relationship. Rather, an account holder deposited money (in the first instance still physical currency) in a bank and relinquished all legal title to that money in exchange for a right to be paid an equivalent sum by the bank (ie a chose in action).

That remains the position. Thus, for example, in *Foley v Hill* (1848) 2 HLC 28 the court was able to describe the relationship between a bank and its customer as 'the ordinary relationship between creditor and debtor'. It follows from the fact of this relationship that, once deposited, a depositor has no proprietary interest in the money he has deposited (and it should be noted in particular that the bank is not a trustee of that money). That is not to say that money in the sense of currency is theoretically incapable of being the subject of a proprietary interest; as Professor Michael Bridge has observed,[43] cash is as amenable as any other kind of personalty to being loaned on terms that the very same coins or notes must be returned. In practice, however, such arrangements are presumably non-existent (clearly a loan on terms that the very same coins and notes have to be returned would in almost all cases be useless to the borrower).

It follows from the above that 'money' is a term that applies both to tangible chattels (ie cash) and intangible chattels (ie 'money in the bank'). This is an analytical observation with at least one important practical consequence, as discussed further below in the context of the conversion of money.

Cash

It would be a very unusual use of the word 'cash' today that did not apply equally to coins and notes. Historically, however, those two forms of physical money had very different origins and functions.

[43] *Personal Property Law*, 4th edition, 22.

Coins in the modern sense were broadly speaking conceived as a repository of value. By virtue of the endorsement of the authority that minted them, the recipient could be confident he was receiving a coin of a given value. Coinage was subject to debasement throughout history, but until fairly recently was intended to have at least some inherent worth.

By contrast bank notes have never had inherent worth, but were promissory notes (as discussed above) of the paradigm kind. It is well known that bank notes bear the legend, signed by an officer of the Bank of England, 'I promise to pay the bearer the sum of …', and that until Britain's departure from the gold standard they could be presented at the Bank of England and redeemed for the equivalent value in gold. Centuries ago (and before the Bank of England was a central bank or owned by the state) it was the practice of various banks to issue promissory notes, seemingly addressed to a named person, 'or the bearer'.

The status of bank notes as promissory notes as distinct from coinage of inherent worth was a matter of utmost practical importance at one time. This is illustrated by the eighteenth-century decision *Miller v Race* (1758) 97 ER 398. The facts concerned an individual, Mr Finney, who sent a bank note through the mail. Before it could reach its intended recipient, however, the mail coach was robbed and the bank note stolen.

In due course, the bank note was used (apparently by the robber himself) to pay an innkeeper for his services. The innkeeper had in no way colluded in the robbery and was not on notice of it; he had simply accepted the bank note in the ordinary course of his business. Mr Finney, on becoming aware of the theft of the note, contacted the issuing bank to arrange the cancellation of the note. As a result of Mr Finney's efforts, when the innkeeper applied to the bank for payment of the note (ie the provision of coin in the value promised in the note) payment was refused and the bank retained the note.

As follows from the facts of this case, a bank note at the time was viewed in a qualitatively different way from the present time. The idea that a person who had had a bank note stolen might contact the Bank of England to arrange its cancellation is little short of ludicrous to modern eyes (albeit of course at the time of *Miller* there was no central bank and no doubt a wide range of private banks issued promissory notes to bearers). Even by the mid-eighteenth century, however, Lord Mansfield in *Miller* was able to draw the equivalence between bank notes and cash:

> It has been very ingeniously argued by Sir Richard Lloyd for the defendant. But the whole fallacy of the argument turns upon comparing bank notes to what they do not resemble, and what they ought not to be compared to, viz. to goods, or to securities, or documents for debts.
>
> Now they are not goods, not securities, nor documents for debts, nor are so esteemed: but are treated as money, as cash, in the ordinary course and transaction of business, by the general consent of mankind; which gives them the credit and currency of money, to all intents and purposes. They are as much money, as guineas themselves are; or any other current coin, that is used in common payments, as money or cash.'

Miller is also authority for an important legal feature of cash, namely that it is excepted from the general rule that good title cannot pass from a person who does not himself have good title – ie it is an exception to the *nemo dat quod non habet* rule discussed above.

This exception dates back at least to the end of the seventeenth century. In *Anonymous* (1698) 91 ER 118, Holt CJ found that an action for trover was not available where a person lost a bank note and another person found it and passed the bank note on to a third person for valuable consideration. Holt CJ reasoned that, although an action would lie against a finder of a bank note, it would not lie against a person who received it in the course of trade, as that course of trade 'creates a property' in the recipient. This was also the reasoning adopted by Lord Mansfield in *Miller*.

In fact, the reasoning in *Miller* and *Anonymous* was targeted at bank notes. Lord Mansfield was able to make the decision he did because he equated bank notes with 'cash' (ie rather than restricting 'cash' purely to coinage). It follows that the exception from the *nemo dat* rule must have pre-dated *Miller* and *Anonymous*; what was new about *Miller* and *Anonymous* was that bank notes were being equated with coinage, and thereby brought within what must have been a pre-existing exception for coinage.

The exception for cash from the *nemo dat* rule is one that can probably be attributed to public policy. A critical purpose of money is as a medium of exchange; that purpose would be dramatically undermined if a recipient of cash was at risk of having to return cash received, or pay damages equivalent to the cash received. This certainly seems to have been Lord Mansfield's reasoning in *Miller*:

> A bank-note is constantly and universally, both at home and abroad, treated as money, as cash; and paid and received, as cash; and it is necessary, for the purposes of commerce, that their currency should be established and secured.

High and comparatively recent authority for this rule is found in *Lipkin Gorman v Karpnale Ltd* [1991] 2 AC 548 at 559. Lord Templeman added to that rule his conclusion that, where the recipient of money had been unjustly enriched by the receipt, he is liable to pay over the proceeds of his unjust enrichment in an action in restitution.

Actions in Conversion for Money

The scope for bringing an action in conversion in respect of money has been complicated by the Torts (Interference with Goods) Act 1977 ('TIGA'). As discussed elsewhere, TIGA creates an umbrella concept of 'wrongful interference with goods', which comprises several common law torts. The torts falling within 'wrongful interference' are regulated by TIGA, such that, for example, the remedies available for them are prescribed by TIGA.

The torts falling within the scope of 'wrongful interference' are defined at s 1 TIGA. One such tort is 'conversion of goods' (as well as 'trespass to goods' and negligence resulting in 'damage to goods').

'Goods' is defined within s 14 TIGA as follows: 'all chattels personal other than things in action and money'. Thus 'money' is specifically carved out of the scheme of the TIGA. This obviously suggests that a claim in conversion cannot be brought in respect of money.

The position is rather more complicated, however, than the wording of TIGA might suggest in this respect. For one thing, the fact that s 1 states that TIGA applies only to 'conversion in goods', when read with the definition of 'goods', on one view means that any common law action that might have existed in respect of conversion of money is not within the scope of TIGA.

Furthermore, extrapolating from the definition of goods in TIGA principles applying to the tort of conversion generally is not necessarily sound. As the authors of *Clerk & Lindsell on Torts* submit,[44] 'this may not be an infallible guide as to the common law position on what kinds of property are amenable to conversion'.

The question of the availability of an action for conversion in respect of money is an issue that greatly pre-dates TIGA. It has long been said that conversion was only available in respect of money that was 'in a bag'. This term (used it seems as a technical term of art) is usually thought to mean money that was physically separate and identifiable as the converted money. The 'in a bag' concept appears to derive from *Holiday v Hicks* (1598) 78 ER 900. The report of that case records that judgment was originally given for the plaintiff in conversion, but this decision was reversed because 'this action lies not for money found, unless it be in a bag or chest'. The total absence of reasoning makes this decision difficult to analyse but from this extract it may be that it was intended to be directed at the law of finding, rather than the law of conversion generally.

In any event, even from the earliest times, it does not appear that the 'in a bag' qualification has ever been a hard and fast rule. In *Hall v Dean* (1599) 78 ER 1068 an action for conversion was brought in respect of money. It was argued on the defendant's behalf that the action could not succeed because it was for conversion of money 'out of a bag'. This argument did not succeed, however, and the action was successful. Again the report is too exiguous to ascertain any reasoning.

In *Draycot v Piot* (1600) 78 ER 1045 a similar question came before the court. An action for conversion was brought in respect of money but was opposed on the basis that the money was 'out of a bag' – the reasoning being, it seems, that the money that was the subject of the action was mixed with other funds.

[44] 22nd edition, paragraph 17-35.

Again, however, this defence was rejected. Again there is no explanation of the court's reasoning.

Very slightly more reasoning was provided in *Kinaston v Moor* (1626) 79 ER 678. Once again a defence was raised to a claim in conversion that money was 'out of a bag'. The report records what appears to be the logical force of the 'out of a bag' defence, namely, 'money lost cannot be known; and so whether it was the plaintiff's money, whereof the trover and conversion was, as is the charge of this action'. In other words, where money was not clearly identifiable by being within some physical container, it was difficult to ascertain what money belonged to the plaintiff and what did not. In *Kinaston*, however, the 'out of a bag' defence was defeated, apparently by the mere fact that the jury had found as a matter of fact that the money to which the claim related was the property of the plaintiff.

Thus, the 'in a bag' principle is perhaps best explained as a factual presumption that it is difficult to determine the ownership of money if that money is not contained within some particular bag or other container. If, however, notwithstanding this difficulty, a factual finding can be made that particular money belongs to the claimant, a claim in conversion can be brought.

Accordingly, the courts have found in favour of plaintiffs in conversion claims. Several early seventeenth-century authorities are mentioned above. Slightly more recently, in *Burn v Morris* (1864) 149 ER 891, the court was called upon to consider a claim for conversion in respect of a lost Bank of England bank note. The bank note had been lost by a bank clerk on the street, picked up by a woman and changed with the Bank of England for coin by the defendant. In the proceedings, and in order to prove its case, the Bank of England produced the note that it maintained had been converted. The question of whether this was indeed the note that had been dropped by the clerk was firmly in issue but the jury decided as a matter of fact that it *was* the same note. The defendant was found liable in conversion. This decision therefore supports the hypothesis that the 'in a bag' principle is in reality nothing more than an evidential presumption.

Even if the 'in a bag' principle does not in reality amount to much more than an evidential presumption, it is still true to say that, when money passes into currency (ie it is given to a third party without notice in exchange for value) no action for conversion is available. That was confirmed by Lord Templeman in *Lipkin Gorman* at 559.

Although there is no authority on the question, the authors of *Clerk & Lindsell on Torts*[45] take the view that the exclusion of 'money' at s 14 TIGA should properly be read as excluding only such money as has passed into currency, rather than as being an attempt at the revival of the always very limited 'in a bag' principle. That construction of s 14 TIGA is one that does much to remedy what would otherwise be a strange and arbitrary limitation of the scope

[45] ibid, paragraph 17-37.

of TIGA and it is to be hoped that it is the construction that the court would adopt if called upon to do so.

It is also to be stressed, however, that even where conversion is not available because the money in question has passed into currency, the prospective injustice that could arise from this principle is ameliorated by the availability of a restitutionary action for money had and received. Per Lord Templeman in *Lipkin Gorman*:

> But the law imposes an obligation on the recipient of stolen money to pay an equivalent sum to the victim if the recipient has been 'unjustly enriched' at the expense of the true owner. In *Fibrosa Spolka Akcyjna v. Fairbairn Lawson Combe Barbour Ltd. [1943] A.C. 32*, 61, Lord Wright said:
>
> > 'It is clear that any civilised system of law is bound to provide remedies for cases of what has been called unjust enrichment or unjust benefit, that is to prevent a man from retaining the money of or some benefit derived from another which it is against conscience that he should keep.'

In appropriate circumstances, of course, equity may also provide a remedy where conversion is barred by the passing into currency principle. In appropriate circumstances a claim may be available in dishonest assistance or knowing receipt.

Conversion of Cheques and Similar Documents

As noted above, s 14 TIGA, as well as excluding money from the scope of 'goods', also purports to exclude choses in action. This is a less controversial proposition because a chose in action per se is not generally thought to be capable of conversion.[46]

This does, however, pose the question of how the law deals with the conversion of documents such as cheques and other bills of exchange, as well as other documents evidencing intangible property such as share certificates. The answer is that generally such documents are valueless, in that the act of conversion entails nothing more than appropriating a piece of paper. In such circumstances an action for conversion is not possible. There are circumstances, however, in which the conversion of the document, particularly when that document is a cheque, has the effect of depriving the owner of the benefit of the chose in action.

A relatively recent example was *International Factors Ltd v Rodriguez* [1979] QB 351. That case involved a claimant that was a factoring company, which had paid a sum of money in exchange for the assignment of certain debts owed to a

[46] ibid, paragraph 17-38 and the Commonwealth authority cited therein. It is certainly hard to see as a matter of philosophy how a right to a debt could be converted as such. Clearly the funds when paid could be converted, but the actual right to be paid is intangible and belongs to the creditor such that it is not at all clear how it could be interfered with.

company called Sound Components Ltd ('SCL'), of which the defendant was a director. A term of the factoring agreement was that, should any payments be made to SCL rather that to the claimant, SCL would hold those receipts on trust for the claimant. In the event, four cheques were received by SCL that the defendant arranged to be paid into SCL's bank account for its own use.

The claimant sued the defendant in conversion. The Court of Appeal found that there was sufficient standing to sue in conversion because, although the contractual right to be paid the cheques was insufficient to found a claim in conversion,[47] the factoring agreement had created a trust.

> In my view, however, there was here something more than a contractual right. Clause 11 (e) of the agreement provided both that the company was to hold any debt paid direct to the company in trust for the plaintiffs and immediately after receipt of a cheque, in the case of payment by cheque, to hand over that cheque to the plaintiffs. Taking together the trust which was thereby set up and the obligation immediately on receipt to hand over the cheque to the plaintiffs, I am satisfied that the plaintiffs had here a sufficient proprietary right to sue in conversion.

[47] *Jarvis v Williams* [1955] 1 WLR 71, discussed elsewhere in the context of conversion.

4

Giving Up Rights in Chattels and Acquiring Chattels that have been Surrendered

ABANDONMENT

As discussed above, the default position is that ownership of a chattel does not pass from its original owner without an intention to transfer ownership. That applies irrespective of what is done with the chattel; an owner can take steps to part permanently with possession, while retaining ownership.

One of the more startling applications of that principle occurred in *Haynes's Case* (1613) 12 Coke Reports 113. In that case the court found that a winding sheet, used to wrap a corpse that had been interred, still belonged to the person who had owned it when it was used to wrap the corpse. The principal question before the court on that occasion was whether the dead person had acquired some ownership of the winding sheet (to which the answer was no because dead people cannot own property). The court's reasoning, however, also shows that wrapping a corpse in a winding sheet and interring it in the ground, with the intention it would remain there forever, was not enough for the original owner to divest himself of ownership.

The law of abandonment also has to be examined through the lens of the law of treasure. Treasure is discussed above. For present purposes, it is enough to say that a necessary (though not sufficient) condition for being 'treasure' under the common law regime[1] is that the original owner hid the items in a secret place with a view subsequently to recovering them.

The term 'abandonment' is capable of referring to two interests in chattels: possession and ownership. Abandonment of these two interests must be considered separately.

[1] As discussed above, there is a separate statutory regime that extends the definition of treasure to include certain specified items.

Abandonment of Possession, Loss and Finding

Lord Browne-Wilkinson gave the following definition of 'possession' in *L.A. Pye (Oxford) Ltd v Graham* [2002] 3 WLR 221 at 233:

> '[T]here are two elements necessary for legal possession: (1) a sufficient degree of physical custody and control ('factual possession'); (2) an intention to exercise such custody and control on one's own behalf and for one's own benefit ('intention to possess'). What is crucial to understand is that, without the requisite intention, in law there can be no possession.'

It therefore follows that possession can be abandoned either by wilfully parting with the requisite level of physical control of a chattel (as in *Haynes's Case*) or by consciously ceasing to intend to exercise the requisite level of custody and control.

It also follows that abandonment of possession occurs where a person intends to exercise custody or control, but as a matter of fact no longer has that custody or control. That is the position where a chattel has been lost.

As has been addressed above, a person who finds a chattel acquires a good title against anyone who does not have a better title. The leading authority is *Armory v Delamirie* (1721) 93 ER 664. In that case the claimant found what was described as a 'jewel', but which appears to have been a ring or other piece of jewellery with precious stones set in it. The finder took the jewellery to a goldsmith, whose apprentice, on the pretence of weighing it, removed the stones and sought to return only the setting to the finder. The court found that the goldsmith (vicariously liable for the actions of his apprentice) was liable to the finder in respect of the loss of the stones. Thus the finder had acquired a possessory title in respect of the stones that was capable of being protected against all others.

The converse of the position in *Armory* can be found in *Moffatt v Kazana* [1968] 3 All ER 271. In that case Mr and Mrs Moffatt had bought a bungalow in 1951. On the journey to the house Mr Moffatt produced a biscuit tin, which he placed between himself and Mrs Moffatt on the front seat of the car. On arrival at the house, Mr Moffatt ascended a ladder with the biscuit tin and disappeared into the ceiling void, returning without the biscuit tin. Mrs Moffatt never saw the biscuit tin again.

In 1961 the bungalow was sold to Mr Kazana. While installing a new aga, Mr Kazana discovered a biscuit tin stuffed with cash in the kitchen flue. Mr and Mrs Moffatt commenced litigation asserting entitlement to the biscuit tin; Mr Moffatt died before the matter came to trial but his estate continued the litigation.

At trial, the judge found that the biscuit tin recovered by Mr Kazana must have been that stowed in the roof by Mr Moffatt, and that Mr Moffatt (odd though it seems) must simply have forgotten about the presence of the biscuit tin in the roof when he sold the house. It followed that Mr Moffatt was the owner of the tin and its contents because even though he had forgotten about it, he had only abandoned possession and not ownership.

In *Moffatt* the court also gave some attention to a case that might prima facie seem authority for the opposite conclusion (and indeed was cited by Mr Kazana in support of his position). That case was *City of London Corporation v Appleyard* [1963] 1 WLR 982.

In *Appleyard* some workmen excavating a basement found a considerable amount of money in a safe. The litigation involved a dispute between the workmen on the one hand and the occupier of the land on the other as to who was entitled to the money. The court concluded that the occupiers of the land had better title than the finders. *Appleyard* is *not* authority, however, (as Mr Kazana's counsel had tried to argue) for the proposition that where possession of a chattel is abandoned ownership goes to the owner of the land on which the chattel is found. As McNair J said in *Appleyard* at 987:

> In my judgment, the notes having been found within the safe which itself formed part of the demised premises, the party in possession of the premises … had, in the absence of any evidence as to the true ownership of the notes, a better title thereto than the finders.

Thus McNair J was expressly affirming the possibility that a person could have better title than the finder – namely the true owner. *Appleyard* is, however, authority for the proposition that when a 'servant' finds a chattel (meaning for modern purposes an employee or a contractor), any interest in the chattel belongs to the 'master'.

The following principles therefore emerge on the subject of abandoning possession of a chattel:

1. It is possible to abandon possession of a chattel without abandoning ownership.
2. Abandonment occurs either (i) (presumably more usually) as a result of accidentally parting with physical control of a chattel (ie the loss of a chattel); or (ii) where a person deliberately relinquishes physical control or the intention to exercise such control.
3. The finder of a chattel in circumstances where possession has been abandoned acquires good title against anyone except the owner.
4. As between a finder and an occupier of land on which the chattel is found, the occupier of the land has, in ordinary circumstances, a better title to the chattel than the finder. An exception exists where an employee or contractor finds a chattel, in which case possessory title will vest in his employer.

Although it is clear from *Appleyard* that, when a servant finds a chattel on his master's land, the chattel belongs to the master, that does not address the consequences of a person who is not a servant finding such a chattel. Who, then, owns the chattel? Is it the finder or the land owner?

This comparatively simple question has been a vexed one in English law for some time, as has been touched on above. Much of the difficulty was instigated by a case called *Bridges v Hawkesworth* (1851) 21 LJ (QB) 75. *Bridges* concerned a commercial traveller who visited a customer, and while on the customer's premises discovered a package containing bank notes. He drew the package to the attention of the shopkeeper and unsuccessful efforts were made to find the owner. The question subsequently arose of who, as between the finder and the shopkeeper (ie the occupier of the land on which it was found), had the better title to the money.

The court found that the finder had the better title to the money. Its reasoning, however, was not at all clear and engendered a good deal of comment and criticism throughout the twentieth century. Those commentators who felt *Bridges* had been correctly decided differed as to the correct interpretation of the court's reasoning. For example, one popular line of thought (supported by the court in *South Staffordshire Water Co* [1896] 2 QB 44 at 47) is that *Bridges* had been decided on the basis that the money had been found in a public place. That is in spite of the fact that no mention of that fact had been made in *Bridges*. On that basis, it was possible readily to distinguish *Bridges* should the judge wish to do so. On the other hand, in other cases[2] the court was content to apply *Bridges* to any circumstances in which a chattel was found on land.

Clarity appears finally to have been introduced to this area by the Court of Appeal in *Waverley Borough Council v Fletcher* [1996] QB 334. That case involved a metal detectorist who found a brooch (which did not qualify as treasure) nine inches under the surface of a public park. Auld LJ drew a distinction between chattels found in land (ie fixed to or under the surface of land) and chattels found on the surface of land. At 343 he approved a previous dictum of Donaldson LJ in *Parker v British Airways Board* [1982] QB 1004 as follows:

> 1. An occupier of land has rights superior to those of a finder over chattels in or attached to that land and an occupier of a building has similar rights in respect of chattels attached to that building, whether in either case the occupier is aware of the presence of the chattel.
> 2. An occupier of a building has rights superior to those of a finder over chattels upon or in, but not attached to, that building if, but only if, before the chattel is found, he has manifested an intention to exercise control over the building and the things which may be upon it or in it.

This of course gives rise to a rather arbitrary distinction. The example given by counsel for the metal detectorist was that of a watch left on a muddy path. It may seem odd that the better possessory title could initially belong to the finder, but after a couple of days of rain, when the watch might have sunk below a thin layer of mud, the better possessory title transfers to the land owner. Nevertheless,

[2] Such as *Hannah v Peel* [1945] KB 509.

the Court of Appeal's view was that, while borderline cases could, as so often, cause oddities, the distinction between finding in land or on land was a justified one. Per Auld LJ at 345:

> In my view, the authorities reveal a number of sound and practical reasons for the distinction.
>
> First, as Donaldson L.J. said in *Parker v. British Airways Board [1982] Q.B. 1004*, 1010, an object in land 'is to be treated as an integral part of the realty as against all but the true owner' or that the finder in detaching the object would, in the absence of licence to do so, become a trespasser. Mr. Munby suggested that this is wrong because if an object is treated as part of the realty the true owner cannot have priority. However, the English law of ownership and possession, unlike that of Roman Law, is not a system of identifying absolute entitlement but of priority of entitlement, and Donaldson L.J.'s rationale is consistent with that: see *Buckland and McNair, Roman Law and Common Law*, 2nd ed. revise (1965), p. 67. It is also consistent with Chitty J.'s reasoning in the *Elwes case, 33 Ch.D. 562*, *567*, which I have quoted. See also *Wake v. Hall (1883) 8 App.Cas. 195*, 203–204, per Lord Blackburn and *Simmons v. Midford [1969] 2 Ch. 415*, 421F–G, per Buckley J.
>
> Second, removal of an object in or attached to land would normally involve interference with the land and may damage it: cf. A. L. Goodhart's view in his article in *3 C.L.J. 195*, 207, that this distinction is not of sufficient importance in principle to warrant separate rules as to possession.
>
> Third, putting aside the borderline case of a recently lost article which has worked its way just under the surface, in the case of an object in the ground its original owner is unlikely in most cases to be there to claim it. The law, therefore, looks for a substitute owner, the owner or possessor of the land in which it is lodged. Whereas in the case of an unattached object on the surface, it is likely in most cases to have been recently lost, and the true owner may well claim it. In the meantime, there is no compelling reason why it should pass into the possession of the landowner as against a finder unless he, the landowner, has manifested an intention to possess it. As to borderline cases of the sort mentioned by Mr. Munby, potential absurdities can always be found at the margins in the application of any sound principle. It is for the trial judge to determine as a matter of fact and degree on which side of the line, on or in the land, an object is found.

It should also be noted that *Parker* establishes the further principle that, for reasons of public policy, in a dispute between a finder and a land occupier over the better possessory title, the law will always favour the landowner where the finder was on the land as a trespasser.

Finally on the subject of the law of finders, there is of course a degree of interplay between the civil question of possessory title in found chattels and the criminal question of theft. This is a work on civil law and no attempt is made to survey the criminal regime that may exist in parallel. It is worth stating, however, as dealt with in more detail elsewhere in this work, that the rights of a finder in respect of a lost chattel are protected in *civil* law by operation of the principles of bailment.

Abandonment of Ownership

In this section we are concerned with the question of whether and when the owner of a chattel can abandon his rights of ownership. As will be appreciated, this goes a step further than merely abandoning possession, and effectively amounts to surrendering any right to recover possession from another person who has acquired possessory title over a chattel.

This kind of abandonment has had a long but at times obscure history within English law. The concept of abandonment is also extremely difficult to disentwine from the specialist areas of the law of wreck and treasure. In some respects the lack of a clear doctrine of abandonment of ownership is not surprising since, as discussed above, English law has always had a somewhat uncertain relationship with the concept of ownership. Rather than treating ownership as an absolute right in itself, it is in reality shorthand for a bundle of rights in respect of that property. In the case of personalty, that bundle of rights does not even include an absolute right to possession (that being, as discussed above, the fundamental original difference between real and personal property).

Under Roman law,[3] there was a clear right to abandon the ownership of property (both moveable and immoveable). That right was called *derelicto* and created property that was *res nullius* – ie ownerless. Abandonment required nothing more than parting with possession with the intention of parting with ownership.

In commentaries of the latter medieval period, in the centuries following the Norman Conquest, there appears to have been an assumption among jurists that the Roman law as to abandonment continued to apply. Thus Henry de Bracton wrote in the thirteenth century:

> A thing taken to be abandoned passes without livery, where the lord at once ceases to be lord; but if it is cast away for lightening a ship it is not derelict for he does not cast it away with the intention of ceasing to be lord or of no longer wishing to be. But if he disposes of it with that intention it will be otherwise.

That analysis was consistent with the existence at the time of the right to 'waifs and strays', commonly granted by the Crown to a landowner in Norman law. A 'waif' was a piece of 'ownerless' property found on land.[4] The right allowed a landowner to claim as his own any waif, having first allowed a period for anyone to assert a right of ownership to it. The very concept of the right to waifs suggests that a concept of abandonment of ownership was known to the law at the time.

A number of authorities subsequently suggest that divestment of ownership is impossible other than by way of passing title to another person. An example

[3] See Anthony Hudson's analysis of the history of the law of abandonment at chapter 23 of the 2nd edition of *Palmer and McKendrick's Interests in Goods*, to which I am indebted throughout this section.

[4] A stray was a domestic animal that had wandered onto the land of the holder of the right.

is *Haynes's Case* referred to above. Although the court was not called upon to decide on facts involving a specific attempt to abandon ownership, it did remark, presumably obiter, that 'a man cannot relinquish the property he hath to his goods, unless they be vested in another'. In the eighteenth century, Charles Viner applied *Haynes's Case* in his *Abridgments*[5] by way of commentary on the law of waifs as follows: 'If a man waives his own good without offence, and says he will not have them any longer, this is no forfeiture and he may take them at his pleasure'.

Thus by the beginning of the nineteenth century the balance of authorities (and certainly if one excludes authorities pertaining to the highly specialist field of wreck) appear to militate against the existence of a concept of abandonment of ownership. From the nineteenth century onwards, however, there is an increase in support for the concept.

In *R v Peters* (1843) 1 Car & K 245 a lady had dropped an item of jewellery in her garden when out walking. The defendant was employed at the house and was asked by the lady's gardener to assist in a search for the jewellery. He found the jewellery but, instead of returning it to the gardener or the lady, he pretended he had found nothing and took it home, presumably with the intention of selling it.

The next morning, the lady and her husband let it be known that they were offering a reward for the safe return of the jewellery. The defendant, in concert with his wife, purported to offer the jewellery for return in exchange for the reward on the pretence that the jewellery had been found in the street near the house.

In directing the jury, the judge allowed for the possibility that a person may be able to abandon his property rights (with the additional common-sense proposition that the more valuable a chattel, the less readily abandonment will be inferred):

> If a man is possessed of a chattel, he does not lose the property in it because he places or drops it in a field. Nay, if he drop it in a street, it still remains his property. The only case where a party can be justified in converting it to his own use is, where it has fallen or dropped where a party may fairly say the owner has abandoned it; or if the party cannot be found to whom it belonged. If I had an apple, and dropped it, it might be presumed that I abandoned it; but if I drop £500, the presumption is, that I do not mean to abandon it.

Similarly, in *R v Reed* (1842) Carr & M 307 the court had to consider the appropriation of a £5 note found on the street. Coleridge J stated as follows in summing up to the jury:

> I am not sorry this case has come here, as it affords an opportunity of setting out the law on a subject of which many people are ignorant. A man who loses anything,

[5] ie his commentary on the common law and equity, at p 409 of Volume 22 of the 2nd edition.

> does not thereby lose his property in it, and the finder is bound to restore it to the owner, if possible; and if he keep it when he thinks it is only lost by the owner, it is larceny in him. If the property be found when it is abandoned by the owner, it is his own who finds it.

A number of other cases arose in the context of criminal law over the following century or so, all of which seemed to accept the proposition that ownership of property could be abandoned, and that taking such property consequently did not amount to theft. The last of these was *Hibbert v Mckiernan* [1948] 2 KB 142. In that case the facts concerned the alleged theft of golf balls from a golf club. The Divisional Court was faced with a case stated including a conclusion that the golf balls had been abandoned by their original owners (ie the golfers). Although the Divisional Court expressed some doubt about the veracity of that conclusion, those doubts appeared to have been predicated on the quality of the first instance reasoning, and there was no sense that the abandonment of personalty was conceptually impossible.

There is, then, a considerable degree of support from criminal cases for the proposition that ownership of property can be abandoned. This raises the question of whether the civil law also recognises the possibility of the ownership of chattels being abandoned.

To some extent that question is still without an authoritative answer. On balance, however, it does seem highly likely that the civil law would recognise the abandondment of ownership rights in property. In support of that view are the following:

1. Although the cases that support abandonment of ownership are criminal cases, they nevertheless draw for their conclusions on civil cases. For example, *Hibbert* applied *Armory* (as well as numerous other cases). It certainly does not appear that those criminal cases sought to create a strand of law unique to the criminal context. It would therefore appear rather illogical for the law of tort not to follow suit.
2. Modern commentators on tort seem to accept the existence of the concept of abandonment of ownership, perhaps most notably the authors of *Clerk and Lindsell on Torts*.[6] The authors rely in support on the decision in *The Lusitania* [1986] QB 384. It must be said, however, that *The Lusitania* seems to concern a specific question of maritime law, namely whether the vessel was a 'derelict', which is a maritime term of art. The question of whether the vessel had been 'abandoned' was relevant to determining whether it was 'derelict'. It may be tenuous, however, to extrapolate from that matter of the law of wreck a principle of applicability to chattels generally.
3. A principle of abandonment of ownership of chattels appeals generally to a sense of natural justice. The notion that ownership of personalty could

[6] Paragraph 17-49 of the 22nd edition.

> continue indefinitely after the chattel is disposed of does not equate to the experience of daily life. It also raises the prospect of injustice if a person disposes of a chattel and then, perhaps some years later, decides he wishes to recover the chattel. If there is no concept of abandonment of ownership, any person who subsequently comes into possession of the chattel is at risk of it being taken away or having to pay damages.

Ultimately, the very lack of authority on the question of abandonment of ownership shows that it is an issue that arises rarely in practice in a tortious context. When the owner of a chattel has taken a step sufficiently drastic as to dispossess himself of the chattel with an intention to surrender all rights over it, it is unusual for a tortious dispute to arise. Nevertheless, so far as can be ascertained, the period of several centuries during which abandonment of ownership of chattels was considered impossible was simply an interregnum. It is highly likely that a civil court would now consider that abandonment of ownership is possible.

BONA VACANTIA

The operation of the concept of bona vacantia, including the circumstances in which it arises, is dealt with in Chapter 2 above. This is an appropriate point, however, to make some more general observations about the principles behind bona vacantia, which affect the way it operates in practice.

In particular, it has been explained in Chapter 2 above that there are certain specific scenarios in which property passes to the Crown bona vacantia (for example property belonging to a company at the time of its dissolution). The question here is whether bona vacantia is confined to those specific scenarios, or whether it is a general principle applying to any ownerless property. Of course, scenarios in which property is ownerless are very rare. There is only one obvious scenario that is not dealt with in the specific bona vacantia instances referred to above. That scenario is where ownership has been abandoned.[7]

As has been discussed in Chapter 1 above, the ultimate ownership of all real property vests in the Crown. Other persons are only able to own estates in land. As a matter of practice, if not of philosophy, this creates a residual right of ownership in favour of the Crown.

It appears to be a principle of Scottish law that chattels that are abandoned pass to the ownership of the Crown.[8] This is a concept that has caused a measure of difficulty in criminal law since its consequence is that a person who takes a chattel that has been discarded by its original owner is guilty of theft from the Crown.

[7] Which, as described above, appears to be possible, although the point has not been decided.
[8] See, for example, *Lord Advocate v Aberdeen University* 1963 SC 533, 549.

Perhaps unsurprisingly, the Scottish courts have been reluctant to find that persons so undeserving of moral censure are guilty of theft. Thus in *Campbell v MacLennan* (1888) 1 White 604 Lord McLaren gave the example of a man who found money on the street and decided to give it to a beggar. In those circumstances the conclusion that the beggar was guilty of theft would be most unpalatable.

The notion that the Crown is the residual owner of abandoned personalty has had a degree of support in English law. Thus in *Middleton v Spicer* (1783) 2 ER 1083 the court found that 'the king is the owner of every thing which has no other owner'.[9]

In *Dyke v Walkford* (1846) 13 ER 557 counsel for the Duchy of Lancaster (who asserted entitlement to bona vacantia on franchise from the Crown) surveyed the commentary on the question as follows:

> In Comyn's Dig., tit. ' Prerogative,' (D.) 49, it is laid down, that the Crown is entitled to all goods which have no owner; and to the same effect is Brook's Abr., tit. 'Prerog. le Roy,' 12, 'Biens;' Bracton, lib. 1, c. 12, s. 10; Coke, 2 Inst. 167. Blackstone (1 Comm. 299) says, besides the particular reason why the King should have treasure-trove, waifs, etc., 'there is one general reason, which holds for them all; that is, because they are '*bona vacantia*,' or goods in which no one else can claim a property.' ... So, by the Civil law, '*bona vacantia*,' went to the State. Cod., lib. 10, tit. 10. Nor is it in that sense unknown to our law; for *[471]* the Vice-Chancellor of England, in *Taylor v. Haygarth*, uses the term '*bona vacantia*,' so in *Middleton v. Spicer*. By the feudal law, also, such goods go to the King. Cragii, in his *Jus Feudale*, lib. 1, c. 16, ss. 30, 43; lib. 2, c. 18, ss. 15, 16; treating ' *de jure regis in feudis et de regalibus*,' includes, among the *regalia*, belonging to the Crown, '*bona vacantia ...*

The Privy Council found as follows at 495:

> The origin of this right shows that, if it existed at all, it must have existed from the foundation of the Monarchy; it is the right of the Crown to '*bona vacantia*;' to property which has no other owner. This is the ground upon which it is plainly rested by Lyndwood, in the reign of Henry the Sixth, and by Lord Thurlow, in his decision in *Middleton v. Spicer*, in the reign of George the Third.

The fundamental principles of bona vacantia were examined again in *Re Wells, Swinburne-Hanham v Howard* [1933] Ch 29. That case concerned a dispute between the Crown and a mortgagee as to the ownership of the equity of redemption of a leasehold property owned by a dissolved company. After summarising the authorities Lord Hanworth MR said as follows at 36:

> It is argued, however, that the right of the Crown is not, as stated above, to take property which has no other owner; but that in the case of a right of property which is

[9] Strictly this was the way in which the law was put in the Attorney General's argument on behalf of the Crown, but it was accepted by the court in its judgment (or at least that was the position as found in *Re Wells* (see below).

> incorporeal, that right will not survive unless it is vested in a trustee and so kept alive; in other words, such a right only survives where there is a trust that fails.

As that extract suggests, the court was called upon to consider whether the principle that the Crown is the automatic owner of otherwise ownerless property should be qualified. However, it only undertook that enquiry into the question of incorporeal rights.

The court considered that it would be a 'curious condition or qualification of the broad rule above stated' (ie the broad rule that the Crown is the owner of otherwise ownerless property) were incorporeal rights only pass to the Crown if first vested in a trustee. That notion was therefore rejected. There is therefore nothing in the decision in *Wells* that restricts the breadth of bona vacantia as a concept embracing all instances in which property is ownerless.

There does not appear to be any authority to the effect that there is any species of ownerless property (with the exception of wild non-royal animals) that does not vest in the Crown. It would therefore appear that, assuming it is possible to abandon ownership rather than merely possession of a chattel (and, as argued above, this does appear to be the position), once abandoned the ownership of the property would pass to the Crown.

Having said that, were chattels indeed to vest in the Crown where ownership is abandoned, that would suggest that some or all of the criminal cases that seem to establish the possibility of abandonment of ownership were wrongly decided. For example, the court would have been wrong in *Reed* to conclude that a person who comes upon ownerless property can make it his own; that property would in fact have belonged to the Crown, absent some further principle.

This issue has apparently never arisen in practice, and the English law has managed to avoid the difficulties caused in Scottish law by the principle that abandoned chattels vest in the Crown. Presumably the reason for this is that if a principle of abandonment of ownership does exist in English law, it will only arise in the plainest of circumstances and, crucially, only where the owner of the chattel has actively indicated an intention to abandon ownership. As discussed above, absent that kind of active indication abandonment will be of possession only, and in those circumstances ownership certainly will not vest in the Crown.

If the court were ever pressed on the point, it is submitted that it is more likely than not that it would conclude that abandoned property (in the sense of abandonment of ownership) does *not* vest in the Crown. The law already recognises at least one type of un-owned potential property, namely wild animals that are capable of being reduced to property by taming. There seems no good reason to interpose a cumbersome operation of bona vacantia, with potentially difficult consequences in criminal law, to prevent other circumstances of ownerless property arising. This approach derives some support from *Blackstone*, Book 1, Chapter 8:

> But a man that scatters his treasure into the sea, or upon the public surface of the earth, is construed to have absolutely abandoned his property, and returned it into the

> common stock, without any intention of reclaiming it: and therefore it belongs, as in a state of nature, to the first occupant, or finder, unless the owner appear and assert his right, which then proves that the loss was by accident, and not with an intent to renounce his property.

It is also the approach that tallies most easily with natural justice and the ordinary perception of the world. Most people would find it surprising if a chattel, ownership of which had been actively relinquished by its previous owner, could not lawfully become owned by its finder. It seems intuitively strange that a person A could gift a chattel to B, but could not abandon a chattel for such unknown person as may wish to take ownership of it on finding it. For example, if someone leaves a newspaper in a pub in case someone else wishes to read it, it would be a most unintuitive state of affairs for ownership of the newspaper to pass at the point of abandonment to the Crown, and for the finder to be infringing the Crown's rights by taking it away.

BAILMENT CREATED WHEN POSSESSION HAS BEEN ABANDONED

Bailment in general is discussed further below. The purpose of this section is to discuss bailment in one particular context, namely the fictional bailment that exists as between a person who has abandoned possession of a chattel (usually in practice by loss) and the finder of the chattel.

That relationship of bailment is described as 'fictitious' because it does not arise from either an agreement or any active or even consensual placing of the chattel in the hands of the bailee. Whether or not it is an example of bailment, or some unique relationship with identical characteristics to bailment, is a matter or no consequence. Per Lord Pearson in the Privy Council in *Gilchrist Watt & Sanderson Pty Ltd v York Products Pty Ltd* [1970] 1 WLR 1262 (PC):

> Both on principle and on old as well as recent authority it is clear that, although there was no contract or attornment between the plaintiffs and the defendants, the defendants by voluntarily taking possession of the plaintiffs' goods in the circumstances assumed an obligation to take due care of them and are liable to the plaintiffs for their failure to do so (as found by the trial judge). The obligation is at any rate the same as that of a bailee, whether or not it can with strict accuracy be described as being the obligation of a bailee. In a case such as this the obligation is created by the delivery and assumption of possession under a sub-bailment. In the English courts the word 'bailment' has acquired a meaning wide enough to include this case.

All types of bailment have somewhat different characteristics as to the use to which the bailee may put the chattel that has been bailed. The fictitious bailment created by finding has its own rules, although their full extent is not yet known.

First, and uniquely by virtue of the circumstances of its creation, the fictitious bailment imposes an obligation on the finder to take reasonable steps to seek the true owner. The case of *Parker v British Airways Board* [1982] QB 1004 (CA) has been discussed above in this chapter and in Chapter 2. Its facts concerned a traveller who found a gold bracelet in the departure lounge at Heathrow Airport. Donaldson LJ made the following observation about the scope of a fictitious bailee's duty:

> A person having a finder's rights has an obligation to take such measures as in all the circumstances are reasonable to acquaint the true owner of the finding and present whereabouts of the chattel and to care for it meanwhile.

From this extract emerges another key facet of the fictitious bailment: it exists to provide a defence to the finder against a claim in conversion brought by the owner. By these means the finder is able to make use of the chattel in reliance on his possessory title without risk of action against him by the owner. That ability has its limits, however. As Donaldson LJ observed, such use of a chattel is subject to a duty to take reasonable care of it until such time, if any, as the owner should wish to recover it. A fictitious bailee is, however, entitled to refuse to hand over chattels of which he is bailed if he is reasonably uncertain that the person seeking the chattel is its true owner.[10]

Bailment traditionally was said to depend on an element of consent on the part of the bailor. The question therefore arises: must there be consent of the owner for a fictitious bailment to come into being? It would to some extent be possible to uphold the concept of consent in such a relationship by presuming consent. For example, a person who loses a chattel could realistically be presumed to consent to a third party taking possession of it and making reasonable efforts to return it to him and safeguard it in the meantime.

The notion that consent, even were it to be presumed, is a fundamental component of all relationships of bailment, however, does not stand up to examination of the authorities. For example, in *Martin v London County Council* [1947] KB 628 a woman was brought into a mental hospital and (in modern parlance) sectioned. The hospital staff took from her various items of worth and stored them in a designated room, from which they were stolen. The local authority, which ran the hospital, was subsequently sued in negligence for breaching its duties as a bailee. The court found against the local authority. There had, of course, on that fact pattern, been no consent to the bailment on the part of the patient.

Indeed, it is apparent from other authorities that a relationship of bailment can come into being against the wishes of the bailor. In *Chesworth v Farrar* [1967] 1 QB 407 the defendant took possession of the plaintiff's premises pursuant to a judgment for rent arrears. The premises was an antiques shop with residential accommodation above. The plaintiff complained that the defendant lost a number of valuable antiques during its time in possession and sued

[10] *Isaack v Clark* (1613) 80 ER 1143.

accordingly, alleging a breach of bailment. It was common ground between the parties (see page 414 of the judgment) that a relationship of bailment existed, yet the bailor had not consented to the bailment, indeed she had opposed it.

The notion that consent on the part of the bailor is a necessary prerequisite of the relationship of bailment seems to have been explicitly rejected by the Privy Council in *The Pioneer Container* [1994] 2 AC 324, albeit in the context of establishing relationships of sub-bailment. Per Lord Godd at 341–42:

> In truth, at the root of this question lies a doctrinal dispute of a fundamental nature, which is epitomised in the question: is it a prerequisite of a bailment that the bailor should have consented to the bailee's possession of the goods? An affirmative answer to this question (which is the answer given by Bell, Modern Law of Personal Property in England and Ireland, at pp. 88–89) leads to the conclusion that, if the owner seeks to hold a sub-bailee responsible to him as bailee, he has to accept all the terms of the sub-bailment, warts and all; for either he will have consented to the sub-bailment on those terms or, if not, he will (by holding the sub-bailee liable to him as bailee) be held to have ratified all the terms of the sub-bailment. A negative answer to the question is however supported by other writers, notably by *Palmer, Bailment*, at pp. 31 et seq., where Professor Palmer cites a number of examples of bailment without the consent of the owner, and by Professor Tay in her article 'The Essence of Bailment: Contract, Agreement or Possession?' (1966) 5 Sydney Law Review 239. On this approach, a person who voluntarily takes another person's goods into his custody holds them as bailee of that person (the owner); and he can only invoke, for example, terms of a sub-bailment under which he received the goods from an intermediate bailee as qualifying or otherwise affecting his responsibility to the owner if the owner consented to them. It is the latter approach which, as their Lordships have explained, has been adopted by English law and, with English law, the law of Hong Kong.'

Thus it is tolerably clear that the consent of the bailor is not a prerequisite of bailment, and so we can say with relative confidence that no kind of consent, whether presumed or otherwise, is required for the fictional bailment in the context of finding to come into being.

Perhaps unsurprisingly, a person who finds a chattel is under no active obligation to take it into his possession and safeguard it. Per Coke CJ in *Isaack*: 'at the first it is in his election, whether he will take them or not into his custody, but when he hath them, one onely hath then right unto them, and therefore he ought to keep them safely'. As always the question of whether a person takes possession of a found chattel is a question of fact, to be decided with reference to the test for possession referred to above. It must follow from *Isaack* that some active step is required to assume the role of fictional bailee. For example, it would no doubt only be on unusual facts that the occupier of land has the duties of fictional bailee imposed on them just because a chattel is lost on their land.

As noted above, it seems tolerably clear from *Parker* that a fictitious bailee owes two principal duties: the duty to attempt to find the chattel's owner and return the chattel, and the duty to take reasonable care of the chattel while it is in his possession. It is sometimes said that a fictitious bailee owes a duty not to convert the bailed chattel, although in truth it is hard to see how that supposed duty adds anything to the duties expounded in *Parker*, or indeed is worthy of comment as somehow different to the various liabilities that private citizens may incur to each other in any event.

It seems possible to form the tentative conclusion that the dictum in *Parker* was intended as a comprehensive summary of the duties owed by the fictitious bailee; it is difficult to see in the context of the judgment why the Court of Appeal would have omitted some other important duty. Authority does not exist, however, enabling a certain statement of the extent of those duties.

Some assistance can be derived from the Australian case *Newman v Bourne and Hollingsworth* (1915) 31 TLR 209. In that case the court was concerned with circumstances in which a woman had visited a clothing shop. Her coat was fastened with a diamond brooch, which she removed and placed upon a display case while she tried on a possible new coat. In the event she left the shop without remembering to take her brooch. One of the shop workers thereafter took the brooch for safe keeping, but subsequently lost it. The owner of the brooch sued the operators of the shop (on the uncontroversial principle that they were vicariously liable for the actions of their employees) for breach of their obligations as bailee.

The court found in favour of the brooch's owner. Unfortunately for the shop, applying the principle in *Isaack*, had the shop worker simply left the brooch on top of the display case, it would probably have avoided liability. As it was, by taking possession of the brooch the shop's operators became liable to take reasonable care of the brooch, which in losing it they failed to do. Significantly for present purposes, the court seemed to equate the duties of a fictitious bailee with the duties of a gratuitous bailee for safe custody.[11] The duties of such a bailee are discussed further below.

Finally it should be noted that it is of the essence of the fictitious bailment discussed in this section that the bailee takes possession of the chattel innocently. That is to say that possession is taken with the intention of returning it to the owner, or at least with some intention other than to appropriate it for the finder's own use. If the owner deliberately takes a chattel with the intention of depriving another of his ownership rights, this will likely be theft and conversion, and the fictitious bailment will not arise to assist him.

[11] An analysis favoured by the authors of the 5th edition of *Crossley Vaines on Personal Property*, 95.

5

Protecting the Rights of Owners and Possessors of Chattels

THE HISTORICAL CONTEXT

THE LAW AROUND the protection of rights in chattels underwent a substantial reform in the late 1970s with the passage of the Torts (Interference with Goods) Act 1977. As will be discussed below, that statute led to an improvement by simplification of the various causes of action available to protect rights in chattels.

It is still useful, however, to understand the way in which English law had protected rights in personalty more historically. This is not least because the cases dealing with the historic protection of property rights are in many cases, as has been seen above, important in understanding how the law might approach relatively novel scenarios arising in the present day.

As has been noted above, the key initial distinction between real property and personal property was that only the former was amenable to an action entitling the owner to recover the actual property. Actions in respect of personalty, by contrast, entitled the owner of the chattel as of right to damages, with only limited or discretionary rights to recover the property itself. That distinction has remained largely constant throughout history.

Historically there have been four principal ways to vindicate a right in personalty: conversion, trespass, detinue and replevin. These will be considered individually, followed by the impact on those causes of action of more modern statute.

Conversion

Conversion is a familiar cause of action to modern lawyers. It is usually described by way of shorthand as the tortious equivalent of theft, although it is somewhat more nuanced than that description suggests. Conversion is a cause of action that protects an owner of a chattel (or a person with a lesser possessory title) from having his rights of ownership interfered with against his will.

In *Ashby v Tolhurst* [1937] 2 KB 242 the Court of Appeal approved what has become the classic definition of conversion at 247 as follows:

> 'The circumstances in which such a dealing amounts to conversion have been stated by Atkin J., as he then was, in *Lancashire and Yorkshire Ry. Co. v. MacNicoll*: 'It appears to me plain that dealing with goods in a manner inconsistent with the right of the true owner amounts to a conversion.' Then he adds these words: 'providing it is also established that there is an intention on the part of the defendant in so doing to deny the owner's right or to assert a right which is inconsistent with the owner's right.'

Notwithstanding the use of the term 'owner', as stated above it is clear that an action for conversion can properly be brought by a person who has only possessory title to a chattel (ie possession of the chattel or immediate right to possess it).

That principle can be seen, for example, in *Moorgate Mercantile Co Ltd v Finch* [1962] 2 All ER 467. In that case a person hired a car under a hire purchase arrangement. The terms of the agreement provided for the hire purchase company to be entitled to possession if the hirer defaulted on payments. The hirer lent the car to a friend 'R', who used it for smuggling. The car was subsequently seized by the UK Customs authorities. Meanwhile, the hirer had defaulted on his payments, which prima facie entitled the hire purchase company to possession. Proceedings were brought against the hirer, but also against R, seeking damages. The court agreed that R should be required to pay damages in view of the hire purchase company's entitlement to possession, notwithstanding that it was not the owner of the car.

The older authorities use the term 'trover' as an alternative to 'conversion'. It does not appear that there is any forensic difference between the terms (at least in recent centuries) – they are apparently interchangeable. Indeed s 1(a) Torts (Interference with Goods) Act 1977 expressly states that 'trover' is a name sometimes used for 'conversion', and to that extent preserves its existence (although in practice the use of the term 'trover' appears to have fallen into obsolescence).

The term 'trover' refers to the fact that the cause of action was originally available only in circumstances where goods had been lost by the claimant and found by the defendant.[1] Latterly, the courts were prepared to allow an action in trover on the basis of a legal fiction that the goods had been found by the defendant. In due course s 49 Common Law Procedure Act 1952 abolished the need for that fiction.

A mark of conversion's history as 'trover' is that for some time the cause of action of conversion was available only in circumstances where the defendant

[1] ie from the French 'trouver' – to find.

came into possession of the chattel other than by taking it from the plaintiff's possession. By contrast, the action of trespass protected a person from having chattels removed from his possession. By the early twentieth century, however, it had been established that a conversion could be committed by taking a chattel from the possession of its owner. It was necessary, however, (and remains necessary) for the taker to intend to exercise a degree of dominion over the chattel, otherwise conversion is not available (although trespass remains a possibility). In *Sanderson v Marsden* (1922) 10 Ll L Rep 467 at 472 Atkin LJ put the position as follows:

> An act of conversion differs from mere trespass inasmuch as the former must amount to a deprivation of possession to such an extent as to be inconsistent with the right of the owner and evidence of an intention to deprive him of that right, whereas the latter includes every direct forcible injury or act disturbing the possession of the owner, however slight the act may be.

The nature of the acts that are capable of amounting to conversion are discussed in more detail below.

Detinue

Detinue was a cause of action that arose where a person wrongly retained possession of a chattel after a demand had been made for its return by a person with a better title. Clearly, then, there is a great deal of potential cross-over between conversion and detinue. Consequently actions tended to be issued in both conversion and detinue and, as discussed further below, detinue as a distinct concept was effectively absorbed into conversion by the Torts (Interference with Goods) Act 1977. There were two principal differences between detinue and conversion, however.

First, a cause of action in detinue was available in circumstances where the defendant did not necessarily deny the claimant's title. This is illustrated by *Clayton v Le Roy* [1911] 2 KB 1031. In that case the plaintiff (or rather his wife) had bought a watch from the defendant jeweller. The watch was subsequently stolen and the plaintiff put the defendant on notice of the theft. Thereafter, the thief of the watch pawned it but did not redeem it from pawn. The unredeemed watch was ultimately put in a consignment of unredeemed items that was sold at auction. The new owner of the watch wrote to the defendant asking its opinion on whether the watch was genuine. The defendant, identifying it as the watch that had been stolen, wrote to both the plaintiff and the new owner explaining the situation and asking them both to express their view on how the defendant should deal with the watch in the circumstances. Those letters did not assert the defendant's own title as against either the plaintiff or the new owner. The plaintiff did not respond to the letter, but some days later a legal representative of his attended the defendant's shop and demanded the watch be handed over.

The defendant refused and the plaintiff's representative there and then served a writ in detinue on the defendant.

The court found that the defendant was not liable in detinue. The reason was that the person who had attended to demand the watch was not the plaintiff himself and had no written or other apparent authority on behalf of the plaintiff. Therefore it would have been remiss of the defendant to have released the watch. The following principles emerge from *Clayton*:

1. A demand by the owner of the chattels that is refused was a prerequisite to an action in detinue.
2. So long as a valid demand is made, it was no bar to an action in detinue that the person in possession of the chattel did not itself assert title to the chattel.

The second principal difference between detinue and conversion was that detinue was an action for recovery of the chattel *in specie* (ie recovery of the chattel itself) as opposed merely to damages. Even in detinue, however, there was no absolute right to recover the chattel[2] and the matter was in the court's discretion; damages could be awarded in the alternative. This is consistent with the traditional distinction between property amenable to actions *in rem* (ie 'real property') and personal property to which there was no such right. A claimant in detinue could also seek damages to compensate him for the period of the chattel's detention.

As is the case with the tort of conversion, it was not necessary for a successful claimant in detinue to own the chattel in question. Nevertheless, self-evidently in the case of detinue, possessory title alone cannot be enough (because a plaintiff was out of possession), and so some degree of proprietary interest was required.

This point was illustrated by the Court of Appeal in *Jarvis v Williams* [1955] 1 WLR 71. In that case, Jarvis sold certain bathroom fittings to a person called Paterson. It appears to have been common ground in the case that Paterson did not pay for the fittings, but that nevertheless title to them passed to Paterson. Rather than taking delivery of the fittings himself, Paterson asked Jarvis to send the fittings to the house of one Williams, which Jarvis did. It appears that Paterson was in some way dissatisfied with the fittings because they remained at Jarvis's house for some time and were never paid for. In the event Jarvis offered to take the goods back if Paterson would pay for collection. Paterson agreed to that proposal by letter dated 14 September 1951. Jarvis then sent his lorry driver to Williams's house with the letter but Williams refused to hand over the fittings. Jarvis claimed against Williams in detinue. The Court of Appeal determined that the claim should fail. This was on the basis that the 14 September 1951 letter had not operated to transfer ownership of the fittings to Jarvis until their

[2] See, for example, *General and Finance Facilities Ltd v Cooks Cars (Romford) Ltd* [1963] 1 WLR 644 at 648.

collection. Therefore, when Jarvis demanded the fittings from Williams, Jarvis was not their owner, and notwithstanding Paterson's agreement that he could take possession of them, Jarvis did not have sufficient entitlement to them to found a claim in detinue. Evershed MR said as follows at 75:

> Although it is, no doubt, true in a sense, and certainly in its original medieval conception, that when speaking of property in chattels there is in mind the right to their immediate possession, nevertheless the sense of property in chattels is now well understood ... Even though, by contract between himself and Paterson, the plaintiff may have had a right which, if infringed, could form the subject-matter of an action for breach of contract, and though he had a right to go and possess himself of these goods, nevertheless, until he has done so, there was in him according to my construction of the arrangement, no proprietary interest in the goods, in the sense in which that term is now, as I think, commonly understood. It seems to me therefore, that he had not, on the authorities which I have mentioned, the necessary foundation on which to sustain an action for detinue against the defendant.

Trespass

Trespass to goods is a cause of action that is available in certain circumstances where the defendant has perpetrated some non-consensual act of physical interference with a chattel belonging to the claimant.

As indicated above, one of the historical features of trespass to goods is that it was able to make good on circumscriptions in the actions of detinue and conversion. For example, in the case of trespass to goods there was never any need to establish that the goods were interfered with when not in the owner's possession. Nor was there any need to show that the owner's true title has been in some way denied or interfered with.

Consistent with those matters, there was historically no *de minimis* level of interference that is incapable of amounting to trespass to goods. The consequences can at times be almost comical. In *Kirk v Gregory* (1876) 1 Ex D 55 a family member of a deceased person took some jewellery from the deceased's drawer and placed it with a watch in a cupboard (where some of it was somehow lost). It was found as a matter of fact that she had done this to keep it safe. Nevertheless it amounted to trespass because it was not reasonably necessary for the property's protection (had it been reasonably necessary for the jewellery's protection, this would have been a legal justification for trespass).

The authors of *Clerk and Lindsell on Tort* assert, at paragraph 17-131 of the 22nd edition, that in the modern era a *de minimis* touching of property belonging to another is unlikely to amount to a trespass to goods. Although there seems persuasive force of common sense behind that analysis, its support from authority is tenuous. The Court of Appeal gave some consideration to that analysis in a family law context in *White v Withers LLP* [2009] EWCA Civ 1122. Ward LJ considered the reasoning of the authors of *Clerk and Lindsell*, and the authorities cited therein, but gave the following indecisive conclusion at 61:

> What conclusions am I to draw from that? It seems to me to still be moot whether or not a slight interference will amount to either trespass or conversion. Common sense suggests that minor infractions especially in this fraught field of divorce should not lead to claims in tort being brought where the action would not be censured by the Family Division judge if it were considered to be, adapting the approach of Robert Goff L.J. in Collins v Wilcock, 'acceptable in the ordinary conduct of everyday life [in the Divorce Courts].' Minor misconduct may be best regulated by the Family Division and should not become the source of satellite litigation in the Queen's Bench Division. The final determination of the question of liability in tort for a minor trespass or conversion must depend upon the facts and circumstances of the particular case and it is, I am rather relieved to say, not a matter which it is appropriate for us to decide on an application to strike out a claim. It must await a decision at a trial when the facts are clear.

However the procedural risks of bringing such a claim were emphasised by Ward LJ at paragraph 62: 'If such a trivial claim is brought, it is difficult to see anything more than nominal damages being suffered and I would encourage and expect such a claim to be struck out for being an abuse of the process'.

Kirk shows that the level of interference required to make out trespass was extremely low. For some time it was unclear whether some element of physical damage or loss was required in order for the tort of trespass to goods to be made out. The question seems only to have been resolved in *Transco plc v United Utilities Water plc* [2005] EWHC 2784 (QB). In that case the High Court considered circumstances in which workmen working underground had mistakenly turned off a stopcock belonging to the claimant. Even though there was no physical damage to the stopcock the court considered that the claimant could make out its claim in trespass to goods.

Replevin

Replevin is said to be[3] one of the oldest actions known to the common law. To modern eyes it looks something more like an interlocutory remedy. The right to 'replevy' goods was the right to regain immediate possession of goods taken by the defendant pending a substantive action. Replevin was both an interim remedy and also a more substantive action.

As an interim remedy, the person seeking replevin (the 'replivisor') brought what appears in effect to have been an interim application to the court. By that application the replivisor would seek the immediate return to him of goods taken by the respondent to the application. The court would require the replivisor to put up security and undertake to issue a substantive claim in replevin. If the replivisor could meet the conditions imposed by the court, the chattels would be returned to the replivisor.[4]

[3] *Crossley Vaines on Personal Property*, 5th edition, 500.

[4] See, for example, *Gibbs v Cruikshank and Others* (1872–73) LR 8 CP 454.

The substantive action in replevin would have to show that the chattels had been taken wrongly by the defendant. As discussed above, historically an action in conversion and detinue would only lie where the defendant had taken possession of the chattels in question other than by taking them from the plaintiff. Therefore, in practice, for most of the history of replevin, a successful substantive action in replevin meant a successful claim in trespass.

After it became clear in the twentieth century (as discussed above) that a claim for conversion was available in circumstances where a chattel was taken with the intention to exercise dominion, there seems no logical reason why replevin might not also have been available in respect of such a claim in conversion (or detinue). That, indeed, appears to be the position of the authors of *Crossley Vaines on Personal Property*.[5] On the other hand, both the authors of *Clerk and Lindsell on Torts*[6] and *Palmer and McKendrick on Interests in Goods*[7] appear to consider that replevin was only available where chattels had been taken by way of trespass. This question will now never be resolved.

It should also be noted that in practice replevin was almost always seen in the context of wrongful distress by a landlord or mortgagee. Distress was likely to be 'wrongful' where, for example, a landlord or mortgagee was mistaken in believing that arrears had accrued. Replevin was not confined to those situations, however. For example, in the Privy Council case of *Canadian Pacific Wine Company v Tuley and others* [1921] 2 AC 417, the replivisor sought the return of whisky, papers and money that had been seized by the police in British Columbia on the suspicion that they were being held for intended sale in the jurisdiction, in breach of prohibition law in being at the time.

As discussed further below, replevin, which in any event seems to have been in very little practical use for some time, has effectively been superseded by statute.

Other Rights

Various other rather more minor rights have historically been available to individuals whose chattels have been infringed in some way. These include the following:

1. *Pound Breach*

This is a cause of action that was available against a thief where goods were distrained and impounded, but then stolen from the impound.[8] To make out pound breach it was necessary to show that the perpetrator knew that he was

[5] 5th edition, 500–01.
[6] 22nd edition, 17-153.
[7] 2nd edition, 860.
[8] See for example *Abingdon RDC v O'Gorman* [1968] 2 QB 811.

taking the goods from impound.[9] Section 3 Distress for Rent Act 1689 provided that a person liable for pound breach was liable for treble damages (ie treble the value of the goods seized). This was to reflect the fact that, once impounded, the goods were technically in the custody of the law and as a matter of important public policy should not be taken from impound.

In 1998 the authors of the second edition of *Palmer and McKendrick on Interests in Goods* felt comfortable describing pound breach as 'of little practical importance'. Pound breach enjoyed a rather surprising curtain call in 2015, however, in *Eyland and Sons Ltd v TSL Turton* [2015] EWHC 3942 (QB). Singh J (as he then was) was called upon to consider a claim relying on pound breach and s 3 Distress for Rent Act 1689. Although that section had been expressly repealed by the time of the decision, it had been repealed as recently as 6 April 2014.[10] Although the defendants maintained that s 3 Distress for Rent Act 1689 was essentially unavailable for obsolescence, Singh J disagreed, albeit his conclusion was that it did not arise on the facts. At paragraph 61 of his judgment he stated as follows:

> The concept of pound breach, as its language would suggest in our period, reflects an earlier period in our legal history when there was not necessarily the strict demarcation line between a tort and a criminal offence, which modern law would readily recognise. Be that as it may, it is clear that there was until recently, still in force …
>
> As I have mentioned and as is apparent from the language used in that provision, pound breach was an offence at common law. The effect of the provision was to entitle the claimant to recover an amount of damages, which was three times the value of the goods.

And at paragraphs 64–66:

> … The claimants submits in the present case that the transitional provision, s.66, clearly applies on the facts, because the power of distrain in this case were exercised on 2 December 2013 and because the alleged pound breach took place in the early part of 2014, before the 2007 Act's material provisions were brought into force by Article 2 of the Tribunals, Courts and Enforcement Act 2007 (Amendment No. 11) Order (SI 2014 No. 768).
>
> 65 The defendants submit that when read as a whole and in particular, having regard to the cumulative effect of s.66, which are not disjunctive but rather constructive ('and'). That the anomalous, at least to modern eyes, remedy of treble damages in s.3 of the 1689 Act no longer should be regarded as subsisting. It is submitted that Parliament paid careful attention to replace the old rules with a modern regime in the commercial property sector.
>
> 66 I do not accept the submissions on behalf of the defendants in this context. Rather, I accept the submission on behalf of the claimants, if the issue of law arose on the events, which, in my judgment, it does not. The intention of the relevant legislation is to preserve the position as it was in cases such as this.

[9] ibid.

[10] By the implementation of the relevant provisions of the Tribunals Courts and Enforcement Act 2007.

The repeal of s 3 Distress for Rent Act 1689 will not technically have extinguished pound breach as a cause of action; it presumably continues to exist at common law. Without the benefit of treble damages, however, pound breach appears to have been deprived of any particular benefit. A claim in conversion and/or trespass to goods will presumably do just as well in any future circumstances when pound breach might have been available. Therefore, notwithstanding its unexpected appearance in *Eyland*, it does seem highly likely that pound breach will now slide into history.

2. *Rescous*

Rescous (ie 'rescue') is comparable to, but even more obscure than, pound breach. As appears from *O'Gorman* (at 819) it is identical to pound breach but is available where a person takes distrained goods before they have been impounded (ie as distinct from pound breach, which applies only where the goods have actually been impounded). Rescous enjoyed the same trebling of damages available to claims in pound breach under s 3 Distress for Rent Act 1689, which was also repealed on 6 April 2014. There appears to have been no attempt to rely on rescous in the last century, and now that treble damages has been disposed of, it is most unlikely ever to be deployed again.

3. *Wrongful Distress*

This is a cause of action that, somewhat self-evidently, arises where a person wrongly exercised the remedy of distress against the claimant. In most such cases, however, the appropriate action will be a claim in trespass to goods. Wrongful distress is available, however, where an act of distress is lawful initially, but becomes unlawful by virtue of some act on behalf of the distrainor. A relatively recent example, albeit an unsuccessful attempt to assert wrongful distress, can be seen in *Wilson v South Kesteven District Council* [2001] 1 WLR 387. The facts concerned a local authority whose act of distress had arguably become unlawful when the bailiffs had wrongly rejected a tender in attempted settlement of the debt. Section 4 Distress for Rent Act 1689 created a right to double damages and costs in actions for wrongful distress (as opposed to triple damages for pound breach and rescous). Again, that provision was repealed on 6 April 2014 by the Tribunals, Courts and Enforcement Act 2007.

4. *Distress Damage Feasant*

This ancient remedy is not strictly a cause of action vindicating a right to a chattel, but rather a cause of action conferring a right over a chattel. The right was described in simple terms by Bingham MR in *Arthur v Anker* [1996] 2 WLR 602 at 571 as follows:

> The first ground relied on was the old, medieval, self-help remedy, adapted to modern conditions, of distress damage feasant. Put in simple English, if a landowner found

> property of another causing damage on his land he could seize the offending property and withhold it from its owner until adequate compensation had been tendered for the damage done. Although the remedy developed primarily as a means of protection against straying livestock, it was not limited to that.

Indeed, the right in the specific instance of animals has been put on a statutory footing by s 7 Animals Act 1971. Distress damage feasant remains available in respect of other chattels. It should be noted, however, that in *Arthur* the court concluded that it was not available to permit clamping of vehicles on private land. This was at least partly on the basis that it would be perverse to permit a self-help remedy against an unwanted chattel present on land if the self-help remedy would actually worsen the situation (ie by making it harder not easier to remove the chattel).

5. *Certain Other Summary Remedies*

At various times throughout history the law has allowed certain specific actions to be brought to deal with specific chattels. For example, various items were exempted from being made the subject of distress (such as clothing worth less than a specified sum), and if distress was executed on those items the Magistrates' Court had the power to order them to be returned to their owner (see, for example, s 4 Law of Distress Amendment Act 1888).

6. *Damage to Reversionary Interest*

This is a cause of action available to a person who does not have either possession of a chattel or else immediate right to possession, but who does have a reversionary interest. Examples include a bailor for a fixed term that has not expired, or a lienor who has not yet paid the sum secured by the lien. Where goods are damaged or destroyed, or disposed of in such a way that the reversionary interest holder cannot recover them, this tort is available. Compensation is by way of damages to compensate the claimant for the damage to or loss of the reversionary interest, not the chattel itself.[11]

STATUTORY DEVELOPMENTS SINCE THE 1970s

Torts (Interference with Goods) Act 1977

It appears that in the latter half of the twentieth century the view began to be taken that the English law on the protection of rights in personalty was in an unsatisfactory state. As the discussion above demonstrates, there were a

[11] *Tancred v Allgood* (1859) 158 ER 910.

considerable number of torts that could be brought to bear on any interference with a chattel, various of which overlapped considerably. It is easy to imagine a fact pattern in which at least three separate torts are committed as a result of one act.

It was presumably this concern that led to the Law Reform Committee's 18th Report on Detinue and Conversion in 1971. The Committee proposed that a new statute should dramatically simplify the law of tort as it related to the protection of interests in goods. The suggestion was that the torts of conversion, detinue, and trespass to goods should be simplified into one new tort called 'wrongful interference with goods'. The proposed new tort would broadly speaking have had the characteristics of conversion.

The product of the Committee's recommendations was the Torts (Interference with Goods) Act 1977 ('TIGA'). In the event the government did not implement the Committee's recommendations in full.

Perhaps confusingly, TIGA introduced, at s 1, a concept of 'wrongful interference with goods'. Contrary to the Committee's recommendations, however, 'wrongful interference with goods' is not a new tort, or a new name for an existing tort. Instead it is a term defined to include conversion, trespass to goods, negligence insofar as it results in damage to goods, and 'any other tort so far as it results in damage to goods or to an interest in goods'. The grouping of those various torts under the umbrella of 'wrongful interference with goods' is intended as a means of conveniently applying various procedural and other provisions of TIGA to all of those torts; it does not alter the substance of the torts themselves. It is therefore wrong to speak of a tort of wrongful interference with goods, which is occasionally done in practice.

Elsewhere, at s 2 TIGA the tort of detinue is abolished. Consistent with that, s 2(2) extends the scope of the tort of conversion to include situations in which a bailee breaches his duty to his bailor by allowing goods to be lost or damaged. In other words, the tort of conversion is expanded to cover the one area in which detinue still had a unique role. Detinue could therefore be safely abolished because it had no features that did not overlap with another tort. This has introduced a measure of simplification of the tortious regime, albeit perhaps not as much as the Committee had intended.

The other significant change brought about by TIGA is at s 3. That section provides that, in the case of any action for 'wrongful interference' in which the defendant is in possession of the goods at issue, the claimant can seek an order for delivery up of the goods themselves. This provision gives the torts of trespass and conversion the historical characteristic of detinue: there is a quasi-right to a proprietary remedy, namely the return of the chattels in dispute. That is described as a 'quasi-right' only because s 3(3)(b) TIGA provides that it is ultimately in the discretion of the court whether to award delivery up of the goods, or whether to award damages instead. As discussed above, the court's discretion as to whether to order damages instead of delivery up always existed in respect of detinue, and so this simply replicates that position.

Tribunals, Courts and Enforcement Act 2007

The Tribunals, Courts and Enforcement Act 2007 ('TCEA') represented a much-needed overhaul of the English law on court procedure and constitution, as well as the enforcement of judgments and awards. As follows from that, it is a wide-ranging statute dealing with many matters beyond the scope of this work. Nevertheless it does have considerable impact on the tortious rights available to a litigant to protect interests in chattels, and those should be observed here.

It has already been noted that the TCEA has repealed s 3 Distress for Rent Act 1689. This has had the effect of depriving pound breach and rescous of any real use as torts distinct from conversion and trespass to goods. It has also repealed s 4 Distress for Rent Act 1689. This means it is no longer possible to obtain double damages in an action for wrongful distress, although (again as discussed above) the tort still remains of some use as the only cause of action available where distress has begun lawfully but become unlawful by the way in which it is carried out.

The other significant development in the TCEA is the implementation of a new regime governing taking control of goods as a means of enforcement (at Part 3 and Schedule 12 TCEA). Section 71 TCEA expressly removes the right to distrain goods for arrears of rent. This in effect removes much of the usefulness of replevin, which, as noted above, tended to arise in practice in the context of distress for rent arrears.

Section 65 TCEA expressly provides that various common law rules, including the rules of replevin, are replaced by the provisions of Schedule 12 TCEA insofar as Schedule 12 overlaps with those rules. Therefore, even the residual instances of replevin falling outside the context of distress for rent arrears have generally been superseded by the TCEA, at least so far as they relate to enforcement actions against goods.

It is presumably possible that replevin still exists outside the context of distress and enforcement against goods – ie in other circumstances where goods have been taken in trespass. The use of replevin in such circumstances has always been rare, however, and may now have petered out to extinction, especially in view of the extensive repertoire of interim remedies provided for at rule 25 of the Civil Procedure Rules ('CPR').

It remains to say that Schedule 12 TCEA and the Taking Control of Goods Regulations 2013/1984 provide a comprehensive statutory framework for enforcement against goods. In place of the old self-help remedy of distress is a carefully structured regime, fully policed by the court, which is much more palatable by modern standards, and much more readily reconcilable with the Human Rights Act 1998.

THE MAJOR MODERN RIGHTS AVAILABLE TO PROTECT INTERESTS IN GOODS

Bailment

One form of quasi-bailment is discussed above, namely the 'fictitious' bailment that comes into being when a finder finds a chattel. It is described as 'fictitious' as a convenient designation of the fact that it is imposed by law to achieve a particular outcome, ie the protection of a finder from a claim in conversion by the owner, but also the imposition on the finder of certain duties and obligations for the benefit of the owner (for example the obligation to take reasonable steps to find and identify the owner).

This section is intended to discuss bailment in its more general and 'non-fictitious' sense and all uses of the term 'bailment' below, unless stated otherwise, are intended to refer to that non-fictitious bailment.

Of course, bailment is a highly detailed subject on which whole works have been written[12] and so what follows can be no more than a general survey.

Prerequisites of Bailment

Broadly speaking, bailment is a relationship in which one person (the 'bailor') passes possession of a chattel to another person (the 'bailee') but without intending to extinguish his own rights as owner.

The exact status of bailment, whether as a source of obligations in its own right, or as a description of a type of relationship giving rise to other causes of action, has historically been uncertain. Certainly, relationships of bailment have been recognised as having legal consequences for many centuries (the concept dates back to Roman law), but the court's view of their fundamentals has not always been consistent. To make matters more complicated, 'bailments' can be of different types arising in different circumstances, each carrying with it its own duties and obligations.

One constant in all relationships of bailment is that physical possession of a chattel must pass from a bailor to a bailee. If physical possession does not pass, there can be no relationship of bailment. This was illustrated in *Ashby v Tolhurst* [1937] 2 KB 242 (CA). In that case the defendant operated a private

[12] Perhaps most significantly *Palmer on Bailment*, which is in its 3rd edition and to which I am indebted in this section.

car park. The plaintiff left his car in the car park and was given a ticket which included a disclaimer of all liability on the part of the car park. Subsequently, while the claimant was away, a thief arrived and was permitted to drive away the plaintiff's car, even though he had neither the ticket nor a key. The plaintiff brought a claim relying, among other things, on an alleged breach of the car park's obligations as bailee. The court found that the car park was not liable because on the facts of the case it had not taken possession of the car. Rather it was a licensor, which had permitted the plaintiff to leave his chattel on its land. As discussed above, the question of possession is one of fact (applied to the relevant test[13]), and in any given case the court will have to decide if the circumstances exist to conclude that possession has been passed to a bailee. It may be in *Ashby* that, had the plaintiff's keys been left with the car park attendant, there would have been sufficient to find a relationship of bailment.

Other prerequisites of bailment have varied over time and depending on the precise nature of the bailment. The present position is as set out by the Privy Council in *The Pioneer Container* [1994] 3 WLR 1 (albeit in a decision that focuses on relationships of sub-bailment). Apart from possession being passed to the bailee, the other essentials of bailment are as follows:

1. The bailee must voluntarily take possession of the chattels bailed.[14] This may in reality be nothing more than a consequence of the core principle that a person must take possession of a chattel for a relationship of bailment to be possible. Since intention to exercise control is a fundamental of possession,[15] a person cannot be fixed with liability when he does not intend to exercise such control. As discussed above, however, although it was once thought to the contrary, it is not necessary for a bailor to consent to the relationship of bailment for it to come into being.[16]
2. The bailee must be aware of the bailor. By that, it is not meant that the bailee must be able to identify the bailor, but he must know that the property belongs to another. This principle, though presumably entirely relevant to ordinary bailment relationships, in practice almost always arises in the contexts of sub-bailments (as in *The Pioneer Container*). For example, in *Morris v CW Martin and Sons Ltd* [1965] 3 WLR a customer gave a fur to a furrier called Beder for cleaning. The furrier then entrusted that fur to a specialist cleaner, which did not offer its services to the public. The cleaner knew that the fur did not belong to Beder, but rather to one of Beder's clients, although it did not know who that client was. Diplock LJ reasoned as follows at 731:

> Duties at common law are owed by one person to another only if there exists a relationship between them which the common law recognises as giving rise to such duty.

[13] *L.A. Pye (Oxford) Ltd v Graham* [2002] 3 WLR 221 at 233.
[14] See, for example, *The Pioneer Container* at 341–42.
[15] *L.A. Pye*, supra.
[16] *The Pioneer Container* at 341–42.

> One of such recognised relationships is created by the voluntary taking into custody of goods which are the property of another. By voluntarily accepting from Beder the custody of a fur which they knew to be the property of a customer of his, they brought into existence between the plaintiff and themselves the relationship of bailor and bailee by sub-bailment.

The case of *Morris* also helps to illustrate one important feature that does *not* need to exist for a relationship of bailment to come into being, and that is a contract. This was not always the case. For example, in *R v Ashwell* (1885) 16 QBD 190 at 223 Lord Coleridge stated:

> [M]my opinion was, and is, that bailment is not a mere delivery on a contract but is a contract in itself … 'The contract of bailment' is not a mere loose and common phrase, but is an accurate expression of a legal idea.

By the time of *Morris*, however, the court was able to find with clarity that a contract was not necessary for a bailment to come into being, per Lord Diplock at 371:

> The legal relationship of bailor and bailee of a chattel can exist independently of any contract, for the legal concept of bailment as creating a relationship which gives rise to duties owed by a bailee to a bailor is derived from Roman law and is older in our common law than the legal concept of parol contract as giving rise to legal duties owed by one party to the other party thereto. The nature of those legal duties, in particular as to the degree of care which the bailee is bound to exercise in the custody of the goods and as to his duty to redeliver them, varies according to the circumstances in which and purposes for which the goods are delivered to the bailee.

Finally on the subject of the prerequisites of a bailment, it should be noted that a bailment can be a bailment at will, in which case it can be terminable at the instance of the bailor, or it can be a bailment for some kind of fixed term or term referable to an event (such as, in the case of a lien, the owner paying the lienee's fees).

Types of Bailment

The starting point in any attempt to prescribe the different categories of bailment is the leading authority of *Coggs v Barnard* (1703) 92 ER 622, which requires some attention. The facts of the case were that the defendant had agreed to transport a hogshead of wine from one cellar to another. Due to the defendant's remiss conduct, however, the hogshead was damaged and the wine was lost. The plaintiff's case had not alleged that the defendant had agreed to carry the wine in exchange for any sum of money; for procedural reasons this was therefore assumed to be true. The defendant accordingly contended that an action in assumpsit (ie, in essence, breach of contract) was not available and nor could the defendant be treated as a 'common carrier', which apparently would have founded a separate cause of action. The defendant's case was consequently that there was no cause of action available against it.

Lord Holt disagreed, holding that there was a 'special undertaking', ie a bailment, and that 'although the defendant might have refused to carry the wine, yet as he made a voluntary undertaking to carry it safely, if he does not do it he shall be punished for the damage which the plaintiff suffers by his neglect'.

The principle significance of Lord Holt's judgment is that it sets out six categories of bailment. Shorn of the anachronistic phrasing of the judgment, they can be formulated as follows:

1. Where a bailor entrusts chattels to a bailee for the bailor's own purposes (for example a coat left in a cloakroom).
2. Where a bailor gratuitously entrusts chattels to a bailee for a bailee's purposes (ie the loan of something useful or profitable for the bailee).
3. Where chattels are hired by the bailee (ie money is paid to the bailor for their use).
4. Where a bailor passes possession of chattels by way of security (for example a pledge in security of a loan or a pawn).
5. Where a bailor entrusts chattels to a bailee to enable the bailee to perform some service on them for which the bailor pays (for example the repair of a car). In those circumstances a contractual relationship comes into being between the bailor and the bailee (and a relationship of lienor and lienee may also arise in the right circumstances).
6. Where a bailor entrusts a chattel to a bailee so that the bailee can perform some gratuitous service.

Lord Holt's judgment goes on to formulate specific duties of care applicable to the various different types of bailment. This is the origin of the notion that the type of bailment is determinative of the extent of the duties of a bailee.

To modern eyes, the nature of the bailee's duties as formulated by Lord Holt is unfamiliar – he speaks of concepts such as 'strict care', 'utmost care' and 'common or public trust'. This is because Lord Holt was speaking of a *sui generis* area of law particular to bailment and was speaking at a time when the modern law of contract and tort did not exist. For some time, Lord Holt's approach to bailment held good (with his key concepts recast as 'strict liability', 'slight liability', 'gross negligence' and 'ordinary negligence').

In due course, however, Lord Holt's approach began to suffer from changing circumstances. In particular, the development and dominance of the law of tort and the law of breach of contract drove the courts to try to understand bailment obligations as belonging to one or other of those systems of law, rather than of comprising a unique area of law in their own right. Moreover, the imposition of defined duties onto Lord Holt's categorisation of the six potential relationships of bailment began to seem unduly restrictive. Thus Ormerod LJ was able to state as follows of the modern law in *Houghland v RR Low (Luxury Coaches) Ltd* [1962] 1 QB 694 CA at 697–98:

> I am bound to say that I am not sure what is meant by the term 'gross negligence' which has been in use for a long time in cases of this kind. There is no doubt, of course, that it is a phrase which has been commonly used in cases of this sort since the time of *Coggs v. Bernard*, when the distinction was made in a judgment of Lord Holt C.J. which has been frequently referred to and cited; but as we know from the judgment of Lord Chelmsford in *Giblin v. McMullen*, that it was said, after referring to the use of the term 'gross negligence' over a long period: 'At last, Lord Cranworth (then Baron Rolfe) in the case of *Wilson v. Brett*, objected to it, saying that he 'could see no difference between negligence and gross negligence; that it was the same thing, with the addition of a vituperative epithet.' and this critical observation has been since approved of by other eminent judges.'
>
> For my part, I have always found some difficulty in understanding just what was 'gross negligence,' because it appears to me that the standard of care required in a case of bailment, or any other type of case, is the standard demanded by the circumstances of that particular case. It seems to me that to try and put a bailment, for instance, into a watertight compartment – such as gratuitous bailment on the one hand, and bailment for reward on the other – is to overlook the fact that there might well be an infinite variety of cases, which might come into one or the other category.

Thus the general position is that the scope of a bailee's duty is analogous to the duty owed in tort – ie to take such care as is reasonable in the circumstances. There are, however, a few surviving aspects to the *sui generis* approach to bailment adopted by Lord Holt. The most important are dealt with briefly below.

1. A bailee's duty of care extends beyond merely avoiding damaging goods; he must also take care to protect the goods from third parties who might damage or steal them. This is not an obligation that is generally imposed at tort, although, as was noted by the House of Lords in *Smith v Littlewoods Organisation Ltd* [1987] AC 241 HL at 271, it might arise in some circumstances. The example given was of a person who entered a house as a licensee and left the door open on his departure.
2. There is at least some support for the proposition that a gratuitous bailee, where the bailment is for the benefit of the bailor, owes a lower standard of care than that for the test in negligence. In *Bullen v Swan Engraving* (1904) 23 TLR 258 CA the Court of Appeal found that such a bailee owed only an obligation to take such steps as a prudent man would take to protect his own goods. There is a school of thought that suggests that *Houghland* has superseded this lower duty of care. Nevertheless, in *The Winson* [1982] AC 939 HL at 960 Lord Diplock seemed quite content with the approach taken in *Bullen*, saying that a lower standard of care required of a gratuitous bailee was 'too well-known and too well-established to call for any citation

of authority'. More recently still, however, the Court of Appeal followed *Houghland* in *Sutcliffe v Chief Constable of West Yorkshire* [1996] RTR 86. The Court of Appeal did not, however, have *The Winson* drawn to its attention. The position is therefore somewhat unclear.

3. When an action is brought against a bailee, the ordinary burden of proof is reversed, in that if the bailor can show that there has been loss or damage to goods it is for the bailee to prove that he did not breach his obligations.[17] The *sui generis* nature of the law of bailment was cited as an explanation for this exceptional rule in the Australian case *Hobbs v Petersham Transport Co Pty Ltd* (1971) 124 CLR 220 at 241.
4. There is some authority that a bailee can expand the scope of the duty of care imposed on him, not merely by accepting an expanded duty in exchange for consideration (which is of course explicable as a matter of contract) but simply by gratuitously agreeing to perform a certain function. This is after all the reasoning underpinning the reasoning in *Coggs*. There seems to be some tentative support for this proposition in *The Pioneer Container* in that, at page 342, Lord Goff contemplated that the terms of a sub-bailee's liability to a bailor could be qualified or otherwise affected by the substance of the sub-bailee's promise to the bailee.

TRESPASS TO GOODS AND CONVERSION

The principal torts that are available under the modern law to protect interests in goods are trespass to goods and conversion. These torts have been addressed above in their historical context and to the extent that they interplay with other historical torts. The purpose of this section is to give a brief overview of the torts which is more focused on their modern context. Again, the usual specialist tort works will provide a more formal detailed analysis than this necessarily brief survey.

Trespass to Goods

The Elements of the Tort

Trespass to goods is available in circumstances where there has been direct and immediate interference with a person's chattels. The requirement for 'direct and immediate' interference means in practice that the contact must be physical. Thus in *Hartley v Moxham* (1842) 114 ER 675 the court found that locking a

[17] See, for example, *British Road Services Ltd v Arthur V Crutchley & Co Ltd* [1968] 1 All ER 811 CA.

person's chattels in a room did not amount to trespass because they had not physically been interfered with.

As discussed above, there is no level of physical contact that is insufficient to found a trespass and nor does there need to be any physical damage. Having said that, the Court of Appeal has understandably indicated that, absent any real damages, a claim in trespass was likely to be amenable to being struck out as an abuse of process.[18]

As well as interference being direct, it appears that there needs to be a degree of culpability on the part of the trespasser for trespass to be made out. The degree of culpability required, however, is not high. It does not matter if the defendant is unaware that the step he is taking is wrong; it is sufficient to found a trespass if the defendant did the act intentionally, or if he did not do the act intentionally but caused injury negligently. Two authorities will assist in illustrating that principle:

1. In *Wilson v Lombank* [1963] 1 WLR 1294 the plaintiff bought a car from a person who (unknown to him) did not have good title to sell it. He then took the car to a garage to carry out some works. After the works were completed, a representative of the defendant took the car from the garage, honestly believing it belonged to the defendant. When it discovered the mistake, the defendant returned the car, not to the garage or the plaintiff but to the true owner. The court found that the plaintiff was in possession of the car and accordingly the defendant was liable in trespass. It made no difference that the defendant had returned the car to its true owner; the plaintiff's possessory title had been interfered with by a deliberate action on the part of the defendant.
2. In *National Coal Board v JE Evans & Co (Cardiff) Ltd* [1951] 2 KB 861 the defendant workmen damaged a cable that had been placed in the ground by the plaintiff or its predecessor as occupier of the land. The person who had laid the cable had not notified the landowner of its presence and so the defendants were entirely unaware. The court found that there was no negligence in the fact that the defendant had damaged the cable, and nor was the act deliberate. It followed that there was no liability in trespass.

As hinted at in the discussion of *Wilson* above, one of the prerequisites of trespass is that the chattel is in the possession of the claimant at the time of the alleged trespass. This is to be contrasted to the position in conversion, where a right to possession, rather than possession itself, can be sufficient to found a claim.[19] As is apparent from the facts of *Wilson*, however, and also *White v Withers*, the courts are sometimes quite lenient to claimants when applying this rule.

[18] Per Ward LJ at paragraph 62 of *White*.
[19] *Ward v Macauley* (1791) 4 TR 489 at 490.

This rule is in any event subject to certain exceptions. Of particular interest to the present work is that a bailor at will has sufficient possessory interest in the bailed goods to sue in trespass.[20]

Remedies

As discussed above, trespass (along with conversion) is one of the torts grouped together under the heading 'wrongful interference with goods' in the Torts (Interference with Goods) Act 1977 ('TIGA'). While this has no effect on the essential elements of the tort, it does afford trespass to goods with the statutorily prescribed remedies for all such torts.

The traditional remedies for trespass to goods were damages or an injunction, and these remedies are still available under TIGA at s 3(2)(c).

Historically, as dealt with above, the cause of action in trespass was capable only of achieving an award of damages. Pursuant to s 3(1)–(3) TIGA, however, a claimant may either seek damages, or delivery up, or give the defendant the option of either paying damages or delivering up. Per s 3(3)(b) TIGA, however, an order for delivery up is ultimately in the discretion of the court. Section 4 TIGA provides a statutory jurisdiction permitting the court to order delivery up of chattels that are subject to a claim for one of the wrongful interference torts. That jurisdiction is subject to rules of the court – ie the procedure for interim remedies contained at CPR 25.

The impact of any improvements to a chattel carried out by a wrongful interferer is dealt with at s 6 TIGA. Section 6(1) applies, in essence, where a defendant to an action in one of the wrongful interference torts improves the chattel in the mistaken but honest belief that he had good title to do so. In such circumstances, an allowance will be made for the value of the improvement when assessing damages. No explicit provision exists governing the interplay of this rule with a claim for delivery up of a chattel (ie a situation where the claimant is not seeking damages). It is to be inferred, however, that where there has been a significant improvement in the chattel by the wrongful interferer, that may well be a situation in which the court exercises its discretion not to make an order for delivery up of the goods, but makes an appropriate award of damages instead.

Finally, s 7 TIGA is a helpful provision with the effect of avoiding the possibility of double liability of a wrongful interferer (ie liability on the one part to a person with possessory title, and on the other to an ultimate owner).

[20] *USA v Dollfus Mieg et Cie SA* [1952] AC 582, 611. For the other exceptions, which relate to executors, trustees and franchise holders for rights in wreck and similar, see *Clerk and Lindsell on Torts*, 22nd edition 17-136.

Conversion

The Elements of the Tort

It is irresistible to begin this section with a gratuitous quotation from Sir John Salmond in 1905: 'In particular the law of trover and conversion is a region still darkened with the mists of legal formalism, through which no man will find his way by the light of nature …'. As recently as 2007 Lord Nicholls said of this remark, 'his observations still have a ring of truth in this area of the law'.[21]

Although conversion is not easy to define, the classic definition of conversion was given by Atkin J in *Lancashire and Yorkshire Railway Co v MacNicoll* (1918) 88 LJKB:[22]

> '[D]ealing with goods in a manner inconsistent with the right of the true owner amounts to a conversion, provided that it is also established that there is also an intention on the part of the defendant in so doing to deny the owner's right or to assert a right which is inconsistent with the owner's right.

As follows from this definition, for dealing with a chattel to amount to conversion, there must be a denial of a claimant's right in that chattel. The leading authority in this area is *Fouldes v Willoughby* (1841) 151 ER 1153. In that case the defendant was a ferryman and the plaintiff wished to travel on the ferry with two horses. The plaintiff boarded with the horses but subsequently began to behave badly, such that the defendant declined to carry the horses over the river. The plaintiff refused to take the horses ashore and so the ferryman took the horses off the ferry himself and left them on the landing slip. The horses were subsequently taken to a hotel run by a member of the defendant's family. The plaintiff refused to disembark the ferry and was carried over the river. The next day the defendant sent for the horses and was ultimately provided with them on the condition that he pay the costs of their board at the hotel. The court found that the defendant had not converted the horses to his own use (or that of a third party) – in other words the plaintiff's rights in the chattel had not been denied.

On the other hand, even a temporary denial of an owner's right can amount to conversion. In *Lord Petre v Heneage* (1706) 88 ER 1491 the wife of an executor wore a pearl that belonged to the deceased's estate and was liable in conversion.

As to property that is capable of being the subject of conversion, s 14 TIGA offers the following definition of 'goods': 'all chattels personal other than things in action and money'. This definition is of somewhat circular nature since it makes no effort to describe what is meant by the phrase 'chattels personal'. No doubt that definition extends to corporeal things, subject to the various exceptions described above that are not capable of amounting to property (such as wild animals).

[21] *OBG v Allan* [2008] 1 AC 1.
[22] And approved by the Court of Appeal in *Oakley v Lyster* [1931] 1 KB 148 (CA).

The definition has caused some difficulty, however, in the context of intangible property. For some time it was unclear whether and to what extent intangible property could be converted. The matter was ultimately settled (notwithstanding two powerful dissenting judgments) in *OBG v Allan* [2008] 1 AC 1 (see especially Lord Hoffmann at paragraph 101). Intangible property rights were said not to be amenable to an action in conversion.

It follows from this that conversion is not available in respect of assets such as documents held on a computer's hard drive.[23] It does appear, however, that a *sui generis* tort exists to protect assets of that type.[24]

As is apparent from the definition of 'goods' in TIGA, money is a special case in conversion. TIGA makes no effort to alter the fundamental operation of the torts it deals with, save perhaps as to remedies. Thus the exclusion of 'money' from the definition of 'goods' does not have any fundamental effect. No doubt this definition is intending to replicate the position generally thought to exist at common law, but it does lack subtlety.

There is ancient but still valid common law authority for the proposition that money can be converted where it is 'out of a bag'[25] – in other words where it has been demarked physically. Therefore a thief of cash or a finder of a lost banknote can be liable in conversion.[26] That only applies, however, until the cash is taken and passed into currency by means of passing it to a third party for value.[27] There is also no conversion of funds held in a bank account. The relationship between a bank and its customer is of creditor and debtor; there is no relationship of bailment or other dealing with goods that is capable of giving rise to a conversion.[28]

The final essential feature of the tort of conversion is one that has been referred to on various occasions above: only a person who has actual possession or immediate right to possession of a chattel has the right to sue.[29] Even an owner cannot sue in possession unless he has actual possession or an immediate right to possession. For example, where title to goods has passed to a purchaser under a contract, but the purchaser is not entitled to possession until he has paid for the goods, the purchaser is not entitled to sue in conversion.[30] The possession or right to possession relied on must exist at the time of the conversion. It is not sufficient that the claimant has reason to believe he would have acquired rights to the property in the future.[31]

[23] *Thunder Air Ltd v Hilmarsson* [2008] EWHC 355 (Ch).
[24] *Armstrong DLW GmbH v Winnington Networks Ltd* [2012] EWHC 10 (Ch); [2013] Ch. 156.
[25] For example, *Kinaston v Moor* (1626) 79 ER 678.
[26] *Burn v Morris* (1834) 2 Cr. & M. 579.
[27] Per Lord Templeman in *Lipkin Gorman v Karpnale* [1991] 2 AC 558 at 559.
[28] *Foley v Hill* (1848) 2 HLC 28.
[29] *Wilbraham v Snow* (1668) 2 Wms Saund 47a.
[30] *Lord v Price* (1873) LR 9 Ex. 54.
[31] *The Future Express* [1993] 2 Lloyd's Rep 542.

Remedies

As discussed above, the remedies for conversion are the same as for trespass to goods since both have been brought within the umbrella of 'wrongful interference with goods' by TIGA. The statutory remedies are discussed above in the context of trespass, and there is nothing further to be added unique to conversion.

Index

abandonment of chattels, 119–27
abandonment of ownership, 124–7
chattel, of and abandonment of possession, 120–1 (case law)
concept of, 124–5
nineteenth and twentieth centuries in, 125–6 (case law)
possession and, 120–1
support for, 126–7
wild animals, and, 129–30
abandonment of possession of chattels, 120–3
bailment and, 130–3
custody or control of goods, 120 (case law)
finder's rights, 121–3 (case law)
ownership of chattel not abandoned, 120–1 (case law)
principles of, 121
accessio cedit principali, 27–9 (case law)
accessory chattel owner loses ownership rights, 27–8
combination of and mixture distinguished, 28
principal chattel owner, ownership transferred to, 27–8
accessory chattel, owner loses ownership rights and access to, 27–8
agreement to marry as contract (LP(MP) A 1970), 91
animals as property, 42–6
Blackstone's categorisation of, 43–4
domestic animals, 43 (case law)
wild animals *see* wild animals as property
annuities, payment of as gifts, 89–90 (case law)

bailees:
fictional, 132–3 (case law)
oral gifts to, 81 (case law)
bailment, 80–1 (case law), 146–51
abandonment of possession and, 130–3
bailer added as party to chattel, 26
categories of, 149
consent and, 131–2 (case law)
contract not necessary for existence of, 148 (case law)
duty of care under, 149–51 (case law)
essentials of, 147–8 (case law)
fictitious, 130–1 (case law)
lost chattels, of, 58 (case law)
prerequisites, 146–8 (case law)
relationships of, 146–7 (case law)
special undertaking (1703), 148–9 (case law)
types of, 148–51
bank notes:
history and development of 113–14 (case law)
bankruptcy and property rights, 12–13 (case law)
banks, money deposited in, 112 (case law)
benefits fraudulently claimed and purchase of property, 85–6 (case law)
bills of exchange, 110
conversion of, 117–18 (case law)
Blackstone, Sir William, 1–2
domestic animals, categorisation of, 43–4
fluid mixtures, on, 37
personal property, definition of, 2
specificatio, definition of, 29
wild animals as property, on, 43–4
body parts as property, 52–3 (case law)
bona vacantia, 42–61, 127–30
property, 42
Scottish Courts' view of, 128
brain as personal property, 51–5 (case law)
breach of promise, 90–2
Law Commission report on (1969), 90, 91
nineteenth-century legislation on, 90

cash, 112–14
chattels personal:
categories of, 11
chattels real, distinguished from, 10
chattels real:
chattels personal, distinguished from, 10
heirlooms as, 10
leasehold interests as, 10
cheques, conversion of, 117–18 (case law)
choses in action, 11–14
choses in possession, differences between, 13
compensation and, 11
definition, 11–12

equitable choses, differences between, 13
rights and shares as, 12
choses in possession, 14, 16
choses in action, differences between, 13
coins, development of, 113
common law defined, 3
common law liens, 97–8, 100–1
lienee's rights against chattel owners, 102–3
companies, dissolved, property of, 60
compensation:
choses in action and, 12
defect in title and, 65–6
distress damage feasant and, 142–3
property and, 32
slaves, for, 49 (case law)
conditional gifts, 78–84
chattels, of and gifts of realty, 78–9
conditions, imposition of, 82–7
conditions precedent:
conditions subsequent and, 82
gift conditions considered, 83–4 (case law)
married persons, benefit to, 84–5 (case law)
conditions subsequent, 83
conditions precedent and, 82
donee to be a Church of England member, 83 (case law)
invalid, 82–3 (case law)
consent and bailment, 131–2 (case law)
contract:
existence of and bailment, 148 (case law)
deposits refunded after payment in advance, 82
'unconditional contract', 68
conversion, 134–6, 154–6
bills of exchange, of, 117–18 (case law)
cheques, of, 117–18 (case law)
definition, 135 (case law), 154–5 (case law)
detinue and, differences between, 137
elements of tort, 154–5 (case law)
power to sue and, 155
principle of, 135 (case law)
remedies for, 156
replevin and, 140
trespass, distinguished from, 135–6
conversion of goods, 115
conversion of money, 114–17, 155
'in a bag', 115 (case law), 116–17 (case law)
'out of a bag', 115–16 (case law)
co-ownership:
chattels, of *see* ownership of chattels
granular mixture and, 41
limits of and mixtures, 39–40
personal property, of, 19–22
Crown:
intestacy and, 60
land, 4
ownership of ownerless property, right to, 128–9 (case law)
ownership of personalty reverts to, 59–61
currency:
title of, 17
virtual, money as, 111

damage:
distress damage feasant and compensation, 142–3
reversionary interest, to, 143
dead bodies or tissue, 49–53
'dead bodies as property', 50 (case law)
disposal of body, 49 (case law)
human tissue as property, 48–54
property, as, 50 (case law)
death bed gifts, 92–4 (case law)
definition, 92
donor predeceases donee, 92–3 (case law)
formality of transferring, 93–4 (case law)
testamentary gifts, differences between, 93
deeds:
gifts of chattels effected by, 70 (case law)
gifts of chattels without, 70–2 (case law)
delivery up of goods (TIGA 1977), 144–5
deposits refunded after payment in advance of contract, 82
detinue, 136–8
abolition of tort of, 144
conversion and, differences between, 137
example of, 136–7 (case law)
proprietary interest requirement for, 137–8 (case law)
distress:
damage feasant, 142–3
replevin and, 140
wrongful, 142 (case law)
Distress for Rent Act 1689, repeal of s 4 and TCEA 2007, 145
divisions, 40–1
definition of, 40
duress and gifts of chattels, 74
duty of care:
bailment, under, 149–51 (case law)
lower, 150–1 (case law)

emptio generis, 40–1
enforcement:
agreement to marry as contract, of, (LP(MP)A 1970), 91
goods, against and TCEA 2007, 145–6
engagement presents, 90–2
LP(MP)A 1970 on, 91–2
English law:
fluid mixtures, of, 37
ownership in, 14–25
specificatio's application to, 31–3 (case law)
English ships, wreck of, 55
equitable choses, 13–14
choses in action and, differences between, 13
equitable liens, 103–6
description of, 103
examples of, 103–4 (case law)
general law of, 105
legal relationships and, 104–6 (case law)
equity and imperfect gifts of chattels, 75–8 (case law)
escheat, 4
estates, 3–4
estoppels and sale of goods, 18

'fee simple' estates, 3–4
nineteenth century, in, 7, 8
'fee tail' estates, 4
finders:
abandonment of possession of chattels and, 121–3 (case law)
possessory title of, 122–3 (case law)
rights over chattels, 58–9
treasure, of, rewards for, 57
flotsam defined, 54–5 (case law)
fluid mixtures (English law):
Blackstone on, 37
case law, 37–9
granular mixtures, applied to, 36–7 (case law)
law of, 37
formality, want of and gifts of chattels, 75–8
found chattels, occupiers' rights over, 59 (case law)
fraud, failure of transfer of goods due to, 95–6 (case law)
future goods and chattels, 107–8 (case law)

gifts:
conditional *see* conditional gifts
conditions precedent and, 83–4 (case law)
death bed *see* death bed gifts
failed, 73–8
illegal purposes, used for, 85–7 (case law)
oral, 81 (case law)
payment of annuities, 89–90 (case law)
rejection of *see* rejection of gifts
title of passed to third parties, 80–1
use of, conditions governing, 87–90 (case law)
gifts of chattels, 68–73
conditional and gifts of realty, 78–9
deeds and, 70–2 (case law)
delivery of, 72–3 (case law)
duress and, 74
imperfect and equity, 75–8 (case law)
loans, considered to be, 69–70 (case law)
presumption of advancement and, 75
requirements for, 68–9 (case law)
undue influence, effect of on, 74
want of formality and, 75–8
gifts of realty and conditional gifts of chattels, 78–9
granular mixtures:
agreement, by, (English law), 34–7 (case law)
co-ownership and, 41
fluid mixtures case law applied to, 36–7

heirlooms as chattels real, 10
human organs as property, 53 (case law)
human tissue as property, 48–54

***in personam* actions,** 5–6
***in rem* actions,** 5
interest:
entire interest of chattel, disposal of, 26
jointly owned interest of chattels, disposal of, 22–3
goods, protection of in, 146–51
reversionary, damage to, 143
transfer of interest in real property, 8–9
interference:
chattels, with, 151–2 (case law)
level required for trespass, 139 (case law)
intestacy and Crown, 60

jetsam defined, 54–5 (case law)
joint bank accounts, purchase of chattels from, 21–2 (case law)
joint owner of chattels, action against third party, 26

'knight's, tenure', 3

land:
chattels are part of, 10–11
Crown, 4
demesne, 4
freehold, 5
ownership of and realty, 123
Land Commission report on breach of promise (1969), 90, 91
landowners:
personalty, right to, 47–8 (case law)
possessory title of, 122–3 (case law)
rights of over found chattels, 58–9 (case law)
Law of Property Act 1925, s 188, 23–5
legal consideration of, 24–5
Law of Property (Miscellaneous Provisions) Act 1970 (LP(MP)A 1970), 90–2
Law Reform Committee's 18th Report on Detinue and Conversion (1971), 144
leasehold interests as chattels real, 10
leases as legal estate, 9–10
legal charges and mortgages, 106–7
legal estate as leases, 9–10
legal papers:
clients' ownership of, 98–100
Court of Appeal ruling on ownership of, (case law), 99–100
legal relationships and equitable liens, 104–6 (case law)
liens 97–106
artificer's, 100
clients' legal papers, of, 98–100
common law *see* common law liens
equitable *see* equitable liens
general and special, 98
possessory, 100
sale of property and, 101–2 (case law)
life interest estates, 3
ligan defined, 54–5
living beings as property, 48–9
living tissue as personal property, 53–4
loans, gifts of chattels considered to be, 69–70 (case law)
lost chattels and bailment, 58 (case law)

market overt, 17–18
marriage and ownership of chattels, 19–22
married couples, joint purchase of chattels by, 20–2 (case law)
'mesnes', 3
lords, 4, 6
***Milroy v Lord* rule,** 76–8
mistake (contract law), 73–4 (case law)
mixtures, 33–4
accessio combination distinguished from, 28
co-ownership limits and, 39–40
definition, 33
fluid, 33
granular, 33
Roman law principles, 33–4
money, 108–18
banks, deposited in, 112
conversion of *see* conversion of money
definition, 108–11
eighteenth century, in, 109 (case law)
recovery of and deposits paid in advance of contract, 82
statutory uses of, 111
stolen, 117 (case law)
twentieth century, in, 109–10 (case law)
virtual, currency as, 111
'money had and received', 81–2
mortgages and legal charges, 106–7

***nemo dat quod non habet* rule,** 17, 22, 25, 62, 114

occupiers' rights over found chattels, 59 (case law)
owners:
co-owners' rights over chattels, 23–6
'particular kind of right', 15
rights available to, 15–16
sale of goods not by, 17–19
ownership, 15, 79
abandonment of *see* abandonment of ownership
changes due to *specificatio*, 29
chattels, of, in marriage, 19–22
conditional, 79–80 (case law)
co-ownership *see* co-ownership; ownership of chattels
Crown's right to ownership of ownerless property, 128–9 (case law)
English law, in, 14–15
'particular kind of right', 15
personal property and, 5–6, 14
plants, of, 46–8
possession and, discussion of, 16–17
real estate, of, 46–8
treasure, of, 57
ownership of chattels, 14–25, 78–9, 119 (case law)
accessory and principal combined, 27–8

common law lienee's rights, 102–3
conditional, 79
co-owners' rights of chattels, 25
co-owner's sale of chattel to third party, 25–6
marriage and, 19–22
single chattel, of, 23–4
spouses' dispute over, 22 (case law)
ownership rights:
protection of in personal property, 5–6
real property and, 3–5, 5–6

Parker v British Airways Board **(1982),** 122, 131
personal property:
Blackstone's definition of, 2
brain as, 51–2 (case law)
chattels and, 9–14
co-ownership of, 19–22
definition and historical development, 2
living tissue as, 53–4
nineteenth century, in, 7–8
ownership and, 14
ownership rights, protection of in, 5–6
real property and *see* real and personal property
recovery of possession of, 8
restrictive covenants and, 9 (case law)
slaves as, 48 (case law)
wedding presents as, 20
personalty:
landowners' right to, 47–8
ownership of reverts to Crown, 59–61
possession of, 58
security over, 96–107
plants, ownership of, 46–8
pledge, 96–7
commercial relationships, in, 97
definition, 96
regulations of, 97
possession of chattels:
abandonment of *see* abandonment of possession of chattels
definition, 120
ownership and, discussion of, 15–17
personalty, of, 58
recovery of and ownership, 15–16 (case law)
possession of goods, sale to third parties, 18
possessory title, 16
landowners', 122–3 (case law)
pound breach, 140–2 (case law)
presumption of advancement and gifts of chattels, 75
principal chattel, ownership of transferred and *accessio*, 27–8
promissory notes, 110–11
property, 6–7
animals as *see* animals as property
body parts as, 52–3 (case law)
bona vacantia, 42
compensation and, 32
dead bodies as, 50 (case law)
human organs as, 53 (case law)
human tissue as, 48–54
living beings as, 48–9
ownerless, Crown's right to, 128–9 (case law)
personal *see* personal property
purchase of and fraudulent benefit claims, 85–6 (case law)
real *see* real property
royal animals as, 45–6
royal fish as, 46 (case law)
sale of and lien, 101–2 (case law)
swans as, 45–6
women as, 48–9 (case law)
property rights:
bankruptcy and, 12–13 (case law)
intangible, 155 (case law)
proprietary interest requirement for detinue, 137–8
protection of goods from third parties, 150 (case law)
protection of rights in chattels, 134–56
historical context of, 134–43
purchase of chattels:
joint bank account, from, 21–2 (case law)
married couples, by, 20–2 (case law)

'quiet enjoyment of goods', 63–4 (case law)
Quistclose trusts, 87–9 (case law)

real actions, 5, 6
real and personal property:
distinctions between, 7–9
succession arrangements, 8
real chattels, 9–10
leasehold interests, as, 10
real estate, 46–8
real property, 1–2, 5
nineteenth century, in, 7
ownership rights and, 3–5, 5–6

personal property and, distinction between, 7–9
transfer of interest in, 8–9
realty:
gifts of, and conditional gifts of chattels, 78–9
ownership of land and, 123
Receiver of Wreck, 55
rejection of gifts, 94–5 (case law)
recovery and, 95 (case law)
rejection of in writing, 95
replevin, 139–40
conversion and, 140
distress and, 140
TCEA 2007 and, 145
trespass and, 140
rescous, 142 (case law)
restrictive covenants and personal property, 9 (case law)
rights:
choses in action and, 12
owner's, 15–16
rights in chattels, protection of *see* **protection of rights in chattels**
royal animals as property, 45–6
royal fish as property, 46 (case law)

sale of goods, 62–8
estoppel and, 18
owner, not by, 17–19
'quiet enjoyment' of goods, 63–4 (case law)
Sale of Goods Act 1979
s 12, prohibited operation of, 64–6 (case law)
salvage, 55–6
rights, 56 (case law)
security over personalty, 96–107
shares:
choses in action and, 12
trust, held on and declaration of trust, 41 (case law)
ships, wreck of English, 55
slaves:
compensation for loss of, 49 (case law)
personal property, as, 48 (case law)
'socage', 3, 4
specificatio, 29–33 (case law)
Blackstone's definition of, 129
English law, application to, 31–3 (case law)
legal significance of, 30–3
'manufacturing' aspect of, 29–30
ownership, changes due to, 29
Statute of Quia Emptores (1290), 5
succession of real and personal property, 8
sue, power to and conversion, 155

tenants, 3
'tenants in chief', 3
'tenants in demesne', 3
tenure, 3
development of, 4
doctrine of, 4
'free', 3
'knight's tenure', 3
'unfree', 3
third parties
car bought from, 64–6 (case law)
co-owner's sale of chattels to, 25–6
joint owner of chattel's action against, 26
possession of goods and, 18
protection of goods from, 150 (case law)
sale to, and possession of goods, 18
single chattel's joint owner's action over, 26
title of chattel obtained from, 62–118
title of gift passed to, 80–1 (case law)
title:
chattels, of, from third party, 62–118
currency, of, 17
defect in and compensation, 65, 66
equitable and 'unascertained goods', 67–8 (case law)
gift, of, passed to third parties, 80–1 (case law)
good title passing, terms as to, 62–6
goods, to, voidable, 18
landowner's possessory title, 122–3 (case law)
passage of, 66–8
terms of, in sale of goods, 62–3
transfer of, 17
void, and voidable, 18–19
Torts (Interference with Goods) Act 1977 (TIGA 1977), 8, 26, 66, 102, 143–5, 153
transfer of goods, failure of due to fraud, 95–6 (case law)
treasure, 56–9
ownership of, 57
rewards for finders, 57
trespass, 138–9
conversion, distinguished from, 135–6
interference level required for, 139
replevin and, 140
trespasser's culpability, 152–3 (case law)

trespass to goods, 138–9 (case law), 151–3
elements of tort, 151–3 (case law)
remedies for, 153
Tribunals, Courts and Enforcement Act 2007 (TCEA 2007), 145–6
trover, 14, 48, 114, 116, 135, 154
trusts:
declaration of shares held on trust, 41 (case law)
failure of, 60–1

'unascertained goods', 67–8 (case law)
equitable title and, 67–8 (case law)
undue influence, effect on gifts of chattels, 74

'villeinage', 3, 4

wedding presents as personal property, 20
'Who Owns the File?' (Law Society practice note 2017), 98–9
wild animals, ownership and abandonment of, 129–30
wild animals as property, 43–6 (case law)
bees as property, 45 (case law)
Blackstone's analysis, 43–4
rabbits as property, 43, 44 (case law)
reversion to wild state, 45
swans as property, 45–6 (case law)
taming of, 44
women as property, 48–9 (case law)
wreck, 54–6
definition, 54–5 (case law)
Receiver of Wreck, 55
'wrongful interference with goods', 114–15, 144